The Everlasting Empire

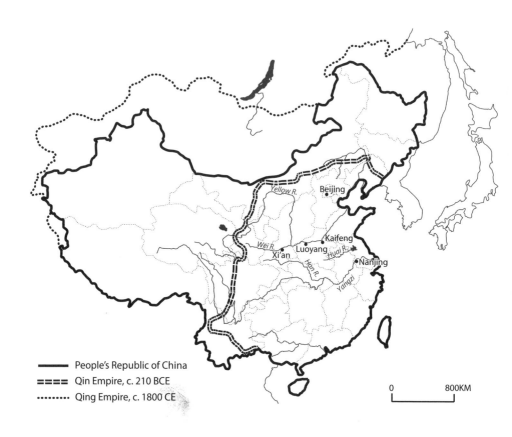

People's Republic of China

==== Qin Empire, c. 210 BCE

.... Qing Empire, c. 1800 CE

Yellow R.

Beijing

Wei R.   Luoyang   Kaifeng

Xi'an   Huai R.

Han R.   Nanjing

Yangzi

0   800KM

The Everlasting Empire

THE POLITICAL CULTURE OF ANCIENT
CHINA AND ITS IMPERIAL LEGACY

Yuri Pines

PRINCETON UNIVERSITY PRESS

Princeton and Oxford

Copyright © 2012 by Princeton University Press
Published by Princeton University Press, 41 William Street, Princeton,
New Jersey 08540
In the United Kingdom: Princeton University Press, 6 Oxford Street,
Woodstock, Oxfordshire OX20 1TW

press.princeton.edu

LIBRARY OF CONGRESS CATALOGING-IN-PUBLICATION DATA

Pines, Yuri.
    The everlasting empire : the political culture of ancient China and its imperial legacy /
Yuri Pines.
        p. cm.
    Includes bibliographical references and index.
    ISBN 978-0-691-13495-6 (hardcover : alk. paper)   1. China—Politics and
government.   2. Political culture—China—History.   3. Political science—China—
Philosophy—History.   4. Imperialism—China—History.   5. Ideology—China—
History.   I. Title.
    JQ1510.P56 2012
    306.20951—dc23   2011036388

British Library Cataloging-in-Publication Data is available

This book has been composed in Garamond Pro

Printed on acid-free paper. ∞

Printed in the United States of America

10 9 8 7 6 5 4 3 2 1

Contents

Acknowledgments

THIS BOOK IS WRITTEN as homage to two eminent scholars. First is my teacher, Professor Liu Zehua 劉澤華 of the Nankai University, Tianjin, whose remarkable ability to combine meticulous study of specific texts, periods, and personalities with bold generalizations and highly original analysis of Chinese political culture throughout the centuries serves as a source of constant inspiration for me. Second is the late Professor Shmuel Noah Eisenstadt, in whose workshops I was privileged to participate in the early 2000s, and who encouraged me to contextualize Chinese history and Chinese political culture in broader global patterns and to think in terms of comparative history. It is to these two great teachers that my book is dedicated.

In preparing this book I have benefited tremendously from the advice of my friends and colleagues: Zvi Ben-Dor, Michal Biran (whose illuminating remarks on nomadic political culture proved exceptionally invaluable), Elizabeth Perry, and Yitzhak Shichor. Paul Goldin and another reviewer for Princeton University Press contributed greatly toward the manuscript's improvement. I am deeply grateful to these scholars—and to many other colleagues whose advice on particular questions I sought and whose studies I have consulted. Naturally, I remain singularly responsible for any possible inaccuracies and imprecise interpretations of secondary research. I am grateful to Yitzchak Jaffe for preparing the map.

I am grateful to Rob Tempio of Princeton University Press for his constant encouragement; to the Institute for Advanced Study, Princeton, where the exceptionally stimulating intellectual atmosphere strengthened my determination to undertake this project back in 2006, and to my wife, Wang Yu, and my friends, who tolerated my partial default on social obligations during the years of writing and revisions.

This research was supported by the Israel Science Foundation (grant no. 1217/07) and by the Michael William Lipson Chair in Chinese Studies.

The Everlasting Empire

Introduction

Stability is in unity.
—*Mengzi*

WESTERN OBSERVERS seem always to have been fascinated with the durability of the Chinese political system. While attitudes toward the Chinese political model changed dramatically over the centuries, reflecting shifts and turns in Europe's political and intellectual history—from the Jesuits' admiration of China's stability to Hegel's derision of its stagnation, from Voltaire's praise of it as an exemplary enlightened monarchy to Karl Wittfogel's detestation of its "Oriental despotism"—interest in the Chinese empire's exceptional longevity persisted.[1] In turn it led Western scholars to investigate numerous aspects of Chinese political thought, values, and modes of sociopolitical behavior—what today may be called "political culture." While in the course of the twentieth century interest in the Chinese imperial model and in China's political culture diminished among nonspecialists, it remained intense among scholars of China who searched in the imperial past for explanations of China's turbulent present. Particularly during Mao Zedong's years in power (1949–1976) and in their immediate aftermath, scholars repeatedly debated the cultural roots of the vicissitudes of Chinese history, investigating imperial patterns of autocracy, dissent, submission, and rebellion and their impact on China's present.[2]

In recent decades this interest in Chinese political culture among Western students of China has gradually subsided. Many factors have contributed to this: emerging scholarly uneasiness with sweeping generalizations that all too often served hidden or overt political agendas; "decentering" shifts in the historiography that redirected scholarly gaze from the center to the periphery and from the rulers to the ruled; and, arguably, the seemingly dull and predictable state of contemporary Chinese politics, which makes the field of political studies of current—and, mutatis mutandis, premodern—China much less attractive than it was during Mao's twists and turns.[3] Yet curiously, just when Chinese politics became less "exciting" and Western scholars lost their interest in Chinese political culture, this topic gained unprecedented prominence in China's indigenous scholarship. Prompted by the need to reassess the traditional sources of manifold malpractices of Mao's (and not only Mao's) era, and encouraged by relative relaxation of academic control, Chinese scholars produced dozens of monographs and thousands of articles on various topics concerning traditional Chinese political ideologies, values, and practices and their modern impact. Few are the topics on which the divergence of interests between Chinese and Western scholars is so marked.

My interest in Chinese political culture had been aroused since my first encounter with the leading Chinese scholar in the field, Liu Zehua, under whose guidance I studied in the 1990s, at Nankai University, Tianjin. It was there that I first began contemplating the need to address anew the political miracle of the Chinese empire—one of the largest political entities worldwide, which endured against all odds for more than two millennia. Unlike my Chinese teachers and colleagues, I was attracted to Chinese political culture primarily not because of its impact on China's current political experience, but as an explanatory framework for the empire's unparalleled durability. I believe that now, as ideological battles in which the Chinese empire served as a model or a foil for the Occident have long ended, the time is ripe to address its history anew, and try to understand how its architects and custodians were able to establish the longest continuous polity in human history.

The Chinese empire was established in 221 BCE, when the state of Qin unified the Chinese world after centuries of intensive interstate warfare. The nascent empire was then roughly contemporary with the Maurya Empire in India and with the Hellenistic and Roman empires in the Mediterranean area. The Chinese empire ended with the proclamation of the Republic in 1912 CE, almost simultaneously with the final collapse of three major empires in the West: the Ottoman, the Habsburg, and the Romanov. Between these termini, for 2,132 years, China underwent tremendous changes in demography and topography, in ethnic composition of the ruling elites and socioeconomic structure, in religion and means of artistic expression. It encountered—like any other comparable polity worldwide—periods of internal wars and foreign incursions, alien occupations, and devastating rebellions; not a few times the very survival of Chinese civilization looked precarious. Yet upheavals and transformations notwithstanding, we may discern striking continuities in institutional, sociopolitical, and cultural spheres throughout the imperial millennia. The monarchic political system; the powerful bureaucracy; the strongly pronounced social hierarchy, usually coupled with considerable social mobility; the extended family system; the uniform written language and continuous educational curriculum—all these features remained valid both under unifying dynasties and under regional regimes during the ages of fragmentation, under native and under alien rule. Moreover, underlying these common features were fundamental ideas and values, which shaped the imperial polity. The emperor should be omnipotent and his rule should be universal; the bureaucracy should be staffed by men of proven talent and merit; and the commoners deserve utmost concern but should remain outside policy making. These ideas guided political actors in China from the beginning to the end of the imperial enterprise, from the Qin dynasty (221–207 BCE) to the Qing (1644–1911).

This study explores the ways in which the Chinese imperial system attained its unparalleled endurance. In this exploration, I outright reject the once-popular environmental deterministic approach, such as that advocated by Wittfogel, or the idea that the empire's success reflected some perennial Chinese "national character."[4] And I do not pretend to provide a comprehensive answer, which would have to take into consideration a variety of geographic, economic, military, religious, and cultural factors, the detailed analysis of which goes beyond the scope of the present study (more on this below). Rather, I shall focus on a single variable, which distinguishes Chinese imperial experience from that of other comparable polities elsewhere, namely, the empire's exceptional ideological prowess. As I hope to demonstrate, the Chinese empire was an extraordinarily powerful ideological construct, the appeal of which to a variety of political actors enabled its survival even during periods of severe military, economic, and administrative malfunctioning. Put in other words, the peculiar historical trajectory of the Chinese empire is not its indestructibility—it witnessed several spectacular collapses—but rather its repeated resurrection in more or less the same territory and with a functional structure similar to that of the preturmoil period. This resurrection, in turn, was not incidental: it reflected the conscious efforts of major players to restore what they considered normal and normative way of sociopolitical conduct—the imperial order.

The peculiarity of China's historical trajectory starts in its preimperial age. In contrast with other imperial polities, the Chinese empire came into existence after a lengthy period of ideological preparation and pre-planning. Centuries of internal turmoil that preceded the imperial unification of 221 BCE, and which are known ominously as the age of "Warring States" (453–221 BCE), were also the most vibrant period in China's intellectual history. Bewildered by the exacerbating crisis, thinkers of that age sought ways to restore peace and stability. Their practical recommendations varied tremendously; but amid this immense variety there were some points of consensus. Most importantly, thinkers of distinct ideological inclinations unanimously accepted political unification of the entire known civilized world—"All-under-Heaven"—as the only feasible means to put an end to perennial war; and they also agreed that the entire sub-celestial realm should be governed by a single omnipotent monarch.[5] These premises of unity and monarchism became the ideological foundation of the future empire, and they were not questioned for millennia to come. Furthermore, the ideological fertility of the Warring States period provided the empire builders with a rich repertoire of ideas from which solutions could be drawn to deal with a variety of problems and challenges. Thus, prior to the imperial unification, an ideological framework was formed within which much of the empire's political life continued to fluctuate.

Preconceived long before it came into existence, the empire remained forever not only an administrative and military entity but also an ideological construct. It was recently defined as "the best illustration of Gramscian hegemony,"[6] and it is certainly true that the imperial idea enjoyed political-cultural hegemonic status. The empire's basic ideological premises were shared by every politically significant social group and even by its immediate neighbors; no alternative political structure was considered either legitimate or desirable; and even those rulers whose ethnic or social background must have encouraged them to be critical of the imperial polity were destined to adopt it and adapt themselves to it, enriching and improving its functioning rather than dismantling it. Until the late nineteenth century, the empire was the only conceivable polity for the inhabitants of the Chinese world. Even during periods of woeful turmoil and disintegration, major political actors—from the emperor and his aides down to local elites and rebellious commoners—all vied to restore and improve the imperial order rather than replace it.

The power of the imperial ideology is undeniable, but it would be grossly inaccurate to reduce the study of the empire's durability to analysis of its ideological guidelines. Rather, the imperial political culture developed amid complex interaction between ideological stipulations and practical requirements. The empire's longevity derived not just from the solidity of its ideological foundations, but also from its leaders' ability to adjust their practices and adapt to changing circumstances. This flexibility—just like the ideological rigidity—was built into the empire's genetic code from its very inception. Preimperial thinkers bequeathed to the empire builders not a ready model, but rather a set of basic principles and a variety of conflicting policy recommendations. The resultant ideological synthesis was fluid enough to allow constant readjustment of manifold policies. When new challenges came into existence—such as the appearance of nomadic tribesmen as the empire's most formidable rivals or the emergence of powerful local elites (see chapters 1 and 4)—the empire's leaders were able to introduce the necessary modifications without compromising the essentials of imperial rule. This flexibility amid preservation of the basic ideological and institutional framework became the true source of the empire's vitality.

In light of this understanding, the present study is built so as to stand at the nexus of intellectual and political history. While my earlier studies focused primarily on the formation of the imperial ideology,[7] here I shall try to elucidate the dynamic interplay between the empire's ideological guidelines and their practical adaptations. Each of the first five chapters starts with a brief analysis of the background on which specific principles concerning the empire's maintenance—the concept of political unity, the idea of monarchism, behavioral norms for politically involved intellectuals, and rules for dealing with local elites and with the commoners—were formulated. After these introductory sections, which largely summarize my previous research, I go on to explore how the ideological principles laid down in the preimperial or early imperial period were implemented and modified in the process of their actualization. The discussion, while roughly chronological, is not intended to present a systematic history of the empire (a task that is beyond this book's scope), but rather provides historical illustrations of the complex pattern of transformation and evolution of ideas and practices throughout the imperial millennia. I have intentionally selected my illustrations from different periods, trying to introduce, even if briefly, every major dynasty (and not a few minor ones), rather than confining the discussion to a few well-known dynasties and personalities. In this way I hope to present a sufficiently complex picture of Chinese history and to avoid haphazard generalizations, which are still quite popular in many synoptic studies of China's past.

It is a crucial premise of this book that Chinese political culture cannot be understood in simplistic, monochromatic, or unilinear terms.[8] Rather, it was full of paradoxes and tensions, reflecting what Liu Zehua aptly names its "*yin-yang* structure."[9] Adoration of monarchism coexisted with extremely critical views of individual monarchs; intellectuals were perceived as both the ruler's servitors and his moral guides; a hierarchical mind-set coexisted with strong egalitarian tendencies; while the commoners, who were declared the "root" of the polity and the kingmakers, were also firmly excluded from participation in political processes. Even such an unshakable principle as the ideal of political unity of All-under-Heaven was sometimes compromised in practice by redrawing the boundaries between the "internal" and "external" realms (see chapter 1). Yet as I shall try to demonstrate, these persistent "creative tensions," to borrow Tu Wei-ming's term, have further contributed toward flexibility of the empire's functioning, its adaptability to a variety of domestic and foreign challenges, and its ultimate durability.[10]

My focus on dynamism and complexity of Chinese political culture, I hope, will allow me to overcome the widespread mistrust of broad generalizations as intrinsically superficial and/or leading to reductionist, essentialized, or ahistorical perceptions of Chinese culture. It is surely not my intention to reduce China's history to a set of immutable principles and rules (see note 8 to this introduction), or to some neat "evolutions" (e.g., toward "ever more efficient authoritarianism"; see chapter 2). Hence, rather than glossing over instances of discontinuities and ruptures, I shall highlight them whenever appropriate, and rather than looking for primordial explanations of basic ideological and institutional patterns, I shall explore their emergence and evolution. I hope to demonstrate that each of these patterns was a product of reasonable choices made by statesmen and thinkers at different stages of the empire's development; and many of these choices were repeatedly reinterpreted, renegotiated, and readjusted in the face of a variety of challenges. However, I also believe that beneath temporal variations we can discern common underlying principles, which, in my eyes, constitute the fundamentals of China's imperial model, and which I hope to foreground in this book.

Aside from the danger of superficial generalizations, my study faces yet another potential pitfall—that of overreliance on traditional Chinese historiography as the major source for understanding the imperial past. As is well known, this historiography in general, and its core, the so-called dynastic histories in particular, suffer not just from political biases but also from ideological conventions that at times result in a skewed presentation of the past. Many historical works tend to perpetuate the illusion of unified rule during the ages of de facto fragmentation, and the illusion of China's superiority over aliens during the ages of dynastic weakness; most of them focus on the center at the expense of the periphery; and the desire of many history writers to seek moral lessons in the past causes some to cross the line between descriptive and prescriptive narratives. More substantial biases permeate not just the official historiography but the entire ideological and historical production of the literati. Thus not just the absolute majority of the empire's subjects—the lower strata, women, ethnic minorities, and the like—remain outside the focus of historical production; what is worse for the study of political culture, even elite and subelite groups other than the literati—military men and alien conquerors, eunuchs and harem women, merchants and monks—remain woefully under- or misrepresented. This intrinsic bias in the writings of the literati dictates utmost caution in the analysis of, for instance, the persistence of fundamental political values, which are explored throughout this book. Is it possible that ideological and political phenomena that did not correspond to the literati's worldview were simply glossed over? Such a question poses an implicit challenge to the validity of my research.

To moderate this challenge, I offer two observations. First, the sheer richness of Chinese historical production and the abundance of primary documents incorporated into historical works allow a sensitive historian to reconstruct a much more nuanced picture than is often assumed. Thus, in addition to official histories, we possess—especially from the late imperial period—a variety of local histories and personal accounts, which were produced outside the court and which elucidate many topics that remain beyond the scope of official historiography. Furthermore, numerous literary works, epigraphic sources, accounts of foreign travelers, writings by members of other ethnic groups (most notably the Manchu archives), and even material objects—all these further enrich our understanding of the complexity of China's past and allow us to go beyond the confines of the official histories, which, as Etienne Balazs derisively said, were written "by officials for officials."[11] Thus, while our picture of the Chinese past may remain incomplete and inaccurate in some details, on balance, I believe, it is possible to restore a sufficiently reliable view of China's political and ideological trajectories.

Second, and most important for the present study, the biases of the literati are less detrimental to an understanding of Chinese political culture than to other research endeavors. Since political culture in China was from the beginning designed by the educated elite, and since this elite retained cultural and ideological (even if not always political) hegemony throughout the Chinese imperial age, its viewpoints naturally constitute the major source for my research. As these viewpoints can be reconstructed with considerable precision from the extant sources, it may be argued that the general picture presented in this study remains largely reliable.

GOALS OF THIS BOOK

My exploration of the strengths and weaknesses of the Chinese empire pursues three distinct goals. The first and perhaps the most audacious of these is an attempt to outline the essentials of China's political culture. I am aware that this undertaking will face the inevitable skepticism of "a generation of historians that has been training its eyes on smaller and smaller temporal and geographical chunks of Chinese history, . . . working to get beyond East/West generalizations."[12] Nonetheless, I hope to demonstrate that historical sensitivity should not preclude readiness to generalize, and that awareness of the immense variability of Chinese history in time and space should not prevent us from discerning long-term patterns and modes of functioning, the combination of which was peculiar to China. I hope that by outlining fundamental principles of the empire's functioning, this study will benefit both historians of China, by providing a possible framework for discussions of specifics of China's imperial history, and colleagues and students who deal with other civilizations and are interested in understanding the patterns of China's past for the sake of comparison.

This brings me to a second goal: namely, to locate the Chinese example more firmly within the nascent but rapidly developing field of "imperiology"—that is, the study of an empire as a historical and sociopolitical phenomenon. Comparative studies of imperial formations were undertaken by both historians and social scientists in the past, and in recent years interest in the topic has visibly burgeoned.[13] With the increasing theoretical sophistication of these studies, particularly evidenced by Goldstone and Haldon's recent insightful analysis of the empires' developmental trajectories, the possibility of creating a viable cross-civilization comparative framework increases as well.[14] Yet while the Chinese case is duly present in most of the comparative studies (and is very prominent in some), research is still overwhelmingly dominated by the Occidental (Roman or, less frequently, Near Eastern) perspective. I think that the time is ripe to reverse this trend, taking into account the Chinese imperial experience in its full complexity. My study in particular may contribute to this end by exploring the importance of the ideological factors behind the empire's sustainability and addressing thereby what appears to be one of the crucial factors behind the differences in the empires' life spans.[15]

To be sure, the present monograph is but a preliminary contribution to comparative "imperiology." Establishing a more rigid comparative framework would require more systematic discussion of a number of questions that are only cursorily dealt with in the present study, such as the impact of geographic, economic, religious, ethnic, and military factors on the empires' different trajectories. To what extent did China benefit from its relative isolation from other civilizations of comparable economic and ideological prowess—for example, those in western and southern Eurasia? To what extent did it benefit from its relative economic self-sufficiency, which allowed China's rulers to moderate contacts with the outside world more efficiently than would be possible elsewhere? How did the Chinese empire escape major religious challenges to its structure and to its mode of functioning? What were the costs and benefits of the empire's strongly pronounced tendency to subjugate the military to civilian control? Were the ethnic identities in the Chinese world more malleable and less politically potent than those elsewhere? These and manifold other questions will require further studies.

My third, and perhaps most contentious goal, is to reassess the role of the imperial experience in the modern history of China. For two centuries, the empire's exceptional stability was reviled as the major impediment blocking China's access to "progress" and "modernization." It is not my intention to dispute the intellectual validity of this perspective, which was—and is—shared by the vast majority of Chinese intellectuals and statesmen throughout the twentieth century and beyond. Nor do I intend to err in a different direction, as a minority of ultrapatriotic Chinese scholars do, obliterating obviously negative aspects of the empire's experience.[16] Yet I think today we should liberate ourselves from teleological perspectives and weigh the empire's strengths and shortcomings on its own terms: that is, against the goals set forth by its architects and custodians. There is no doubt that many of these goals were never realized: periodic disastrous collisions, widespread corruption, the inadequacy of many rulers and of their officials—all these persistent weaknesses of the empire were readily recognized not only by modern but also by traditional scholars. On the positive side, however, few if any premodern polities worldwide were able to provide such a fair degree of stability, peace, and relative prosperity to so many people as did the Chinese empire. The very fact that China—despite obvious ecological challenges[17]—remained the most populous country on earth through much of the imperial period speaks highly of its success.

Eschewing a "modernization" perspective does not mean, however, ignoring altogether the question of imperial China's disastrous performance vis-à-vis Western (and Japanese) challenges in the nineteenth–twentieth centuries. The empire's collapse was very real, and it involved profound changes in the structure and underlying ideological norms of the Chinese polity. In the final chapter I address these events by offering a new assessment of the fate of the imperial political culture in the modern age. I focus in particular on the following questions: Which aspects of the imperial model were abandoned altogether? Which were modified, and which were retained? Does the end of the monarchy in February 1912 mark the end of imperial China or just another—more radical than ever—modification and readjustment of the traditional system? Is it permissible to speak of political continuities during the age of revolutions and rupture that spanned most of the twentieth century? What—if any—are the lessons that the current Chinese leadership may draw from the imperial experience, especially in the early twenty-first century, as China appears to be irresistibly advancing toward an age of renewed global prowess and self-confidence? Inevitably tentative, my answers, so I hope, will add another dimension to the ongoing debates about China's cultural identity in the modern age and the connections between its past and its present.

Today, as the economic center of gravity of the modern world shifts back toward Asia, and Western narratives of historical progress are increasingly questioned, blind faith in the supremacy of European sociopolitical and intellectual models gives way to more sober reflections. While we remain deeply enmeshed in our own hegemonic discourse—that of democracy, equality, and human rights—it may still be refreshing to weigh the advantages and disadvantages of alternative political formations and alternative hegemonic ideologies, of which the Chinese empire presents one of the most interesting examples. Without either embellishing or disparaging it, we may reflect upon its strengths and weaknesses and reassess its value, not only for a better understanding of the history of political ideas and political formations, but also for coping with the ever-changing political challenges of our own time.

Note on References and Translations

Throughout this study, I have tried to keep references minimal, limiting these either to those studies that exercised major influence on my research or to those that provide convenient explanations for the historical examples that I present. Since the book targets nonspecialists as well as established scholars, I avoided whenever possible references to non-English sources, limiting those to an absolute minimum. The only exceptions are direct citations from Chinese primary sources, which I have translated myself; in these cases the reference is to the original text.

CHAPTER 1

The Ideal of "Great Unity"

They say that the great forces of All-under-Heaven after prolonged
division must unify, and after prolonged unity must divide.

THE PHRASE IN THE EPIGRAPH, taken from the preface to a classical
Chinese novel, *The Romance of the Three Kingdoms*, may serve as an
excellent summary of Chinese history. An ostensibly endless chain of
unifications, subsequent disintegrations, and renewed unifications of the
oikoumenē, "All-under-Heaven" (*tianxia*), is a distinctive feature of the
Chinese empire. While there is nothing exceptional about periodic disintegrations of the empire, its repeated resurrection in a more or less similar
territorial framework and with a mode of functioning similar to that of
the preceding unified dynasty clearly distinguishes China from other continental empires. It seems that the Chinese found a remedy to what elsewhere became a terminal illness of vast empires. What was their secret?

To answer this question we should first dismiss the once-popular deterministic explanations of the Chinese empire's vitality as reflecting an
unusually convenient topographic or demographic setting. The Chinese
terrain, crisscrossed by mountain ranges (especially in the south, but also
in the north) and huge rivers, was as conducive to the emergence of small
independent polities as any other part of the world, with many regions
(e.g., Shanxi, Sichuan, and parts of Fujian) easily defensible against outsiders' attacks. China's population was similarly heterogeneous: not only
did ethnic minorities continuously occupy important pockets within so-
called China proper, but also the core "Han" population remained highly
diverse in terms of spoken language, customs, modes of life, and even
religious beliefs and the pantheon. Clearly, preserving the empire's unity
was as challenging a task in the Chinese case as it was for other continental empires.[1]

What are the reasons, then, for the sustainability of the unified empire,
and, most of all, for its regeneration after periods of division? In what
follows I would like to propose that the answer should be sought primarily in the realm of ideology. The idea that "All-under-Heaven" should be
unified under the aegis of the single monarch predated the imperial unification of 221 BCE and directly contributed to it. As I shall demonstrate
below, it became the true cornerstone of traditional Chinese political culture, and decisively shaped political dynamics during ages of unity and

fragmentation alike. Although in the course of imperial history the quest for unity had to be qualified to accommodate domestic and foreign political realities, it was never essentially compromised. Indeed, it may be argued that this belief remains the single most important legacy of the traditional political culture well into our own day.

Fragmentation: China as a Multistate System

Archaeological discoveries of recent decades have revolutionized our understanding of China's past. A previously widespread uncritical acceptance of Chinese political mythology, which postulated the existence of a single legitimate locus of power on China's soil since the very inception of civilization there, gave way to a polycentric perspective. It is widely accepted nowadays that multiple Neolithic and Bronze Age cultures interacted for millennia in the basins of the Yellow River, the Yangzi, and beyond, none of them obviously superior to the others. Even the first historical royal dynasty, the Shang (ca. 1600–1046 BCE), might have enjoyed only a relative cultural, military, and political superiority over its neighbors, but by no means ruled the territories beyond its immediate sphere of influence in the middle reaches of the Yellow River.[2]

The overthrow of the Shang by the Zhou dynasty (ca. 1046–256 BCE) became an important turning point. The victorious Zhou leaders utilized their success to rapidly expand the territory under their direct and indirect control, establishing a military and civilian presence beyond their original Wei River locus to the middle and low Yellow River basin, and even further to the south, to the Huai and Han Rivers area. Notably, while the conquest of the Shang and the immediate crushing of the pro-Shang rebellion were accompanied by considerable violence, the subsequent expansion of Zhou rule, including the establishment of new settlements ruled by royal kin and allies, the relocation of the subjugated Shang population, and the imposition of the Zhou elite over the indigenous inhabitants of the eastern parts of the realm, appear to have been accomplished relatively smoothly. While the dearth of reliable sources and obvious biases in later narratives make many details of early Zhou history unverifiable, it seems certain that the Zhou rulers succeeded in establishing their position as the single legitimate locus of power in the northern part of what was to become China.[3]

From the very beginning, the success of Zhou rule derived not only from the dynasty's administrative and military prowess, but also from its peculiar legitimating devices. The Zhou kings succeeded in positioning themselves as exclusive mediators between the supreme deity, Heaven, and the people below; and in their capacity as "Sons of Heaven" (*tianzi*) they continued to enjoy obvious superiority over their allies and subordinates, the regional lords (*zhuhou*). Most interestingly, currently available textual and paleographic evidence suggests that even the leaders of non-Zhou polities, who appropriated the royal title, dared not proclaim themselves "Sons of Heaven," recognizing thereby the ostensible superiority of the Zhou kings.[4] This position of the kings at the apex of the ritual (and, supposedly, sociopolitical) pyramid allowed the battered dynasty to endure for centuries, becoming the longest royal dynasty in Chinese history. More importantly for our discussion, this persistent symbolic superiority of the Zhou house might have inspired the quest for political unification during the generations of turmoil, which followed the collapse of effective Zhou rule.[5]

This said, one should not assume, as is frequently done in Chinese scholarly publications, a kind of lineal progression toward an ever more strongly pronounced quest for unity from the beginning of Zhou rule. To the contrary, the disastrous defeat of the Zhou dynasty by a coalition of internal and external foes in 771 BCE, its ensuing relocation to the crippled eastern part of the royal domain, and subsequent loss of effective royal power ushered in a lengthy period of political fragmentation, which was initially accepted by most political actors as a fait accompli. Especially during the so-called Springs-and-Autumns period (Chunqiu, 770–453 BCE), statesmen focused their efforts on creating a viable multistate order rather than seeking renewed unification. During that period, the Zhou kings retained only symbolic superiority, while their nominal underlings, the regional lords, became for all practical purposes independent political players. Regional polities invaded each other, established alliances, signed treaties, and annexed weaker neighbors. Powerless Sons of Heaven gradually became hapless spectators of internecine struggles, in which they could occasionally intervene but the outcome of which they could not determine.[6]

In retrospect, the seventh and sixth centuries BCE appear to have been an exceptional period in Chinese history, when political fragmentation was considered an acceptable state of affairs and efforts were made to attain stability within the framework of the multistate system; and it is the failure of these attempts that ultimately led to the rejection of the multistate world altogether. Initially, a certain degree of stabilization was attempted under the so-called system of hegemony. The most powerful regional lord acted as a surrogate of the Zhou king, combining the legitimacy of the royal representative with the fearsome power of his armies. This system, which presupposed the ongoing existence of a single locus of military superiority, however, was not sustainable in the long term. By the late seventh century BCE it was replaced by a bipolar system of two competing alliances, each led by a powerful state (Jin in the north, Chu in the south). The alliance leaders tried to stabilize their coalitions, acting as arbiters in inter- and intrastate conflicts, and pretending to be protectors of the old sociopolitical order. They perpetuated ties with allied states through vigorous diplomatic activities, including periodic meetings of the state leaders and the swearing of solemn alliance covenants. Moreover, the ongoing commitment of the ruling aristocratic elites in each of the competing polities to Zhou cultural norms, particularly to the Zhou ritual system, perpetuated cultural ties across state boundaries, moderated the cruelty of military conflicts, and contributed toward the establishment of certain common rules of interstate relations, becoming a surrogate for international law.[7]

The age of covenants and alliances was relatively short-lived, however. Alliance leaders too frequently favored the narrow interest of their polity at the expense of their commitment to their allies; and increasing cynicism with regard to the validity of treaties and alliance oaths undermined the effectiveness of the system of covenants. Moreover, the fierce interalliance competition between Chu and Jin amid ongoing military deadlock caused the leaders of both polities to seek expansion of their alliances by alluring or forcing the enemy's allies to switch sides. This, in turn, generated repeated invasions of intermediate states, sandwiched between Jin and Chu, whose situation, according to a contemporary testimony, was grave indeed:

> Everything is ravaged and destroyed and there is no one to appeal to. People lose either their fathers and elder brothers, or sons and younger brothers. All are full of sorrow and sadness and do not know how to protect themselves.[8]

This plight of the tiny states generated the most curious attempt to institutionalize the multistate system: namely, two "disarmament conferences" in 546 and 541 BCE. The organizers proposed the creation of a mega-alliance, led simultaneously by Jin and Chu, legitimating thereby the bipolar world.[9] This initiative, however, failed miserably owing to the lack of mutual trust between major powers, and also to internal crises in both Chu and Jin and the rise of new "peripheral" powers, which further jeopardized the fragile interstate order. By the end of the sixth century BCE, the multistate system of the Springs-and-Autumns era was on the verge of collapse. On its ruins, the war of all against all ensued, giving the period following the breakup of the state of Jin in 453 BCE, and prior to the imperial unification of 221 BCE, its ominous name, the age of Warring States.

As the name suggests, the Warring States period was an age when diplomats were overshadowed by generals. Alliances were inevitably short-lived; treaties were routinely violated—sometimes immediately upon being concluded—and the increasing cynicism further diminished the appeal of diplomatic means of settling conflicts. A contemporaneous observer noted:

Despite clear pronouncements and manifested principles, weapons and armor arise ever more; [despite] outstanding and compelling arguments, battles and offensives never stop; [despite] gorgeous sayings and refined words, the world lacks ordered rule; tongues are worn off and ears deafened, but no achievements are seen.[10]

This gloomy summary explains why the multistate order was no longer seen as sustainable. As war became ubiquitous, attempts to preserve peace among rival polities were discontinued. In the meantime, a series of military innovations, and particularly the replacement of the aristocratic chariot-based armies of the past with massive infantry armies manned by peasant conscripts, changed the nature of warfare. Wars became longer and harsher; the size of the armies and the number of casualties steadily increased; and the texts of the late Warring States period inform us of dozens, and sometimes hundreds of thousands, of casualties in a single campaign. Slaughter of prisoners of war and of civilians, massive plunder, deliberate destruction of the enemy's civilian infrastructure, and forced relocation of the hostile population—all exacerbated the sense of despair, eventually fueling the quest for unification.[11]

While devastating warfare contributed in the long term to the quest for unity, in the short term it strengthened centrifugal rather than centripetal forces. Each of the newly reformed Warring States was more cohesive internally than the aristocratic polities of the preceding age, and this internal consolidation occurred in tandem with increasing estrangement from neighbors. The separation was spatial, marked by long protective walls; administrative, as suggested by legal distinctions between native and foreign subjects; and cultural, as is indicated by the increasing divergence in the material and, to a lesser extent, written culture of major states. The decline of the aristocratic elite of the Springs-and-Autumns period meant partial abandonment of the Zhou ritual culture, which had once served as a common cultural denominator of the elite members. The new elite, some of whose members had risen from the lower social strata, was more diversified culturally than its predecessors. This diversification is particularly evident in the changing image of powerful "peripheral" states, Qin in the northwest and Chu in the south, which had once been considered members of the Zhou *oikoumenē* but by the fourth–third centuries BCE were treated as cultural strangers.[12] Cultural separation followed the lines of political fragmentation, indicating that centuries of division might well have resulted in the complete disintegration of the Zhou world into distinct quasi-national entities.

The process depicted above of internal consolidation of large territorial states, and their political and cultural separation from neighbors, unmistakably recalls similar developments in early modern Europe, where, as is well known, these developments resulted in the formation of nation-states. In China, however, the development trajectory was markedly different. The potential transformation of the Warring States into full-fledged separate entities never materialized. Instead, these polities were submerged by the unified empire in 221 BCE, becoming thereafter a locus of ethnographic curiosity rather than of political separatism. Below we shall see how and why this happened and focus specifically on the extraordinary role of the thinkers of the Warring States period as promulgators of unification.

"Stability is in unity"

The Warring States period was a formative age of China's intellectual tradition. This was an age of bold intellectual departures and remarkable ideological pluralism, unhindered by either political or religious orthodoxies. Thinkers competed freely for the rulers' patronage, moving from one court to another in search of better employment. They proposed distinct remedies to social, political, economic, and military maladies, their views ranging from harsh authoritarianism to anarchistic individualism, from support of a laissez-faire economy to advocacy of state monopolies, from blatant militarism to radical pacifism. Yet this immense pluralism notwithstanding, the competing thinkers held core beliefs in common. Among these, the commitment to the universal benefit of All-under-Heaven—eventually through political unification—stands as one of the most remarkable features of the Warring States period's intellectual discourse. An individual state never appears as the ultimate beneficiary of the thinkers' proposals, but, if at all, as a springboard for attaining the highest aim of resolving "universal" problems.[13]

This remarkable universalism ostensibly stands at odds with the dominant tendency during the Warring States period of individual states to strengthen their sociopolitical cohesiveness. The contradiction reflects a major difference between the lives of members of the educated elite, or at least its highest segment, and those of the rest of the populace. In an age when most states actively discouraged emigration, the intellectually active elite members, the so-called *shi* (whom I shall hereafter dub "intellectuals," for heuristic convenience; see more in chapter 3) were free to cross boundaries in search of better careers. Any known thinker of that age served more than one court; and this very flexibility of movement through the interstate "market of talent" broadened the intellectuals' horizons, causing their concerns to transcend the confines of individual states. Eventually, this breadth of horizons became associated with high elite status, while localism—local customs and identities—was viewed as characteristic of culturally impaired commoners.[14] Lacking the intellectuals' endorsement, the local identities of the Warring States never developed into a politically meaningful factor, as happened elsewhere, for example, in modern Europe.

The proclaimed universalism of the Warring States period's intellectuals had immediate political implications: namely, their common commitment to the attainment of peace in All-under-Heaven. In an age of escalating warfare, of endless bloodshed and inherent lack of stability, in an age when rival states routinely tried to undermine domestic order in the neighbor polities, it was all too clear that the internal problems of an individual state would never be resolved unless the entire *oikoumenē* was settled. And, insofar as diplomatic means of stabilizing All-under-Heaven were inadequate, political unification became the only feasible way out of unending disorder. Therefore, the quest for unity became a peculiar intellectual consensus of the thinkers of the Warring States period, legitimating the universal empire long before it came into being.

The pro-unification discourse of the Warring States period developed gradually, with early voices being somewhat hesitant. Thus Confucius (551–479 BCE), the earliest and arguably the most prominent thinker of the preimperial age, proposed curbing political disintegration by restoring the early Zhou system, in which "rites, music, and punitive expeditions" were initiated by the Son of Heaven and not by regional lords.[15] Confucius's later intellectual rival, Mozi (ca. 460–390 BCE), embedded his vision of unity even more deeply in the past. He claimed that in an unspecified antiquity, "when the people had just arisen," there was a beastlike war of all against all, which ended only when "the worthiest and the most able [man] in All-under-Heaven" was established as Son of Heaven, creating thereafter a perfectly centralized and uniformly ruled universal state.[16] Mozi's audience may well have understood that his narrative "invoked the past to serve the present": this political myth aimed to demonstrate that unification was the only way out of current disorder and devastating mutual strife.

Whereas Confucius and Mozi embedded their quest for unity in appeals to the past (either the early Zhou or some unspecified primeval age), other thinkers proposed alternative justifications for the unification of the realm. Thus an exceptionally influential fourth-century BCE text, the *Laozi*, provides metaphysical underpinnings for political unification. Just as the universe is ruled by the uniform and all-penetrating force of the Way (*Dao*), so should society be unified under a single omnipotent leader. These ideas appear in the *Laozi* in a nascent form, but they were duly developed in later texts that utilized them to buttress the need for unity and also to lionize the future ruler of the unified realm to superhuman proportions (on which see chapter 2).[17] Yet intellectually engaging as they are, these and other philosophical justifications of unity mattered little

for the evolution of the drive for unification in the second half of the Warring States period. The more devastating the interstate warfare became,
the clearer it was that unity was needed not just because of historical
precedents or metaphysical constructs but primarily as the only means of
avoiding further bloodshed. This understanding is vivid in the following
dialogue between one of the most important followers of Confucius,
Mengzi (Mencius, ca. 380–304 BCE), and one of the regional kings:

> [The king] asked: "How can All-under-Heaven be stabilized?"
> [Mengzi] answered: "Stability is in unity."
> —"Who is able to unify it?"
> [Mengzi] answered: "He, who has no proclivity to kill, is able to
> unify it."
> —"Who will be able to follow him?"
> [Mengzi] answered: "Nobody under Heaven will not follow him.
> ... If there is [a ruler] who has no proclivity to kill, then the people of
> All-under-Heaven will crane their necks looking at him. If this really
> happens, the people will go over to him as water runs downward: who
> will be able to stop this torrent?"[18]

Mengzi's dictum, "Stability is in unity," may be considered the common motto of the intellectual discourse of the Warring States period; but
his moralistic idealism—expressed in the belief that only a benevolent
and nonmilitaristic ruler, "who has no proclivity to kill," would attain
final unification—was pathetically naive. It was duly rejected by some:
for instance, Mengzi's elder contemporary and ideological antipode,
Shang Yang (d. 338 BCE), argued that unity can be attained only through
resolute and merciless military action against rival rulers. Shang Yang
was notorious in his advocacy of attaining victory through "performing
whatever the enemy is ashamed of."[19] Yet blatantly militaristic Shang
Yang and radically moralistic Mengzi, who considered aggressive war a
"crime for which even death is insufficient punishment," clearly shared
the conviction that "stability is in unity"; Shang Yang explicitly stated
that war is needed simply to "eradicate wars."[20] The commitment of intellectual antipodes to the same goal is revealing. By the middle of the
Warring States period, the only true issue at stake was *how* to unify the
world, not *whether or not* it should be unified.

Aside from explicit calls for unity, the discourse of the Warring States
period facilitated the future imperial unification in a variety of other
ways. For instance, the political mythology of that age backdated the notion of unity to the remote past, implying thereby that political fragmentation is an aberration and not an acceptable state of affairs.[21] Ritual
compendia postulated the existence of a universal sociopolitical pyramid

headed by the Son of Heaven as the singular ritually appropriate situation. The very language of political discourse, with its repeated postulates of the superiority of universality to particularity, was conducive to the goal of unification.[22] Yet perhaps the single most important feature of pro-unification discourse is the firm association of the ruler's legitimacy with his ability to attain universal unification. In the next chapter, we shall analyze the concept of a True Monarch, created by the thinkers of the Warring States period; here suffice it to say that the most pronounced consensus with regard to this quasi-messianic figure was that under his aegis the world would be firmly unified. Thenceforth and until the end of the imperial period, it was tacitly understood that a ruler who failed to attain unity was not "real Son of Heaven."[23]

Finally, to understand fully the contribution of the intellectuals of the Warring States period to the imperial unification, we should note not only what they said but also what they did not say. That not a single individual is known ever to have endorsed a goal of regional state's independence is most remarkable. Denied ideological legitimacy, separate polities became intrinsically unsustainable in the long term. Having been associated with turmoil, bloodshed, and general disorder, these states were doomed intellectually long before they were destroyed militarily. In retrospect, it seems that centuries of struggle could not have ended differently: insofar as everybody expected unification, it became a self-fulfilling prophecy. The zero-sum game of the Warring States ended, amid tremendous bloodshed, in 221 BCE, when the most powerful of the regional states, Qin, wiped out its enemies in a series of brilliant military campaigns. The proud king of Qin proclaimed himself the First Emperor (r. 221–210 BCE), ushering in a new era in China's history.

Sustaining Unity

Unification was attained through resolute military action; but how to sustain it? The experience of the first unified imperial dynasties, the Qin (221–207 BCE) and the Han (206 BCE–220 CE), is particularly illuminating with regard to both challenges that faced the empire's unifiers, and the ways developed to cope with those challenges. As ideological, administrative, and social patterns of the first dynasties had a lasting impact on Chinese imperial history, in what follows I shall focus on their experience before proceeding to analyze broader trends throughout the imperial millennia.

It seems that the empire's most powerful asset was its uniform acceptance by its subjects. While imperial unifications were invariably achieved by force, establishing the empire was not a purely military enterprise. Let us focus on the Qin example. The wars of unification, in which Qin wiped out its six formidable eastern foes, lasted for ten years, during which huge armies of hundreds of thousands of soldiers operated simultaneously in the freezing Liaodong Peninsula in the northeast and the humid areas of the Yangzi delta in the southeast. Success would have been impossible had organized resistance on the part of the newly conquered population slowed the Qin armies. Yet, despite widespread hatred of Qin, frequently designated by its rivals as a "land of wolves and jackals," the people of the vanquished states made no significant attempts to regain independence.[24] Why was this the case? How did Qin succeed in imposing its will on the subjugated population? A brilliant analyst, Jia Yi (200–168 BCE), who lived a generation after the Qin's collapse, explained:

> Qin appropriated all within the seas, annexed the regional lords; [its ruler] faced south and called himself emperor. Thus, he nourished all within the four seas, and the gentlemen of All-under-Heaven docilely bowed before his wind. Why did this happen?
>
> I would reply that recently the world had for a long time been without [a true] monarch. The Zhou house had sunk into insignificance, the Five Hegemons have passed from the scene, and no commands were obeyed under Heaven. Hence, the regional lords governed relying on strength alone, the strong impinging on the weak, the many lording it over the few; arms and armor were never set aside, and the people grew exhausted and impoverished. Now, after Qin faced south and ruled All-under-Heaven, this meant that there is a Son of Heaven above. The masses hoped that they would obtain peace and security and there was nobody who did not whole-heartedly look up in reverence. This was the moment to preserve authority and stabilize achievements, the foundations of lasting peace.[25]

An astute thinker, Jia Yi realized that widespread support of the long-expected unification was a greater factor in Qin's final success than sheer force. After the long period of turmoil and wars, the people obtained peace and security; hence they acquiesced in Qin's domination. The First Emperor shrewdly appealed to these feelings to bolster the legitimacy of his rule. In his tours through the newly conquered realm, the emperor established stone steles on the tops of sacred mountains, on which he proudly proclaimed his achievements. In these inscriptions, the emperor repeatedly addressed the universal quest for peace and stability, reminding his subjects that "warfare will never rise again," that he "brought peace to All-under-Heaven," and that "the black-haired people [= the commoners] are at peace, never needing to take up arms." By "uniting All-under-Heaven, he put an end to harm and disaster, and then forever he put aside arms," ushering in the "Great Peace" (*tai ping*). The imperial propagandists even inscribed the newly issued weights and measures with a uniform text that began with the words "In his twenty-sixth year, the Emperor completely annexed all the regional lords under Heaven; the black-haired people are greatly tranquil." Thus, even in the marketplace, each customer was reminded that the emperor fulfilled the venerable aspirations of the Warring States period thinkers: "Stability is in unity"![26]

Aside from pure propaganda, Qin sought to convey to its subjects the feeling of stability and uniform orderly rule through a variety of practical and symbolic means. For example, they imposed unified systems of measures, weights, coinage, orthography, laws, and calendar, establishing thereby a standard repertoire of unification measures for the subsequent dynasties. Equally important was the incorporation of members of the conquered states' elites into the imperial regime. While Qin rulers naturally mistrusted members of the ruling lineages of the enemy states (whom they reportedly transferred to the vicinity of the Qin capital in order to control them), this mistrust did not pertain to other elite members of the eastern rivals. Even before unification, Qin, like other contemporaneous polities, routinely employed foreign advisers in high positions, notwithstanding occasional protests from the members of the ruling lineage. The "foreigners" were crucial for Qin's success: thus the administrative architect of the empire, Li Si (d. 208 BCE), was of Chu origin; the eminent general Meng Tian (d. 210 BCE) came from the eastern state of Qi, and many of the "erudites" at the Qin court came from Qi and the neighboring Lu. By promoting these men to the top of the administrative and military apparatus, the First Emperor vividly demonstrated to the inhabitants of the eastern states that they were not second-rank subjects but legitimate participants in the imperial project.

Attaining acceptance for a newly established universal empire was only one of manifold tasks that faced the Qin regime. A more challenging issue was sustaining the hard-won unity. How was the huge realm to be preserved intact? What did it require administratively? Here, there were no clear answers. One ready model, that of the Zhou kings who exercised suzerainty over highly autonomous regional lords, enjoyed a respectable pedigree; but in the eyes of many pre-Qin and Qin thinkers, it was too lax and could not prevent renewed disintegration. An alternative model of centralized rule emerged in many of the Warring States, most notably in preimperial Qin itself: it endowed the court with a much higher degree of control over the localities than in the Zhou case. However, the unified empire was immeasurably larger than any of the regional states; and it was unclear whether the tightly centralized Warring State model was applicable to the enormously expanding realm. The debates over proper administrative settlement began immediately after the unification had been accomplished. Several leading Qin ministers proposed reestablishment of autonomous princedoms in the eastern parts of the realm, emulating thereby the Zhou model. However, the Emperor, backed by Li Si, rejected this proposal:

> The world suffered immensely from incessant strife and warfare because of the regional lords and princes. Now, with the help of my ancestral spirits, All-under-Heaven has just been pacified. To reestablish princedoms means to sow weapons. Will it not be difficult then to demand peace and tranquillity?[27]

The Emperor's views prevailed: Qin extended its preimperial two-tier system of local administration to the entire realm, dividing it into thirty-six (later forty-two) commanderies (in later dynasties, prefectures) and numerous counties. The commanderies were headed by a triumvirate—a governor, a military commander, and a superintendent, whose tasks were primarily supervisory; this system of "checks and balances" prevented undue concentration of power in the hands of a single executive. Beneath was a horde of officials and clerks, who reached downward to the smallest hamlets, performing their tasks under the tight control of their superiors. Recently unearthed Qin legal and administrative documents disclose amazingly powerful mechanisms of control over local officials. An overseer of the subcounty unit applied to the county head to approve the appointment of a village chief and a postman in a local hamlet in the recently conquered southwestern territory. After four days, he received an answer: the application was rejected owing to the negligible size of the hamlet (only twenty-seven households). That the affairs of such a minor unit in a huge county were handled so swiftly and efficiently defies imagination; but as we shall see, this amazing efficiency came at a price.[28]

Several factors hindered the applicability of the Qin model in the long term. First, the sheer magnitude of the empire with its huge distances and highly heterogeneous local conditions made an ideal of uniform centralized rule very difficult to attain. Qin duly tried to improve internal communications by creating a series of radial "highways" from its capital, Xianyang, to the frontiers; but this was of no avail when major rebellions, which broke out soon after the death of the First Emperor in 210 BCE, disrupted communications and profoundly shattered the empire. Second, and more importantly, centralized control was a costly affair. Huge amounts of written information had to travel back and forth, imposing an undue burden on the locals, who had to provide post services and whose taxes had to support local officials. We cannot estimate accurately the weight of this administrative burden, but there is little doubt that it was enormous, and that it contributed indirectly to the flurry of popular uprisings that brought about the first imperial dynasty's swift demise.[29]

The breakup of Qin and the ensuing collapse of the sociopolitical order caused the pendulum of centralization to swing in the opposite, "Zhou," direction. First, the imprudent rebel leader Xiang Yu (d. 202 BCE) attempted restoration of a modified version of the multistate system. Having briefly tried to maintain a loosely unified empire under the puppet emperor, Xiang Yu then opted for an even looser model, in which he was to govern All-under-Heaven from the position of a "hegemon-king." Immediately, the void of legitimate power led to chaos, and the renewed war of all against all devastated most of the Chinese world. Then the more centralized model reemerged. Xiang Yu's rival and the founder of the Han dynasty, Liu Bang (d. 195 BCE), had skillfully posed as the only candidate able to restore unity and bring an end to war and turmoil, and this attracted many outstanding advisers and generals to his camp. Eventually, Liu Bang had to compromise his goal of centralized control by agreeing to reestablish highly autonomous princedoms, which were granted to some of his most powerful allies. Yet immediately after the establishment of the Han dynasty, Liu Bang and his successors diligently undertook the reduction of the princedoms' autonomy, moving steadily in the direction of ever-stronger centralization.[30]

Throughout the imperial millennia, the empire's administrative structure fluctuated between the two models depicted above. On the one hand, bureaucratic logic and political theory alike generally favored tighter control over local potentates, to prevent both potentially subversive political activities and power abuse in the localities. The imperial government developed an impressive repertoire of control techniques over local officials, ranging from the Qin-related "checks and balances" system, to the "rule of avoidance" that prevented an official from serving in his home province, to frequent rotation of officials among different localities. Central government gradually increased its intervention in appointments of low-level officials in counties and prefectures; and it established an elaborate inspection apparatus to monitor local administrators. These and a variety of other means were supposed to solidify unified rule.

Against these tendencies, there was a recurring pattern of decentralization and establishment of semi-independent satrapies under the nominal suzerainty of the emperor. These satrapies, like the Zhou fiefs, were ruled by lifelong or hereditary potentates, who controlled local economic, human, and military resources with minimal intervention from the emperor's court. There were several reasons for the resurrection of these autonomous units. The emperor could use them as an alternative to the regular system of local government if he mistrusted the officialdom, or when he had to reward his most powerful allies or kin. These considerations were particularly important under the rule of nomadic tribesmen, whose political operational mode was generally less centralized than was common in China proper. Furthermore, relegation of power to local potentates could cut the court's expenses and diminish the burden on the central apparatus. Moreover, local autonomy could allow greater flexibility in the ruling of remote territories or areas inhabited by ethnic minorities, where Chinese administrative practices were at odds with local conditions. Finally, decentralization could be helpful when the regime had to cope with extraordinary economic, or, more often, military situations. It may be argued that in terms of pure efficiency, the dispersal of royal authority might have been more attractive than excessive centralization.

This said, the dominant tendency, especially during the empire's second millennium, was toward increasing centralization of power, even at the expense of military and economic flexibility. In a pattern that we shall encounter in later chapters, the empire's leaders opted for stability at the expense of efficiency. The accumulated historical experience taught them that substantial devolution of the court's authority would sooner or later lead to the emergence of alternative loci of power and would inevitably bring about a new round of civil wars. Most imminently dangerous was relegation of military power to regional potentates. In the Han dynasty, it was employed to deal with internal rebels after 184 CE; in the Tang (618–906), to deal first with external and then with internal enemies; in the Western Jin (265–316), the Southern Dynasties (420–589), and, very briefly, in the beginning of the Ming dynasty (1368–1644), it was undertaken to enhance the imperial family's control over the military. The results invariably were the same: local military potentates, including the emperor's closest kin, were soon raising arms either to defend or to expand their autonomy or even to replace the ruling dynasty. It is not surprising, therefore, that in the second imperial millennium the general tendency was to reduce the power of regional military leaders, even when this effectively left the court barely defended against external or internal foes. The First Emperor's motto, "To reestablish princedoms means to sow weapons," became a lasting, albeit not unanimously accepted, lesson of China's history.

The overall commitment of the empire's leaders to stability did not preclude experiments aimed at enhancing the efficiency of regional rule within the rigidly centralized framework. One of the most interesting breakthroughs in this regard was achieved at the very end of the imperial period, when the Qing dynasty (1644–1912) introduced the system of provincial governors as mediators between the imperial center and the lower tiers of local administration. Leaders of earlier dynasties were generally averse to permanent administrative units above the prefecture (commandery) level; and when such units were formed, this usually signified the weakness of the imperial center (see, below, the example of the Tang dynasty). Yet a series of experiments that began under the Mongol Yuan dynasty (1271–1368) and continued throughout several centuries brought about the formation of a supraprefecture tier, the province, as a fully functioning unit of regional rule. The Manchu (Manju) Qing emperors, who, like the Mongols, were habitually inclined to delegate their power to the underlings, proved that controlled decentralization is workable: eventually, Qing provincial governors played a crucial role in the overall success of that dynasty in the first half of its rule. After two millennia, the empire's builders seem finally to have discovered a proper balance between the dictates of administrative efficiency and those of stable centralized rule.[31]

FROM DISINTEGRATION TO REUNIFICATION

The architects of the Chinese empire provided it with sophisticated ideological justification and with elaborate administrative tools aimed at sustaining unity, but none of these means could permanently prevent repeated disintegrations. Two political players were latently subversive of the imperial unity: regional elites and local potentates. The first of the two were less dangerous politically, since their goal was usually to protect local interests through enhancing their representation in the empire's administrative apparatus rather than disengaging from it. However, during periodic crises when local elites felt that the government did not heed their voices and the tax collectors disregarded their vested economic interests, they could shift their support to a local rebellious leader and challenge the court. Without their support, few local potentates could succeed in their "subversive" activities.

These local potentates—either military or civilian leaders, either the emperor's kin and fellow tribesmen, or even former rebels who were granted provincial authority in exchange for their submission—were the most formidable rivals of the central government in times of crisis. Normally, local governors were not natives of the area under their control and were not supposed to serve lengthy terms in a single locality. In times of lax control, however, a governor could occupy his position long enough to ingratiate himself with local elites, for instance by appointing their members to positions in his administration and by reducing the amount of tax revenue sent to the central government. Such a governor could emerge in an age of domestic turmoil as a natural leader of his province (or quasi-provincial territorial unit), a position that he could then turn into a springboard for establishing a new dynasty. Thus the de facto secession of provinces remained an almost inevitable outcome of major domestic crises well into the twentieth century. However, as I shall demonstrate below, centrifugal forces were of limited vitality; and after disintegration reached its apogee, a move back to the center invariably ensued.

To illustrate the cycle of disintegration and reunification in Chinese history, I shall focus on the Tang dynasty, the long decline of which exemplifies many of the empire's basic functioning principles. Tang suc ceeded to and inherited the centralizing tendencies of the preceding Sui dynasty (581–618), which had reunified China after a long period of fragmentation. The political elite of the Tang was strongly disinclined to allow renewed decentralization, and even succeeded in thwarting the plans of the second Tang emperor, Taizong (r. 626–649), who proposed establishing autonomous princedoms.[32] During the first century of its rule, the Tang may have been more centralized than any preceding dynasty since the Qin.

The decentralization of Tang rule came about as a by-product of its initial military and diplomatic successes, which brought about unprecedented territorial expansion. The need to provide swift military response to mobile enemies at the remote northern and western frontiers facilitated the establishment of a system of military commissioners (*jiedushi*). The commissioners controlled a relatively large area comprising several border prefectures; they were allowed to mobilize the human and economic resources of the subordinate prefectures, combining thereby military and civilian functions; they served for lengthier periods than ordinary officials, had the right to appoint subordinates, and enjoyed a high degree of operational autonomy. In its quest for military effectiveness, the Tang court thus sacrificed much of the empire's traditional caution with regard to autonomous power-holders.[33]

The court soon had to pay a high price for its lenience. When a powerful *jiedushi*, An Lushan (d. 757), found himself in a rivalry with the prime minister, he rebelled in 755 and dealt the dynasty a dreadful blow, briefly occupying both capitals, Luoyang and Chang'an (modern Xi'an). To survive, the court had to build a coalition of loyal military commanders, which eventually brought about a proliferation of the *jiedushi* system into the interior provinces. For the next century and a half, the emperors of the Tang dynasty faced a new situation characterized by the rise of powerful military leaders who evolved into full-scale governors of the newly formed circuits (or "provinces," a supraprefecture tier of local administration). The degree of the governors' loyalty to the court varied considerably, but they uniformly acted to expand their power at the court's expense: specifically, they tried to monopolize civil and military appointments in the area under their control, to reduce tax remittance to the central court, and to secure lifelong or even hereditary tenure for themselves. While not all of them were equally determined to pursue this course, the empire nonetheless soon developed into a conglomerate of more or less autonomous territorial units, with separate armies, and to a lesser extent separate systems of administration and financial management. Powerless, the court could manipulate the governors and employ them against one another, but it was no longer able to abolish completely the system of provincial autonomy.[34]

The beleaguered dynasty responded to the crisis with remarkable inge-
nuity, reforming its financial system and effectively employing alien
tribesmen, most notably the Uighurs, to augment its weakened military
forces.[35] Yet it seems that the primary reason behind its survivability in
the prolonged struggle against the governors was its exclusive position as
the supreme arbiter, even if not necessarily the true manager of "All-
under-Heaven." Insofar as there was no alternative to the principle of a
singularly legitimate "universal" monarch, autonomous governors could
not "secede" in a modern sense. Unless they were willing and able to position themselves as founders of a new dynasty (an exceptional step), the
governors continued to recognize the superiority of the Tang emperor,
even when defying his orders. They continued to employ the Tang calendar, ritual paraphernalia, and administrative vocabulary, and sought imperial confirmation of their position. Even the rebellious governors of
Hebei, the hotbed of An Lushan's uprising, continued to maintain relations with the Tang court, seeking a position akin to that of foreign tribu-
taries, whose ritual submission to the emperor had to be recompensed
with imperial recognition of their full-scale autonomy in domestic affairs
(more on this below).

Scholars sometimes understand the autonomous governors' ritual submission to the emperor as a mere veneer of full-scale independence, but
this is imprecise. Ritual inferiority significantly impaired the possibility of
a local unit's long-term autonomy. In exchange for his recognition of a
local potentate's legitimacy, a prudent emperor could demand the potentate's military assistance, increased tax remittance, or acceptance of the
imperial center's nominees to some of the posts within the restive province. Indeed, the Tang court was skillful enough to translate its symbolic
power into partial regeneration of centralized control; by the second
third of the ninth century, the center reestablished a meaningful presence
in all but a very few circuits.[36] However, beginning in the 870s, a series of
military mutinies and popular uprisings shattered Tang's sociopolitical
fabric anew, facilitating the reemergence of full-scale regional autonomy
under ruthless military leaders, many of whom came from among the
rebel ranks. Once again a coalition of loyal governors crushed the rebels;
but this time the court was unable to regain the initiative and restore its
fortunes.[37]

The major reason for the Tang dynasty's final demise was internal:
mired in the debilitating struggle between eunuchs and officials, the imperial court failed to utilize its ritual superiority to subdue the governors.
The last decades of Tang rule were a sad story of inadequate emperors
languishing as hapless pawns in the hands of rival potentates. Disintegration intensified: dozens of rival military governors became entangled in
an endless game of wars and alliances, in comparison to which even the

turmoil of the Warring States period looks like orderly rule. On the evidence of contemporaneous historical chronicles, one might easily conclude that reunification of the completely fragmented realm was utterly impossible.[38]

The de facto disintegration became a fait accompli in 907, when the powerful governor and former rebel Zhu Wen (852–912) delivered the coup de grace to the Tang, establishing his new, Later Liang dynasty (907–923). Zhu Wen's coup was ill-timed, however, coming after several military setbacks. Zhu Wen tried to bolster his position with an elaborate legitimation campaign, but neither performance of imperial rituals, nor manipulation of portents and omens, nor even his belated—and somewhat surprising, in light of his notorious ruthlessness—display of respect for Confucian scholarship could compensate for the weakness of his armies. Zhu Wen's foes refused to recognize his rule and established several independent regional regimes, elevating themselves to the positions of kings or emperors, and inaugurating thereby the de facto disintegration of the realm.[39]

The ongoing disintegration had been briefly checked in 923, when the Shatuo Turk leader, Li Cunxu (885–926), the self-proclaimed restorer of the Tang dynasty, inflicted a surprising defeat on the Later Liang, unified much of northern China, and even established partial or full authority over some of the southern parts of the realm. However, Li's ineptitude in domestic affairs caused his regime to disintegrate rapidly, and the reunification momentum was lost. Even in the northern part of the realm the unification remained thereafter highly vulnerable owing to ongoing internecine struggles among local military leaders, which ended only with the ascendancy of the Song dynasty in 960. More interesting were political dynamics in the south, where seven relatively stable states emerged in the Yangzi basin and southward. Although founded mostly by former rebels, these states gradually attained relative, even if never lasting, stability; their economy (and occasionally arts and culture) prospered, population increased, and their general situation remained more attractive than that of the war-plagued north. In terms of size, topography, economic and military resources, and the like, each of these states could well have become an independent and well-functioning unit. Nonetheless, this transformation did not occur, as eventually all these states were easily destroyed by the Song. What factors hindered their independence and allowed swift Song victory?[40]

I believe that lack of viability characterized not just regional states as such but the multistate order itself. This order was moribund not only because it was ideologically unacceptable, but no less significantly because it time and again proved to be unsustainable. The problem was not just the lack of adequate means to ensure long-term peaceful coexistence between rival regimes (on which, see the discussion above and more below) but also the impossibility of attaining domestic stability within each of these regimes. As noted by Naomi Standen, among others, the coexistence of several loci of recognized authority allowed any disgruntled official, and, worse, general, to shift sides and to begin serving his former master's bitter foe. Any domestic crisis within a regional state— for example, a succession struggle—could bring about mass defection of officials, governors, and generals, causing an immediate and dramatic shift in the balance of power among rival regimes. Since in the age of division "changing allegiance was readily justified and rarely criticized,"[41] it was extremely difficult for most of the leaders to impose their will on their underlings. In these conditions statesmen could not but revert to Mengzi's dictum: "Stability is in unity."

Given the common conviction that reunification is the only viable outcome of an age of division, leaders of regional regimes had two possible modes of action. The first was to proclaim themselves dukes, princes, or kings, while recognizing the nominal suzerainty of one of the self-proclaimed emperors. A local "king" (*guo wang*, the highest possible degree of autonomy) could even establish a separate ritual and administrative system and employ his own reign names, indicating thereby his possible intention to elevate himself to the position of emperor. Alternatively, he could adopt these symbols of sovereignty within his realm and in relations with weaker neighbors, while reverting to an inferior status when contacting an emperor whom he nominally recognized. Whatever course he chose, insofar as the "king" acquiesced in his inferior status vis-à-vis an "emperor" elsewhere, his regional state was doomed. It was all too clear to every political actor that the existence of autonomous kingdoms was but a temporal aberration, justifiable only insofar as there was no "true monarch" above. Sooner or later, a truly powerful emperor would emerge, and it would be his duty to abolish deviant kingdoms and turn them back into prefectures and counties. Thus recognition of one's ritual inferiority implied recognition of the provisional character of one's dynastic rule.

An alternative to submission—and the only act that meant real "independence"—would be to proclaim oneself an emperor, a new "Son of Heaven," second to no one. This, however, implied that a local leader sought the unification of All-under-Heaven under his aegis, which meant that he could neither coexist with other self-proclaimed emperors nor tolerate autonomous kingdoms, at least in the long term. As mentioned above, from the Warring States period on, it was universally accepted that only he who was able to unify the realm would become the "True Monarch." Therefore, an aspiring "universal" emperor had to adopt an aggressive stance toward other regional potentates, or at the very least to display his determination to reunify the realm through a variety of symbolic means.[42] Alliances and coalitions between the "emperors," or other policies aimed at attaining "partial [rather than universal] peace" (*pian'an*), were possible only as an ad hoc measure; it was well understood by all that the competition was a zero-sum game. A saying attributed to Confucius, "There are neither two suns in Heaven nor two Monarchs on earth,"[43] required a life-and-death struggle from which only one legitimate winner could emerge.

Ironically, therefore, the idea of the singularity of imperial rule as the guarantee for peace ruled out the peaceful coexistence of two or more "emperors," dooming the fragmented world to a bitter struggle, which allowed no real compromises, no territorial adjustments, and no sustainable peace agreements. Predictably, the strife between aspiring emperors turned into a nightmare of bloodshed and cruelty, which, in turn, enhanced expectations of renewed unification as the only feasible way out of mutual extermination. The notion that "stability is in unity" acted therefore as a self-fulfilling prophecy.

This peculiar situation of inevitable warfare preceding successful reunification immensely benefited the most powerful and resolute of the contenders. Whenever an aspiring emperor succeeded in inflicting substantial defeats on his rivals, this could create an avalanche of successes, as minor leaders with limited ambitions would flock to his camp, exchanging their status as regional princes or kings for firm positions in the newly evolving hierarchy of the unified empire.[44] Even if local kings remained defiant, many of their underlings, including generals and top officials, would switch sides to ensure their safety in anticipation of their state's inevitable demise. And, usually, local elites would not defend the regional regime unless the unifier was so imprudent as to alienate them by exceptionally cruel or avaricious behavior. Hence, after a lengthy period of division, "the great forces of All-under-Heaven" would indeed inevitably unify.

The post-Tang history of the South serves as a good illustration of this trajectory. Among southern rulers, the weakest preferred the position of regional king, recognized by the northern emperor, which allowed many of them to attain relative stability for their states; while stronger leaders fluctuated between, on the one hand, adopting the imperial title and taking the inevitable aggressive stance toward their neighbors, and, on the other, temporarily recognizing the suzerainty of northern emperors. Of these regimes only the Southern Tang dynasty (937–975) under Li Jing (r. 943–961) became fully engaged in the competition to unify the realm, successfully annexing two of the neighboring principalities and planning northward expansion. Yet Li Jing's fortunes were reversed after the north was reunified under energetic leaders of the Later Zhou dynasty (951–

960). The second Zhou emperor not only succeeded in substantially reducing the Southern Tang territory but also forced Li Jing to relinquish the imperial title. When the Song dynasty succeeded the Later Zhou, it promptly renewed southern campaigns. These were surprisingly swift: aside from the Southern Tang, which resisted the Song armies for fifteen months, other kingdoms were annexed within a few months, difficult terrain and formidable armies notwithstanding. By 978, the last of the southern kings had voluntarily yielded his position, facilitating the bloodless annexation of his state of Wu-Yue (907–978). A century-long fragmentation was over.[45]

The success of Song, just like that of most other unifying regimes before and after it, would never have been possible had most of the elites and the general populace of the vanquished states not accepted the annexation. When they did resist, military campaigns changed drastically. Thus it took the Song armies only two months to conquer the state of Later Shu (934–965) in Sichuan; but then widespread pillage and killings by the Song troops caused a massive rebellion, which took almost two years to quell. The Song founder, Zhao Kuangyin (927–976), learned the lesson; thenceforth he imposed strict discipline on his troops and rebellions never recurred. Evidently, inhabitants of southern states realized that swift surrender would be preferable to a protracted war of resistance that would deplete local resources and turn everyday life into a nightmare. Insofar as conquerors acted prudently, allowing the elites of the occupied states to join the ranks of national officialdom, and did not overburden the local population with unreasonable taxation, the acquiescence of the regional regime's subjects could be taken for granted.

Another major factor that made reunification inevitable was the determination of northern leaders to pursue the course of full-scale integration of regional states into a newly unified empire. This determination was itself dictated by the realization that the preservation of autonomous loci of power would be detrimental both to future stability and to the overall legitimacy of the newly formed imperial regime. Hence, when approached by the Southern Tang envoy who pleaded for the retention of his state as Song's faithful vassal, which would serve the Song as a son serves his father, Zhao Kuangyin pointedly remarked: "Would the so-called father and son maintain two separate households?" The question was demagogic (to be sure, separate familial households existed throughout Chinese history, even if never lauded); but the envoy understood the message: he "had nothing to offer in response and withdrew."[46]

The pattern depicted above recurred with only minor variations throughout most of Chinese history. The inherent understanding that political fragmentation must inevitably be reversed encouraged fierce competition among the would-be unifiers. While chief contenders exhausted themselves, minor players were warily watching, prepared to support the winner. Richard Mather summarizes these dynamics with regard to the minor states established by non-Chinese ethnic groups in northwestern China in the late fourth and early fifth centuries:

> There is even something pathetic in the eagerness with which the various non-Chinese groups would offer their allegiance [to succeeding local potentates] always in the hope that at last a leader had appeared who would bring unity and a measure of stability.[47]

In this atmosphere, reunification became an inevitable outcome of the period of disunion. As the multistate order was considered neither sustainable nor legitimate, separatist tactics were doomed, and indeed were never pursued. Each of the players knew well that "the great forces of All-under-Heaven after prolonged division must unify."

Limits of All-under-Heaven

Up to this point I have been employing primarily Chinese traditional terminology, speaking of the unity not of "China" (a modern term, of course), but of "All-under-Heaven." It is time now to ascertain which areas belonged to this "subcelestial" realm. Should the unification involve only the lands of China proper (i.e., roughly the territory under the control of Qin, sometimes referred to as "Nine Provinces," *jiu zhou*),[48] or those of Greater China, as formed under the Han and (briefly) Tang dynasties; or was the referent the entire known world? To reformulate the question politically: in which parts of the known world would the emperors tolerate the autonomy or outright independence of local potentates, and where would they consider such independence to impugn the emperor's legitimacy? Changing answers to these questions determined to a great extent the empire's foreign policy.

When discussing the intellectuals of the Warring States period, I emphasized several times their perceived universalism; and this claim may have irritated some readers. After all, it is often presumed that the Chinese were chauvinistic and "culturalistic," if not outright nationalistic; that they despised outside peoples as "barbarians"; and that their view of the world was exclusive rather than inclusive.[49] These suppositions, however, even if applicable to certain thinkers and intellectual currents during the imperial age, are largely invalid for the formative age of China's intellectual and political tradition, the Warring States period. Although most contemporaneous texts treat alien tribesmen as morally and culturally impaired, they invariably share an optimistic view about their ultimate mutability. If—and when—the aliens of the four quarters were incorporated into the realm ruled by the sage monarch, their backward customs would be modified and they would join the civilized world. This all-inclusiveness became a touchstone of the sage's rule; hence legendary sage rulers of the past were either hailed for having attained the submission of all "from within the Four Seas" or criticized for having failed to do so. In any case, the extension of the sage's rule to the entirety of humankind was understood as a normative state of affairs.[50]

The optimism of the intellectuals of the Warring States period with regard to the ultimate attainability of truly universal unification derived not only from their idealism but from their good historical and limited geographical knowledge. With regard to the first, thinkers might have been aware of the relatively easy absorption of alien ethnic groups who lived on the fringes of or within the Zhou world during the Springs-and-Autumns period. By the Warring States period, these groups—for example, the Rong and the Di, some of whom had repeatedly challenged the Zhou polities in the past—almost disappear from historical accounts, which suggests their overall amalgamation within the Zhou cultural *oikoumenē*. It was reasonable, therefore, to expect that similar processes would in due time encompass other neighboring tribes.

In addition, the universality of Chinese thinkers' outlook may also have derived from their limited geographic horizons. Unlike the inhabitants of early Europe, the Near East, or South Asia, who were well aware of the existence of powerful civilizations elsewhere, thinkers and statesmen of the Warring States period apparently lacked any knowledge of civilization centers beyond the Zhou world. Even the nomadic pastoralists, whose presence shaped Chinese political, military, and cultural life during the imperial millennia, were marginal players in China proper prior to the imperial unification.[51] This explains why the thinkers could consider the creation of a state unifying the whole known world to be a feasible goal. This belief is duly reflected in the stele inscriptions erected by the First Emperor, in which he boasted:

> Within the six directions, / this is the land of the Emperor. / To the west it ranges to the flowing sands, / To the south it completely takes in where the doors face north, / To the east it enfolds the eastern sea, / To the north, it goes beyond Da Xia. / Wherever human traces reach, / There is none who did not declare himself [the Emperor's] subject.[52]

This piece of political propaganda might in this specific case have reflected the Emperor's genuine belief that the entire world had indeed been unified;[53] yet this belief was shattered a few years after the stele was erected. Having decided to expand his boundaries farther toward the barely known, the First Emperor sent his armies southward and northward. In the latter direction, Qin repulsed the nomadic Xiongnu tribes, who theretofore had been of limited significance in Chinese politics. Chinese expansion northward had already begun in the Warring States period, when nomads were gradually pushed into ever more arid areas.

Now, as the victorious Qin armies occupied the strategically important Ordos area, driving the Xiongnu further to the north, the emperor decided that this would be the limit for further expansion and ordered the construction of a lengthy wall to protect his new lands. This wall, which joined earlier walls built by the Warring States on their northern frontier, was erected shortly after the demolition of numerous internal walls that marked the boundaries of the former Warring States. The act was symbolic: the First Emperor distinguished in the most visible way China proper, in which no internal walls would be tolerated, from the outside world, which was to remain beyond Chinese control. The limits to All-under-Heaven had been set.[54]

The encounter with the nomads became the single most significant event in the political, cultural, and ethnic history of the Chinese. Not a single ethnic group on China's frontiers had a comparable impact on China's life, or was able to challenge Chinese political culture as the nomads did. This challenge was threefold. First, the arid steppe zone was basically unconquerable and ungovernable, and its nomadic and seminomadic dwellers remained largely inassimilable to the sedentary, Chinese, ways of life. Second, the nomads swiftly established their independent tribal confederations, the very existence of which undermined the notion of the singularity and universality of the Chinese emperors' rule. Third, the nomads gradually became involved in Chinese domestic affairs, eventually conquering parts of China and much later the whole of the country. As we shall see in the next section, in this latter endeavor, the nomadic rulers actually benefited from China's pervasive adherence to the principle of political unity.[55]

China's nomadic nightmare began immediately after the collapse of the Qin dynasty. The recently organized Xiongnu tribal confederation, the very emergence of which may have been a response to Qin's northward expansion, reversed the nomads' fortunes. The Xiongnu took advantage of China's internal turmoil and reoccupied much of the territory they had lost, inflicting in the process heavy blows on the Han imperial armies. Frustrated, the Han emperors recognized the Xiongnu as a "rival state" (*di guo*), that is, China's equal; established marriage alliance with the Xiongnu leader, the *chanyu*; and bestowed lavish gifts on him to prevent further clashes. Unfortunately for China and the nomads, this "peace of relatives" (*he qin*) proved unsustainable: the unruly tribesmen repeatedly raided the Chinese frontiers, resulting in renewed military tension, renegotiation of the treaties, and a steady increase in the value of China's "gifts" to the Xiongnu. This mode of relations was humiliating to the Han and indicative of the weakness of its ruling house. Not surprisingly, a leading early Han thinker, Jia Yi, complained that appeasing the Xiongnu meant "letting legs be up, and the head—down."[56] Jia Yi and many other Han courtiers demanded decisive change in relationships with the aliens to demonstrate the superiority of the Son of Heaven.[57]

Han Emperor Wu (r. 141–87 BCE), the single most energetic Han ruler, reversed the tide once again. His armies inflicted a series of blows on the nomads, dramatically expanding the Han realm to an extent that dwarfed even the Qin empire. Emperor Wu's exceptionally vigorous expansion appears to have been driven, among other considerations, by his peculiar type of imperial ideology. A previously marginal text, the *Gongyang* commentary on the canonical *Springs and Autumns Annals*, was suddenly elevated in Emperor Wu's court to almost sacral status; and insofar as this text advocated the eventual incorporation of the aliens into the realm of the True Monarch, it provided Emperor Wu's expansionist endeavors with an excellent ideological excuse.[58] Indeed, only a very few Chinese emperors could match Emperor Wu's enthusiasm for military expeditions to the remotest corners of the realm: from North Korea to Yunnan and from the Ferghana valley to Hainan Island. Not only were the Xiongnu repulsed; scores of smaller polities were annexed or subjugated.

Ideology and enthusiasm aside, Emperor Wu, his aides, and his successors eventually realized that incorporating remote territories within the empire would be economically unfeasible and militarily unsustainable. The solution, which had a lasting impact on China's ties with its neighbors, was to focus on the ritualistic facade of the Chinese emperor's superiority. The so-called tribute system, which had been devised to maintain diplomatic and commercial ties with alien polities, turned into an important asset for preserving the image (sometimes entirely fictitious) of China's supreme position vis-à-vis the foreign states, while simultaneously allowing the aliens to maintain domestic autonomy, if not outright independence. Through a combination of economic enticement, military intimidation, and skillful diplomacy, the Han dynasty and most of its heirs succeeded in preserving the vision of the Son of Heaven's unrivaled position at the apex of the universal ritual pyramid without inciting much resentment in foreign leaders. Even the proud Xiongnu, who engaged the Han in a lasting conflict for more than eighty years, had finally succumbed to Han demands, recognizing its superiority in 53 BCE. Once again, it was possible to speak of the Chinese emperor as a "universal" monarch.[59] Indeed, not just the Han but incomparably weaker dynasties, the rule of which was limited to a small portion of China proper, such as the aforementioned Southern Tang, could at times utilize tribute relations to maintain their self-image as a "universal" dynasty, which "possesses the four quarters" and "leads Chinese and barbarians" alike.[60]

Throughout subsequent Chinese history, one can discern a constant tension between what Wang Gungwu terms the rhetoric of the inclusiveness of the emperor's rule and of China's superiority over alien polities,[61] and that of tacit—and yet quite recognizable—division between the "internal" realm, where the power of the emperor had to be comprehensive, and the "external" one, where compromises were tolerable. The boundaries between the "internal" and the "external" realms constantly fluctuated, reflecting the shifting balance of power between China and its neighbors, and the changing demographic and cultural composition of the extensive frontiers of China proper. At times, such as during the peak of territorial expansion under the Tang dynasty, intermediate areas under military rule could be established, expanding well into the Central Asia heartland, while the "external" realm was defined as an area of "loose rein" (*jimi*), where the superiority of the Chinese monarch remained primarily symbolic. At times of weakness, the designation "external" could be applied not only to border areas once under Chinese control, but even—scandalously—to the Chinese heartland itself, the Yellow River valley, ruled by the Jurchens since 1127.[62] Regions once rendered "external" could be firmly reincorporated into "China proper," as happened to the Gansu and Yunnan Provinces under the Ming dynasty, while other areas could move in the opposite direction, as happened to North Vietnam, once an imperial province, which turned into an "external subject."

Most Chinese dynasties refrained from active attempts to expand the "internal" areas in which the real unity was maintained; it was cheaper to preserve the nominal "universality" of the monarch's rule, as represented primarily in the tribute system, and not to attempt the military and administrative incorporation of alien lands and their hostile populations. Nonetheless, the desire for real mega-unification remained latently observable throughout imperial history. Not incidentally, some of China's nomadic rulers, whose dynasties fared much better than native ones in projecting their rule beyond China proper, considered this success to be one of the major foundations of their dynasty's legitimacy. Thus the Yongzheng Emperor (r. 1723–1735) of the Manchu Qing dynasty proudly proclaimed:

> Unity of the Central Lands [China proper] began with Qin; unity beyond the border passes began with [the Mongol] Yuan [1271–1368], and peaked under our dynasty. Never before were Chinese and foreigners one family and the country so expansive as under our dynasty![63]

These words, pronounced in the midst of bitter polemics with a dissenting Chinese subject over the legitimacy of Manchu rule, are revealing. The Yongzheng Emperor was not a warmonger; actually at the beginning of his career he contemplated withdrawal from some of the territories acquired under his father, the Kangxi Emperor (r. 1661–1722), most notably Tibet.[64] Yet he might have apprehended that the remarkable territorial expansion of the Qing and their incorporation of the alien periphery into the empire proper would be hailed by many Chinese subjects as a hallmark of Qing's success. These sentiments were echoed by the Yong-zheng Emperor's son, the Qianlong Emperor (r. 1736–1795), who appealed to the "greatness of All-under-Heaven" to silence critical voices of those advisers, who feared that the Qing ongoing expansion would overstretch its human and material resources.[65] Insofar as the emperors' expectations that appeals to universality would be a convincing argument in domestic debates were correct (and we have no reasons to assume otherwise), they indicate that a latent desire for attaining truly universal unification remained intact—or was reproduced—a full two millennia after the First Emperor ordered the construction of the Great Wall, which was supposed to set limits to "All-under-Heaven."

GREAT UNITY UNDER NOMADIC RULE

The Yongzheng Emperor's invocation of the "Great Unity" ideal to bolster the legitimacy of his "alien" dynasty brings us to the last point of the present discussion: the impact of the ideal of unified rule on China's nomadic rulers. What was the degree of their commitment to the unification of All-under-Heaven, and how did this commitment (or the lack thereof) influence their position vis-à-vis their Chinese subjects? The answer to this question, I hope, will help elucidate a rarely noticed aspect of the complex process of the nomads' adaptation to Chinese political culture.

The nomadic and seminomadic neighbors of China conquered significant portions of China proper, including its historical heartland in the Yellow River and Wei River basins in the early fourth century CE, ushering in the period of "Northern and Southern dynasties" (318–589). The nomads were drawn into China's internal affairs almost incidentally; but once in charge of northern China, the conquerors had to adapt themselves to their new role as rulers of sedentary society.[66] This adaptation was a multifaceted process that cannot be discussed here in full; but it is important to note that the nomads did not mechanically copy Chinese practices but rather adjusted them to the peculiarities of their native society and to their own political culture. This complexity is duly observable in their employment of the idea of unified rule.

The nomads had their own concept of Great Unity: they believed that the high god of the steppe, Heaven/Tengri, confers the right to rule on a single charismatic clan. This notion had already emerged vividly in the Xiongnu empire, and it surely influenced the nomadic rulers of China in their endorsement of the Chinese idea of unified rule. However, ostensible similarities notwithstanding, the nomads' idea of unity differed from that of the Chinese in three marked respects. First, Tengri did not bestow his mandate on every generation; hence, in contrast to the Chinese case, the unity of the pastoralists was not conceived of as a natural state of affairs but rather as a peculiar situation attainable only under truly charismatic leaders or in times of crisis; political fragmentation was therefore a tolerable situation. Second, demographic and economic peculiarities of the pastoral economy precluded the establishment of a tightly centralized Chinese-style empire in the steppe; hence the nomads' "unity" was intrinsically lax and, with a few exceptions, tolerant of a much greater degree of regional autonomy than was acceptable in China proper. Third, for most nomadic rulers (Mongols are a notable exception) ruling "All-under-Heaven" actually meant ruling "the felt tent dwellers," that is, the steppe world only. Therefore they were usually satisfied with establishing their rule over the pastoralists but did not seek to rule sedentary China, and their notion of unity was intrinsically more limited than was the Chinese ideal.[67]

This background explains why the nomadic rulers of the northern dynasties in the fourth–sixth centuries did not wholeheartedly commit themselves to the goal of unification, despite occasional proclamations of their intention to unify the realm. Their hesitation derived in part from practical considerations: nomadic cavalryman could not easily penetrate the Yangzi barrier, and there were fears that a military adventure in the south would benefit enemies in the north. Yet it is also likely that in the eyes of many northern leaders, southern China was not supposed to be conquered at all: the coexistence of northern and southern regimes might have been seen as a continuation of the bifurcation of power between the steppe and China proper, like that, for example, between the Han and the Xiongnu. Thus, despite their obvious military superiority, northern leaders did not allocate sufficient resources to conquer the south. It may be not incidental, therefore, that the two most serious efforts to attain true unification under the Northern Dynasties occurred under the rule of those leaders who were most deeply committed to Chinese political culture, namely, Fu Jian (338–385, r. 357–385) of the Former Qin (350–394) and Emperor Xiaowen (r. 471–499) of the Northern Wei (386–534). Eventually, unification was attained only when the late sixth-century Sino-nomadic leaders of northwestern China, who combined the military skills of the nomads with the Chinese determination to achieve unity, finally allocated sufficient resources to subdue the South and put an end to centuries of division.[68]

The nomadic challenge to the notion of unity recurred in the tenth century, in the aftermath of the Tang dynasty's demise. The northeastern Khitan tribesmen formed the new Liao dynasty (907–1125), which swiftly established its hegemony over the eastern section of the steppe belt, and over sixteen northeastern prefectures of China proper. Unlike other nomadic states, the Liao from its inception acted as a proper "Chinese" dynasty: its rulers adopted the Chinese imperial title and claimed to be true heirs of the great Tang dynasty. As such they were expected to try to unify all of China under their aegis; and their active involvement in the affairs of northern China in the post-Tang era could have suggested precisely this course of affairs. In 947, Liao briefly occupied Kaifeng, the capital at the time of northern China, and for a short while—before their rapid withdrawal—it seemed that China faced a new period of nomadic rule in the north, and potentially in the whole of the country.[69]

These expectations notwithstanding, Liao rulers resisted the temptation to enter the nightmarish politics of divided China. They continued to maintain a dual identity, combining nomadic and Chinese traditions in their administration, and appeared to be satisfied to rule over just the sixteen prefectures of China proper. Liao remained the most powerful state in East Asia even after the Song dynasty reunified most of China in 960; and its military prowess enabled it to negotiate an exceptionally favorable treaty with the Song in 1005. According to the Treaty of Shanyuan, the Song emperor recognized his Liao counterpart as his equal; Liao retained the sixteen prefectures and received huge annual payments from the Song court. The treaty proved remarkably viable: aside from brief conflicts in 1042 and 1074–1076, both sides maintained peace, even if, at times, grudgingly.[70]

In terms of realpolitik, the Shanyuan Treaty was a good bargain for the Song: even annual payments to Liao were minuscule in comparison with the costs of war, and lasting peace allowed Song rulers to create a remarkably stable and efficient state. And yet the treaty undermined the very foundations of dynastic legitimacy. Recognizing the equal status of the Liao emperor was bad enough; but it could be tolerated if the Khitans remained pure aliens, like the Turks, Uighurs, or Tibetans, whose independent and equal status had been recognized by China's rulers in the past. Yet Liao presented itself as a Chinese dynasty; it demanded equality in terms of Chinese diplomatic protocol; and it ruled Chinese-inhabited territories to the south of the Great Wall. Its persistence meant that the Song emperors failed to complete the unification of the realm, and this challenged their position as "True Monarchs." To aggravate the matter, the normalization of two concurrent emperors encouraged new players, most notably the Tangut Xi Xia kingdom (1038–1227), to attempt to create yet more loci of recognized authority on a par with the Song and the Liao. The notion of the singularity of the Chinese Son of Heaven had been greatly compromised.[71]

Members of the Song political and intellectual elite faced a difficult task in trying to come to terms with the new situation. While the practical advantages of the Shanyuan Treaty and the lasting peace on the vulnerable northern frontier were self-evident, and while the exceptionality of the Liao in comparison with earlier nomadic polities was readily recognized, the idea of lasting parity with the Liao was nonetheless considered abnormal. In the short term, Song intellectuals were ready to admit the inevitable bifurcation between the imperial rhetoric and the reality; but in the long term the insistence on the universality of the emperor's power could not be dismissed.[72] Suffice it to mention that two of the leading Song intellectuals, Ouyang Xiu (1007–1072) and Sima Guang (1019–1086), argued in influential essays that the only true criterion of dynastic legitimacy is the ability to unify "All-under-Heaven."[73] Clearly, the Song rulers failed to do so. What impact did this have on their legitimacy?

Ouyang and Sima did not pose the question directly; they were not warmongers, after all. However, their writings and others of that ilk created an atmosphere of deep dissatisfaction with the Shanyuan Treaty and fueled latent hopes for change. Even after a century of largely peaceful coexistence with the rival court, this was considered an aberration, to be corrected whenever conditions permitted. "Irredentism" (or, more precisely, the drive to finalize unification) had deeply influenced the Song court since the second half of the eleventh century; and it eventually caused the dynastic disaster: Emperor Huizong (r. 1101–1125) chose to ally with Liao's foes, the Jurchen Jin dynasty (1115–1234).[74] The Jurchens overpowered the Liao but almost immediately moved against Song, driving it south of the Yangzi and eventually enforcing a much more humiliating treaty, in which the Song emperors recognized their inferiority vis-à-vis Jin.

Song history, especially the history of Northern Song (960–1127), poses therefore an intriguing alternative to the common narrative of the advantages of unification for ensuring peace. Pragmatically, the Shanyuan Treaty was a more efficient means of preserving peace than "irredentist" war; and had the Song emperors agreed to discount the sixteen prefectures from "All-under-Heaven," they might have enjoyed peace and stability for a considerably longer period. It was the ideological determination to attain "full" unity rather than practical considerations that led the Song to denounce the Shanyuan Treaty and try to regain the lost lands. The resultant debacle was extremely costly: although the crippled dynasty succeeded in preserving an impressive degree of internal stability and economic prowess for another century and a half, its position in continental East Asia remained precarious. An attempt to eliminate the Jurchen menace eventually led it to cooperate with the Mongols, and it was the Mongols who put an end to the Song dynasty after a prolonged and heroic war of resistance, which ended with the dramatic drowning of the last Song emperor and many of his courtiers after the naval defeat near modern Hong Kong, in 1279.[75]

The Mongols' rule opens a final chapter in my discussion of the impact of the "Great Unity" paradigm on Chinese history. The Mongol conquest of China (especially of its northern parts) was as violent as Mongol victories were elsewhere; of all rulers of China the Mongols were the least inclined to assimilate within the Chinese culture; and their policy of relying on foreigners and ethnic minorities at the expense of native cadres should have deeply alienated the Chinese elite. Nonetheless, the Mongols were deemed during their reign and thereafter—including nowadays—legitimate rulers of China, and despite occasional anti-Mongol diatribes, their image in China was considerably better than in other parts of their worldwide empire.[76] The reason for this is not difficult to find: as unifiers of the Chinese world, the Mongols put an end to the long-term ambiguity of the Song period coexistence of two or more "Sons of Heaven." Chinggis Khan (ca. 1162–1227) was the first steppe ruler to commit himself to the literal unification of the *entire* world (the steppe and the sown areas alike); and when his grandson, Khubilai Khan (r. 1260–1294), had brought the entire Chinese realm under Mongol rule, this enhanced his legitimacy both among his tribesmen and among the Chinese subjects.[77] Thenceforth, "All-under-Heaven" remained unified, albeit mostly under alien rule. The advantages of unification in the eyes of the Chinese elite (and probably of the whole population) clearly outweighed the disadvantages of alien rule.

This final observation suggests that the "Great Unity" paradigm was not just an essential feature of Chinese political culture but the most foundational of all. Even the explicitly discriminatory conquest regime fared relatively well in China's history owing to its attainment of unification, unprecedented in its geographic scope. The Mongols might have dismissed many Chinese cultural norms; but their blending of nomadic and Chinese ideas of Great Unity into a coherent whole made their accommodation possible both in real time and long after their dynasty was overthrown. The Yongzheng Emperor, whose statement in favor of mega-unification I cited above, was right: steadfast commitment to the goal of the unification of "All-under-Heaven" was the sine qua non for any dynasty—be it native or "alien"—to be accepted.

EPILOGUE: FRAGMENTATION REVISITED

The notion of Great Unity is probably the most distinctive production of China's political ideology. Having been formed long before the empire came into existence, it was repeatedly reinforced through official rhetoric, imperial historiography, and other means of ideological production, turning into the pivotal principle of Chinese political culture. While at times the need to accommodate political and military constraints re-

quired the leaders to refrain from actively pursuing the goal of unification, such pursuit of "partial appeasement" (*pian'an*) was invariably conceived of as a temporary compromise, not as abandonment of the goal of
the realm's unification. Lasting compromises were acceptable—if unwelcome—only with regard to the territorial extent of the due-to-be-unified
realm, but not with regard to the elimination of alternative loci of power
within China proper.

In the late twentieth century, several scholars opined that the quest for
unity in China is primarily a historiographic construct, which reflects the
common predilection of imperial history-writers to emphasize the legitimacy of a single monarch and to denigrate regional rulers as illegitimate.[78] I hope that in the preceding pages I have marshaled enough evidence to show that, beyond obvious historiographic bias, the quest for
unity was very much a reality: this ideological paradigm deeply influenced political behavior in the ages of unity and division alike. And yet it
is useful to readdress the biases of traditional historians. Was the period
of fragmentation indeed as gloomy as most of them tend to depict it? Or
rather, echoing Rafe de Crespigny, should we steer clear of the assumption "that grand centralized authority was an advantage to the people or
the culture of China"?[79]

The answer is not simple. On the one hand, there is no doubt that the
ages of division were not just periods of stagnation and despair. To the
contrary: the ideological richness of the Warring States, the Buddhist
flowering under the Southern and Northern Dynasties, and economic expansion and technological innovativeness under many of the post-Tang
regional kingdoms are undeniable. On the other hand, we should not
forget that what most people wanted was peace and stability—and those
were unattainable in the ages of division. Interstate war was far more
devastating than the incursions of foreigners. Pillage, indiscriminate killings, enforced mobilizations, deliberate destruction of civilian infrastructure, the burning of the enemy's granaries, and, of course, mass-scale
murder and rape: all those turned political fragmentation into a nightmare. Moreover, since internecine wars were commonly waged in China's
fertile heartland, their destructiveness dwarfed the human and economic
costs the population had to pay under even the most cruel and tyrannical
regime. Suffice it to cite Shen Yue's (441–513) description of the grave
results of the mid-fifth-century wars between the states of Northern Wei
(386–534) and Liu Song (420–479):

> The strong were killed, the weak—imprisoned. Of several dozens of
> thousands of households in the area from the Yangzi and Huai to the
> Qing and Ji rivers, even one in a hundred could not flee to lakes and

marshes. Villages became wasteland, wells were empty; none will return to hear the dogs' barking and the cocks' cries.[80]

This gloomy picture was all too common during the periods of disunion. Although astute regional rulers, such as the kings of Wu-Yue (907–978 CE), succeeded at times in ensuring relative stability and peace for their subjects, this was an exception, not the rule. As China never developed adequate means of peaceful coexistence between contending regimes, and as their conflicts were not confined to border incidents but were wars of mutual extermination, the only way to stop such bloodshed was unification. Neither the splendor of local courts, nor technological innovations, nor economic expansion under contending regimes could reduce the immense suffering of the populace. The saying "Stability is in unity" was self-evident for the people of China throughout the imperial millennia and beyond.

CHAPTER 2

The Monarch

> There is no turmoil greater than the absence of the Son of
> Heaven; without the Son of Heaven, the strong overcome the
> weak, the many lord it over the few, they incessantly use arms
> to harm each other.

> From the earliest generations, multiple states were
> extinguished in All-under-Heaven, but the Way of the ruler did
> not decline: this is because it benefits All-under-Heaven.

BOTH EPIGRAPHS are taken from the *Lüshi chunqiu*, the major ideological compendium composed on the eve of the imperial unification of 221 BCE. The ideas they convey, namely, the fear of sociopolitical disintegration without a single powerful monarch and the belief that a ruler-centered polity is the only normal and normative situation on earth, can be considered a succinct summary of the ideological consensus that crystallized during the Warring States period and remained unshaken until the very end of the imperial age. Throughout the intervening two-odd millennia, China was ruled by an immense variety of individuals: dreadful tyrants and weaklings, capable autocrats and mediocrities. Almost every single emperor was bitterly criticized by his underlings and his inadequacy mercilessly exposed by subsequent historians, but the fundamental idea of monarchic rule as the singularly acceptable form of government was not questioned. It is not surprising, then, that many leading historians consider monarchism to be the quintessential feature of Chinese political culture.[1]

In theory, the Chinese emperor was the single most powerful human being in the world. His exaltedness was, above all, symbolic: by the mere fact of his singularity, the emperor personified the supreme principle of the realm's unity, while in his capacity as the "Son of Heaven," he acted as the sole mediator with and representative of the highest deity, Heaven. The emperor presided over the elaborate system of state rituals and performed (personally or through substitutes) manifold sacrifices through which he supposedly ensured his subjects' well-being. His sacredness was conceived of as "matching" (*pei*) Heaven itself; hence he could promote or demote any deity or abolish any cult. He was venerated as the supreme regulator of time and space: years were counted according to his reign titles, and the annual ritual calendar was invalid without his approval. Elaborate rites elevated him to superhuman heights; his body and his paraphernalia were considered sacrosanct and any harm to them regarded as the gravest crime; even his personal name was tabooed. The emperor's august presence was disseminated throughout society down to its lowest levels through a variety of ceremonies, legends, and even proverbs.[2] The institution of emperorship was the ritual pivot of the Chinese polity from 221 BCE until the early twentieth century; during that lengthy period China without an emperor was as inconceivable as the Catholic Church without a pope.

The symbolic importance of the emperor was duly matched by the magnitude of real power that he was expected to hold. The emperor was the chief administrator, legislator, and judge of the realm; he was its commander in chief, supreme pontiff, and top educator; he was the nominal possessor of all the property "within the seas"; no important decision or major appointment could be valid without his explicit approval. There were no institutional limitations to his power; no group enjoyed legal autonomy from his will; and the official discourse often referred to him as a superhuman Sage (*sheng*), postulating the emperor's moral and intellectual, in addition to political, superiority over his subjects. Few if any monarchs in human history could rival the theoretical power of their Chinese counterparts.[3]

In the eyes of many Western observers, such as Montesquieu (1689–1755), the hugeness of the Chinese emperor's power turned him into the paradigmatic "oriental despot"; and this view eventually gained prominence in China as well, with the advent of republicanism in the early twentieth century.[4] There is no doubt that there was significant despotic potential in the institution of the emperorship, and that at times it was fully realized; yet, as I shall show below, reducing the Chinese empire to a millennia-long tyranny would be far too simplistic. First, the emperor's whims were normally checked—with varying degrees of success—by the members of the powerful and self-aware bureaucratic stratum, who could employ such means as moral suasion, active or passive noncompliance, or even veiled threats of rebellion to discourage the monarch from abusing his power. Second, and more significant, the imperial bureaucrats developed a subtle and yet efficient system of "checks and balances" through which they were able to direct all but the most strong-willed monarchs toward collegial modes of decision making and relegation of power to the ministers. Quite surprisingly, the supposedly omnipotent monarch was more often than not reduced to a nullity, a rubber stamp in the hands of his nominal aides, a person with limited impact even on his family affairs, to say nothing of the concerns of "All-under-Heaven."

In retrospect, Chinese emperorship appears as a curious construction that combined the principle of the monarch's limitless power with multifarious attempts to prevent this power from damaging the sociopolitical fabric. This coexistence of two conflicting impulses was maintained through a subtle and yet discernible bifurcation between the monarchy as an institution and the monarch as an individual. Institutionally speaking, the emperor was omnipotent, omniscient, and omnipresent—in other words, all but divine. Personally, however, it was tacitly recognized that his abilities might be limited and his morality flawed, and that his individual input in political processes should therefore remain circumscribed. The solution was not neat: the complete depersonalization of the emperor was neither practical nor desirable, and the precise degree of tolerable intervention by the emperor in everyday administration was never agreed upon. Nonetheless, amid continuous tension, the Chinese variant of "checks and balances" proved to be viable enough to survive for more than two millennia, occasional malfunctions notwithstanding.

THE EMERGENCE OF MONARCHISM

Like the idea of the unity of "All-under-Heaven," the notion of an omnipotent monarch is often traced to the earliest stages of China's political history. As early as the Shang period, the kings were exceptionally influential political players, leading the armies, initiating public works, maintaining friendly ties with neighboring polities, and—arguably most important of all—performing a variety of divinations and sacrificial rituals to ascertain the deities' attitudes toward royal undertakings and to ensure their support through appropriate offerings. In the Shang, as in many primordial polities elsewhere, there was no clear demarcation between "the state" and its leader: the king was his polity's sole center of gravity. To maintain their authority, the Shang kings had to travel continuously throughout their realm, personally displaying their majesty to subjects and allies alike. The importance of the king's personal abilities for the proper maintenance of the realm may explain the Shang's complex system of lateral succession (passing the throne from an elder to a younger brother and then back to the elder brother's son), which ensured that the throne was occupied by a mature leader. Arguably, more than any later monarchs in China's history, the Shang kings could proclaim, "L'État c'est Moi" (I am the State).[5]

It would be tempting to draw a direct line from the Shang kings to later emperors and to claim that monarchism has been an essential feature of Chinese civilization since time immemorial; but this assertion would run counter to historical evidence. Actually, as time passed and a more sophisticated state apparatus came into existence, the king's per-

sonal impact on political affairs declined. The political and military significance of the kings from the middle to late Western Zhou period appears markedly lesser than that of their Shang and early Western Zhou
predecessors; even in religious terms the kings lost part of their power, as
they no longer held a monopoly on performing divination. Nonetheless,
the idea of the rulers' preferential access to the divine, and of their ability
to mediate between the superhuman Powers and the community of the
living, remained intact. Adopting the proud title of "Sons of Heaven," the
Zhou kings claimed that they ruled by Heaven's Decree (or Mandate),
and maintained the exclusive right to perform sacrifices to this supreme
deity. In addition, they had preferential access to the deified ancestors of
the ruling clan, whose support was essential for the living kin. Rulers on
the lower levels of the Zhou sociopolitical pyramid similarly possessed
supreme pontifical power within their communities.[6]

In these supreme, exclusive, lifelong, and nondispersible pontifical
powers of the community's leader, it is not difficult to identify the foundations of the monarchistic mind-set that became characteristic of Chinese
civilization for millennia to come. Yet in the short term, the rulers' preferential access to the supramundane powers did not suffice to ensure
their earthly authority. As described in the previous chapter, the Springs-
and-Autumns period was marked by progressive disintegration of the
sociopolitical order, and nowhere was this process manifested with
greater clarity than in the sovereigns' declining power. First, the authority
of the Sons of Heaven was eclipsed by regional lords; then these lords
were in turn challenged by powerful aristocrats, who appropriated most
of the military, economic, and administrative power in the regional states.
As the lords' religious prestige could no longer ensure their effective authority, many of them were assassinated, expelled, or otherwise humiliated by their nominal underlings. The plight of regional lords is exemplified by the offer made in 544 BCE by the ousted Lord Xian of Wei to the
local potentate Ning Xi: "If you let me return [to Wei], all the administration will be in the hands of the Ning lineage, while I shall [only control
the] sacrifices."[7] In dire straits, a lord was apparently willing to embrace
the position of a ritual figurehead!

The aggravating deterioration of the ruler's power during the sixth–
fifth centuries BCE contributed to what turned into the deepest systemic
crisis in China's long history. Most polities throughout the Zhou world
became entangled in a web of debilitating power struggles between powerful nobles and the lords, among aristocratic lineages, and among rival
branches within some of these lineages, in addition to endless wars with
foreign powers. Weakened rulers were unable to rein in the forces of disintegration, which threatened the very survival of the polity. In 453 BCE,
the crisis reached its nadir, as one of the richest and militarily most suc-

cessful states of the Springs-and-Autumns period, Jin, disintegrated and was divided among three major ministerial lineages. Yet this collapse of the erstwhile superpower marked the turning point in preimperial history. The "scheming ministers" who dissolved the state of Jin—heads of the Wei, Han, and Zhao lineages—were determined to avoid the mistake of their mother state and to prevent further disintegration. They were the first to launch a series of reforms aimed at solidifying the ruler's authority, weakening alternative loci of power, and establishing centralized control over the localities. These successful reforms were emulated and deepened in other polities, bringing about an entirely new entity, which Mark E. Lewis aptly names a "ruler-centered state."[8]

It is not my intention here to analyze the practical aspects of the resurrection of politically potent rulership during the Warring States period, as this analysis has been successfully performed elsewhere.[9] What is important for our discussion, however, is that the administrative and social reforms were paralleled by a deep ideological transformation, namely, the advent of the ideology of monarchism. Thinkers of various convictions put forward a variety of ideas to bolster the ruler's authority. Thus ritual specialists, associated with Confucius and his followers, emphasized the importance of preserving the exclusive ritual prerogatives of the rulers on each of the levels of the Zhou sociopolitical pyramid, and facilitated the widening of sumptuary distinctions between the ruler and his underlings. Moralistic thinkers from Mozi to Mengzi promoted the idea that the ruler should serve as the ultimate source of moral inspiration for his subjects; and while criticizing current immoral sovereigns, they unhesitantly adopted the view that universal morality could prevail only in a strictly ruler-centered political order. Other thinkers provided metaphysical underpinnings for the ruler's exaltedness: they averred that the ruler's superiority, like that of Heaven above, reflects fundamental cosmic laws; hence, while an individual ruler or even a dynasty may be replaced, the monarchic political order remains inviolable. Thinkers' arguments differed, and so did their practical proposals, but all of them—from the staunchly authoritarian Han Feizi (d. 233 BCE) to the relentless critic of the reigning lords, Mengzi—agreed that monarchy was the only conceivable political system, and that only the monarch could represent the common good of his subjects and constrain divisive private interests. It is their consensus, violated only by a radical critic of organized society, Zhuangzi (d. ca. 280 BCE), that turned monarchism into a perennial feature of Chinese political culture.[10]

Of the manifold ideological developments during the period under discussion the one that deserves utmost attention is the strong authoritarian trend in administrative thought of the Warring States period. Amid a great variety of divergent and at times mutually exclusive administrative proposals, not a single one was put forth to impose institutional limitations on the ruler's power. While most thinkers urged the ruler to consult his aides, and none considered the sovereign's decisions to be intrinsically infallible, it was nonetheless universally agreed that the ruler should have the final say on any matter of importance, and that nobody should have the right to overrule his decisions. Thus, despite the strong self-confidence of the intellectuals of the Warring States period (see chapter 3), and despite their widespread dissatisfaction with current rulers, none of these proud thinkers ever suggested a kind of "constitutional monarchy" with a "council of worthies" routinely approving or disapproving the ruler's policies. We find no ideas of oligarchy or of other collective modes of rulership; strict monarchism remains the singularly acceptable mode of rule.

This consensus during what was surely the most creative period in the history of Chinese political thought is indicative of the depth of the thinkers' commitment to the principle of monarchism. Their aversion to decentralization and fear of the coexistence of competing loci of power—either in an individual state, or, as discussed in the previous chapter, in the entire subcelestial realm—brought them to the conviction that only under a single omnipotent sovereign would the political system become truly sustainable. Like the army, the state should be structured by an unbreakable chain of command headed by an unquestioned leader, and as in the army, preserving the leader's authority is essential, even when the leader's individual abilities can be questioned. Numerous texts of that period reiterate: "Oneness [of the ruler] brings orderly rule; doubleness brings chaos."[11] The first of the epigraphs heading this chapter succinctly presents this view.

In retrospect, this almost unanimous adherence of preimperial thinkers to the principle of monarchism appears as significant as their consensus in favor of a politically unified realm. Monarchism was promulgated under an exceptional "open-ended" situation, when no government was able to impose political orthodoxy, and when divergent ideas were freely aired at competing courts. It is exceptionally significant that during that period of intellectual openness and creativity we know of not a single philosopher or intellectual, aside from Zhuangzi, who opposed the ruler-centered political order. Throughout the two subsequent millennia many thinkers raised their voices against the excesses of the monarchic system, and some of them, such as Deng Mu (1247–1306) and Huang Zongxi (1610–1695), made sweeping accusations against dynastic rule as a whole, but even they never departed from the ideological framework established during the Warring States period: the common good is attainable only under the morally impeccable and selfless emperor.[12] Having become singularly legitimate long before the formation of the unified empire, the monarchic principle of rule remained virtually unchallenged until the very last years of the imperial polity.

SAGES, MEDIOCRITIES, AND INACTIVE RULERS

Ritual and institutional empowerment of the monarch was a reasonable solution to the ongoing disintegration of the sociopolitical order in the centuries preceding the imperial unification; but it was also a dangerous gamble, insofar as the enormous monarchical power could be abused by a malevolent ruler. The awareness of the dangers that a bad ruler might inflict on his subjects was embedded already in one of the foundational myths of Chinese political culture: the story of the last king of the Shang dynasty, Zhouxin (d. ca. 1046 BCE), whose atrocities brought about Heaven's withdrawal of its Decree from the Shang, and the resultant overthrow of the tyrant and collapse of his state. This event was rationalized in the concept of the transferability of Heaven's Decree, which served throughout Chinese history as a powerful warning to the rulers to mend their ways, and as justification of the occasional overthrow of a dynasty and/or the replacement of an erring ruler.[13] We shall return to the concept of legitimate rebellion in chapter 5; but here it should be noted that hideous tyrants who deserved to be overthrown were an exception rather than the rule. Much more frequent were average, inadequate rulers, who were neither as depraved as Zhouxin nor as good, intelligent, and moral as the ideal envisioned by most thinkers.

The question of the ruler's potential ineptitude became increasingly acute during the Warring States period. With the rapid adoption of the meritocratic principle of rule—the appointing of officials according to their abilities rather than their pedigree—an odd situation ensued: the monarch came to be the only power-holder who owed his position exclusively to his birth rather than his merits. This added a paradoxical dimension to the contemporaneous monarchistic discourse: the same thinkers who committed themselves to enhancing the ruler's authority commonly considered themselves to be morally and intellectually superior to their sovereigns. Accommodating this inherent contradiction became one of the most challenging tasks for political thinkers of the preimperial, and, mutatis mutandis, the imperial age.[14] It is against this background that the discourse of the True Monarch came into existence, adding another, extraordinarily important dimension to the emerging culture of monarchism.

The idea of the True Monarch as a person who unifies political with moral and intellectual superiority burgeoned in the second half of the Warring States period, in tandem with the increasing interest in the concept of a Sage. The Sage was a semidivinized person whose ability to develop his mental and moral qualities to the utmost would allow him to subdue human beings and possibly the cosmos itself. This construct was an outgrowth of the increasingly intensive search for individual perfection; and it had manifold ramifications in the realm of ethical, metaphysical, and political thought.[15] Occasionally, the discourse of sagehood, with its focus on a hierarchy of abilities and morality separate from the sociopolitical pyramid, could become subversive of the political order, especially as thinkers unanimously refused to identify current rulers as sages. Yet it was also widely recognized that the bifurcation between sagacity and rulership was a temporary aberration: the two had presumably been unified in the age of legendary sage rulers of the past and would reunify in the figure of the future True Monarch. The latter's all-penetrating intellect and paradigmatic goodness would eventually enable him to put an end to war, turmoil, and bloodshed, and to establish an era of universal peace and orderly rule.

The towering figure of the True Monarch—a quasi-messianic savior, "who arrives once in five hundred years," and whose coming is long overdue[16]—overshadowed the political discourse of the century that preceded the imperial unification. This monarch was conceived of as essentially distinct from the current, inadequate sovereigns, not only in terms of his individual abilities but also in terms of his expected achievements. It was widely agreed that only the True Monarch would be able to unify the world at last after centuries of bloodshed and turmoil; only he would bring about tranquillity, a perfect sociopolitical order, universal compliance, and, in some texts, moral and intellectual uniformity. Only under the True Monarch would the utopian dreams of thinkers finally be realized. These high expectations of the future savior are evident, for instance, in the writings of Xunzi (ca. 310–230), arguably the single most important political thinker of the Warring States period:

> The [True] Son of Heaven is the most respectable in terms of his power and position and has no rivals under Heaven. . . . His morality is pure; his knowledge and kindness are extremely clear. He faces southwards and makes All-under-Heaven obedient. Among all the people, there is none who does not politely hold his hands following him, thereby being compliantly transformed. There are no recluses under Heaven, the goodness of no one is neglected; the one who unites with him is good, the one who differs from him is bad.[17]

Under the rule of the perspicacious, kind, and moral True Monarch there is no room for injustice, for neglect of one's duties, for noncompliance. Even independent-minded intellectuals of Xunzi's ilk will not be needed: indeed, if the only criterion of goodness and badness is identification with the monarch, then members of the educated elite lose their importance as the ruler's guides. The future sage ruler, whom Xunzi identifies elsewhere as a counterpart of Heaven and Earth, deserves nothing short of absolute obedience.

Panegyrics to the True Monarch at times may fuel the misconception that Xunzi and his fellow thinkers were empty flatterers whose support of the monarchic principle of rule blinded them to its potentially negative consequences. This impression is patently wrong, though. In the *Xunzi* and elsewhere exaltation of the future unifier coexists with strong criticism of contemporaneous inept sovereigns.[18] Actually, idealization of the True Monarch served here and in other texts primarily to underline the inadequacy of current rulers, whose mediocrity was contrasted with the superb abilities of the future Sage. Insofar as reigning rulers fell short of that superhuman hero, they could not expect the degree of obedience and submissiveness that would be owed to the True Monarch.

Inasmuch as the reign of the True Monarch remains a distant and barely attainable possibility, how should the monarchic system function in the meantime? Here Xunzi proposes what appears at first glance to be a brilliant solution: the sovereign, while ostensibly omnipotent, should relegate most of his everyday tasks to meritorious aides: he should reign but not rule:

> The enlightened sovereign endorses the guiding principles, while the benighted ruler endorses the details. . . . The ruler selects one chancellor, arranges one law, clarifies one principle in order to cover everything, to illuminate everything, and to observe the completion [of affairs]. The chancellor selects and orders heads of the hundred officials, attends to the guiding principles of the hundred affairs, and thereby refines the divisions between the hundred clerks at court, measures their achievements, discusses their rewards, and presents their achievements at the year's end to the ruler. When they act correctly, they are approved; otherwise they are dismissed. Hence the ruler works hard in looking for [proper officials] and is at rest when employing them.[19]

In this passage Xunzi speaks of an "enlightened sovereign": one who is able to select a truly worthy aide and to relegate to him everyday tasks. Elsewhere Xunzi argues that a capable chancellor would successfully run the state even under an inadequate (infantile or senile) monarch.[20] This appears to be an effective merging of the principles of monarchism and meritocracy, both of which Xunzi cherished: while the ruler will enjoy ritual supremacy and also preserve the crucial right to appoint, inspect, and, naturally, dismiss his aide, it would be the latter, a man of proven capabilities, who would run everyday affairs. The appeal of this approach to members of the educated elite was considerable: even two millennia later Huang Zongxi viewed it as the best solution to the problem of a monarch's inadequacy.[21] But why should an "enlightened monarch" relegate much of his power to an underling? Would the promise of "being at rest" suffice to entice the sovereign to give up active intervention in policy making?

Xunzi leaves this question unanswered. Perhaps he did not consider his proposal to be threatening to the ruler: after all, Xunzi repeatedly reiterates his assertion that the ruler's ministers would forever be morally upright men whose actions would benefit the monarch. Not all of Xunzi's contemporaries shared his belief in harmonious relations between the ruler and the ministers, though: Xunzi's dissenting disciple, Han Feizi, for example, compares the ruler's underlings to hungry tigers, who are ready to devour the sovereign unless he is able to overawe them into submissiveness, and who seek nothing but personal gain. Yet despite their diametrically opposed assumptions about ruler-minister relations, Han Feizi's practical recommendations curiously resemble those of Xunzi. Han Feizi warns the ruler that excessive engagement in the tasks of government would expose him to scheming ministers: it is better, then, to display impartiality, to avoid overengagement in administrative routine, and to allow the ministers to rule the realm while closely supervising them and mercilessly exposing their machinations.[22] Differences aside, Han Feizi and Xunzi agree that the ruler should rein in his whims, limit his intervention in everyday administration, and enjoy the utmost prestige and absolute power without actually realizing it. In the final account, both thinkers propose radical reduction of the monarch's personal involvement in routine government affairs.

The ultimate convergence of two supposedly antithetical approaches is not incidental. Texts from the late Warring States period, whatever their ideological affiliation, repeatedly advocate the ruler's impartiality, his lack of emotion, and his refraining from action as the quintessence of political wisdom. Rationalizations for these suggestions differ, but the bottom line appears to be surprisingly similar for all: the ruler is supposed to retain his ritual prestige, the right to appoint chief ministers, and the final say on major political matters; but he is not expected to exercise his will directly. In this fashion the thinkers apparently hoped to ensure that even an inept ruler would not cause irreparable damage to his state. Only under the morally and intellectually superb True Monarch would this situation have to change. What most thinkers might not have anticipated is that their ideal of the sage monarch would be appropriated by one of the most powerful—but also one of the most ruthless—rulers of China: the First Emperor of the unifying Qin dynasty. Having proclaimed himself the True Monarch, the First Emperor brought about a radical change in ruler-minister relations and forever altered China's monarchism.

THE FIRST EMPEROR: THE REIGNING SAGE

The First Emperor of Qin is arguably the single most important ruler in China's long history. His reign became a crucial historical juncture: both because he creatively appropriated aspects of the monarchistic discourse of preceding centuries, molding them into a novel image of a reigning True Monarch; and because the new pattern of emperorship that he established lasted, with certain modifications, for two millennia.[23] Moreover, his reign is important not only for its positive but also for its negative impact on subsequent dynasts: those rulers adopted many of his institutional and ideological innovations but distanced themselves—at least declaratively—from his alleged hubris, harshness, and arbitrariness. This complex legacy highlights the essentially contradictory nature of Chinese emperorship, with its simultaneous emphasis on the ruler's omnipotence and on the desirability of limiting his personal impact on political affairs; and, as I shall argue below, the First Emperor's reign exacerbated this contradiction.

The First Emperor's reconceptualization of his position was primarily a result of his truly unprecedented success. Having put an end to centuries of warfare and having unified the entire known civilized world, he fulfilled the major requirement for becoming the True Monarch. Indeed, his propaganda efforts focused on stressing his identity with the True Monarch, both in terms of his individual features, such as sagacity and morality, and in terms of his achievements—most prominently, peace, perfect sociopolitical order, universal prosperity, and the populace's total compliance with the emperor's will. "Wherever human traces reach, / There is none who does not declare himself subject"; "men and women embody compliance"; "there is none who is not respectful and submissive"; "all live their full life and there is none who does not achieve his ambitions"; and even "horses and oxen" receive the emperor's favor.[24] All this means that the dreams of generations of thinkers had been realized: the First Emperor became the savior of humankind!

Exaltation of the emperor to the position of the True Monarch had immediate political consequences. First, it tremendously elevated the monarch above other human beings, including his closest aides. The new superhuman status of the emperor was duly buttressed by the newly designed imperial title, with its explicit sacral connotations (*huangdi*, "emperor," meaning literally "the August Thearch"); by the new imperial vocabulary; by the emperor's propaganda; and, most notably, by his megalomaniac construction activities, traces of which can still be seen at the site of his staggering burial complex, where the famous Terracotta Army was unearthed. Second, in his capacity as the True Monarch, the First Emperor was expected to rule and not just to reign, which he duly did—fervently traversing his new realm, ascending sacred mountains, re-shaping the imperial pantheon, and managing the everyday affairs of the state, reportedly to the degree of self-denial.[25] Third, and most conse-quentially, the emperor declared himself the Sage, boldly appropriating this most prestigious designation, which had theretofore been applied exclusively to legendary and semilegendary rulers of the remote past, but never to living monarchs. Having declared himself Sage, the First Em-peror radically redefined his position vis-à-vis members of the intellectual elite. Gone was the age of passive and deferential sovereigns for whom intellectuals were respected teachers: now the emperor held not just po-litical but intellectual authority. This was the beginning of a new era in the history of China's rulership.

By his bold appropriation of the position of the sage True Monarch, the First Emperor had decisively empowered himself and future rulers vis-à-vis their entourages and society as a whole. This may explain why, despite persistent criticism of the First Emperor's excesses, his model of the emperorship remained intact for more than twenty-one centuries. Nonetheless, rulers of subsequent dynasties did not miss another lesson from Qin's short history: namely, the swift disintegration of the empire under an inept and intemperate Second Emperor (r. 209–207 BCE). This rapid collapse of the first imperial dynasty had taught future statesmen and rulers that excessive monarchism may be no less damaging to the social fabric than the absence of a powerful sovereign. The Qin model was alluring, but some of its details had to be modified.

The modification of the Qin model was subtle but nonetheless sub-stantial: it can be summarized as renewed awareness of the difference between the institutional power of the throne and the power of an indi-vidual ruler. Nominally, every emperor from the Han dynasty on was conceived of on the model of the First Emperor as an embodiment of the True Monarch and the Sage; yet practically, most emperors learned not to take their sagacity at its face value. They duly adopted a more modest stance, disclaiming their abilities and endorsing a more cooperative and collegial attitude toward their aides than the First and Second Emperors had done.[26] And yet, the persistence of fundamental aspects of the Qin model meant that any monarch who took his sagacity literally could im-pose his will on his subjects in the most resolute and ruthless way. This added yet another dimension to the ongoing tension between the mon-arch's institutional omnipotence and the courtiers' persistent desire to avoid Qin-like abuses of power.

The appropriation of the imperial title by the king of Qin in 221 BCE marks a watershed in Chinese history. Thereafter, despite tremendous variability in the personal qualities and actual power of individual mon-archs, no major changes were made in the institution of emperorship, of which Qin—as both admirers and bitter critics of dynastic rule recognized—served as a fountainhead.[27] At this point it may be useful, then, to shift from a chronological discussion to a more generalized one, in which I shall analyze interactions between the institutional and individual powers of China's monarchs throughout the imperial millennia.

THE INSTITUTIONAL POWER OF THE MONARCHS

The paradoxical coexistence of the image of omnipotence and an abundance of passive and weak emperors explains modern observers' highly contradictory assessments of Chinese emperorship. A scholar can choose to focus on despotic rulers, who mobilized millions of people for controversial military and civilian projects, who indulged in a life of luxury amid overall poverty and devastation, who terrorized their subjects and tortured or executed outspoken officials, and who defied any attempt to rein in their whims. Such a scholar may well concur with Montesquieu's identification of the Chinese emperor as a paradigmatic despot: "a single man, unrestrained by laws and other rules, dominates everything by his will and caprices."[28] Another scholar might focus on those emperors who were completely overpowered by their officials, unable even to change the status of their concubines or leave the capital without having difficult bargain with restive courtiers; hapless sovereigns who knew nothing of the real situation in their realm and had to humbly rubber-stamp memorials and policy proposals, the content of which they rarely could fully understand. This scholar might well agree with Ray Huang that the emperor was a nullity on the throne, a "living ancestor," who "remained the Son of Heaven only because everybody believed that he was."[29] Yet these ostensibly contradictory assessments are reconcilable. In what follows, I shall suggest that the paradoxes of emperorship can be resolved through the distinction between the institutional omnipotence of the monarchy and individual limitations on the emperor's power. I shall analyze first the institutional aspects of imperial power and demonstrate that its omnipotence was not just a meaningless convention but a potentially powerful stabilizing force. Next, I shall focus, conversely, on the limited power of individual monarchs and show how invisible "checks and balances" prevented imperial China from sinking into the abyss of senseless autocracy.

My analysis of the emperors' institutional authority will start with their ritual supremacy rather than with their administrative powers. This choice is not arbitrary; actually, it reflects the understandings of many Chinese thinkers from Xunzi on. Indeed, as we shall see below, while all of the emperor's endless administrative tasks could be relegated to his underlings, his ritual supremacy normally remained inviolable; any infringement of it was viewed as a major step toward usurpation of the throne. Not incidentally, one of the most brilliant historians and political thinkers of the imperial age, Sima Guang (1019–1086), opted to start his magnum opus, *The Comprehensive Mirror to Aid the Government* (*Zizhi tongjian*), by explaining that the preservation of the emperor's ritual power was the most essential precondition for proper monarchic rule:

> In the office of the Son of Heaven, nothing is more important than ritual. . . . After, all, in the vastness of four seas, among multitudes of people, [all] are ruled by a single person. Even among those whose power suffices to sever the norms and whose knowledge exceeds that of their age, none will not hurry to serve—is not it due to the basic norms of ritual? . . . Unless [the ruler] is as evil as [the paradigmatic tyrants] Jie and Zhou[xin], and [the subject] is as benevolent as [the founders of the Shang and Zhou dynasties,] Tang and Wu, one to whom the people flock and who is decreed by Heaven—one should preserve the separation between the ruler and the minister even at the expense of prostrating [oneself and accepting] death![30]

Sima Guang's message is clear: ritual distinctions between the ruler and his subjects allow the monarch to preserve his authority even vis-à-vis the most powerful of his underlings; only under truly exceptional circumstances can these distinctions be ignored and the ruler overthrown. This statement is surely prescriptive rather than descriptive, but insofar as it comes from the single most important imperial historian, it deserves some scrutiny. What does Sima Guang mean by "ritual" here? In the context of ensuring the monarch's authority, this term cannot be reduced to its surface referent, the manifold regulations that distinguished the emperor from his subjects, such as sumptuary rules, specific forms of address to the ruler, and the ceremonial display of reverence to the monarch, i.e., the performance of obeisance. Surely, all these regulations were essential in displaying the emperor's majesty; but there were also deeper aspects of this majesty, what I would refer to as the sacredness of the throne. This sacredness, the elevation of the emperor to superhuman heights, was arguably the single most important dimension in ensuring the emperor's authority.

My discussion of the sacredness of the throne will not focus on what is often conceived of as its immediate manifestations, such as the emperors' position as the exclusive intermediaries with the supreme deity, Heaven, or their occasional acquisition of divine features borrowed from Buddhism, Daoism, or other creeds (e.g., presenting themselves as Buddhas, bodhisattvas, Daoist deities, or the Buddhist Wheel-Turning King, Chakravartin).[31] While these divine features of the emperors, especially their role as Sons of Heaven, surely bolstered the monarchs' authority, my interest lies in a deeper dimension of the emperors' sacredness. I believe that the emperorship as an institution possessed a sort of sacral aura, the acceptance of which by all social strata can be interpreted as a Chinese variant of "civic religion," which transcended the diverse creeds and faiths of emperors, courtiers, and the populace at large. This aura turned any emperor ex officio into a semidivine person, sharply differentiating him from other human beings.

To understand the sacredness of the emperor, we should distinguish him from Chinese gods, although at times among the lower social strata this distinction may have been blurred.[32] Unlike most Chinese gods the emperor was not understood to possess individual superhuman qualities nor posthumously to join the popular pantheon. Rather, his godlike position approximated certain features of the God Almighty of the Abrahamic religions, with its aura of singularity and omnipotence. In what resembles a conceptual inversion of medieval Europe—where multiple loci of secular authority were tolerated, but there could be only one God, one Church, and one legitimate pope—in China, conversely, multiple gods and creeds were legitimate, but only one legitimate monarch could exist. The first biblical commandment, "Thou shalt have no other gods before me," is perfectly applicable to the emperor of China, whose subjects were free to worship any deity but could not possibly contemplate simultaneous recognition of two competing emperors. Among segments of the elite, the imperial institution could at times generate truly religious zeal, as is exemplified in mass loyalist suicides—China's equivalent of religious martyrdom in Western Eurasia.[33]

Further resembling the Jewish God, the Chinese emperor remained aloof, mysterious, inscrutable, and invisible for the vast majority of his subjects. He was generally enclosed behind the walls of the Forbidden City; and even when he left it for ritual or other purposes, he was usually not supposed to intermingle freely with his subjects (although some rulers did so—often incognito). Normally, no statues or paintings of the emperor decorated temples or individual dwellings;[34] his name was tabooed; his image was not reproduced on coins; and individual communication with him was difficult even for the majority of officials, not to speak of the public in general. This position might not have ignited strong religious feelings in the populace, but it evidently strengthened the emperor's mysterious majesty.

The concept of the emperor's sacredness permeates multiple aspects of Chinese culture: from rituals to laws, from court life to popular legends and tales. The emperor's body, his seals, his edicts, his ritual paraphernalia—everything was sacrosanct. Among the "ten abominations"—the gravest and most unpardonable crimes under imperial law—we find "great irreverence" (*da bu jing*), a term that refers, among other acts, to stealing the emperor's sacrificial utensils, mislabeling his medicine, or mishandling his chariot. Whenever an imperial edict, written in vermillion ink on yellow silk, was read by an imperial envoy, the recipient—be he a fearsome general, a proud tribal chief, or a meritorious official—could not but prostrate himself before the emperor's supreme power, even if he knew that the edict had been drafted by a hated regent or, worse, by a eunuch secretary acting on behalf of a child ruler.[35] Any display of irreverence signified open rebellion and could have the gravest consequences.

The emperor's sacredness pervaded his entourage and officials; occasionally, it could empower the inner court or the emperor's in-laws. It subverted other sociopolitical norms, including gender and age hierarchies. The immortal eighteenth-century novel *A Dream of Red Mansions* tells of an imperial concubine who is permitted to visit her natal home. During the visit, her father, a stern high official who would never talk to his progeny as equals, let alone as his superiors, turns to the daughter from behind the door curtain:

> Your subject, poor and obscure, little dreamed that our flock of common pigeons and crows would ever be blessed with a phoenix. Thanks to the imperial favor and the virtue of our ancestors, your Noble Highness embodies the finest essence of nature and the accumulated merit of our forebears. . . . His Majesty, who manifests the great virtue of all creation, has shown us such extraordinary and hitherto unknown favor [by allowing his concubine to visit her parents] that even if we dashed our brains we could not repay one-thousandth part of our debt of gratitude. All I can do is to exert myself day and night, loyally carry out my official duties, and pray that our sovereign may live ten thousand years as desired by All-under-Heaven.[36]

Such deference to a daughter would be unimaginable in a normative family in any other situation save the particular case in which the daughter shared some of the aura of the Son of Heaven and, on that basis, was her father's superior. This short passage is perhaps more indicative of the emperor's exaltedness than volumes of historical, philosophical, legal, and ritual writings. If the emanation of the emperor's sacral aura could turn his minor concubine into a "phoenix," while diminishing her proud father to the position of a "pigeon and crow," little else needs to be said of the inconceivable loftiness of the monarchy in the subjects' eyes.

Having clarified the sacral status of the emperorship, we are in a better position to understand Sima Guang's above-cited statement. While not every subject invariably opted to "prostrate himself and accept death" when facing the emperor, it is true that compliance with the emperor's orders was a norm even during a dynasty's periods of weakness, when the court possessed neither efficient coercive apparatus nor sufficient material resources to reward their supporters. This ability of the imperial court to generate compliance allowed many dynasties to survive for decades against great odds.[37]

The sacral status of the emperor could be instrumental not just in preserving centralized rule, but also in strengthening its despotic potential. Insofar as the emperor was sacrosanct, any assault, however indirect, on his position could be interpreted as lèse-majesté, one of the "ten abominations." Thus, while Chinese court etiquette welcomed and even at times prescribed "loyal criticism" directed against the throne, an outspoken critic always had to be wary of crossing an invisible line between legitimate remonstrance and criminal "great irreverence." At times, the definition of this crime was broadened to produce some of the gloomiest manifestations of arbitrariness: the death penalty could be inflicted for a poem, for a careless usage of the emperor's tabooed personal name, for insufficiently strict observation of mourning rules for an empress, for a potentially subversive examination question, and even for the "crime of criticizing [the ruler] in the stomach" (fu fei zui), or mere unspoken but presumed dissent.[38] Although, as we shall see below, imperial tyranny was moderated through a variety of means, its intimidating presence behind the scenes of normal political life chilled the court atmosphere throughout the centuries.

Aside from its short-term impact in strengthening the imperial regime, the emperor's superhuman status could contribute to long-term political stabilization, most notably in controlling the religious life of the realm. In this regard the emperor's power exceeded that of monarchs elsewhere: he had the right to appoint, promote, or demote any deity of the official (and supposedly popular) pantheon; he could patronize or outlaw any cult, any type of religious ceremony, any scripture; he could approve or disapprove of the establishment of monasteries and temples, or demolish them altogether.[39] While these prerogatives usually had only a marginal impact on popular religious activities, and even strict regulations with regard to monasteries and temples were rarely implemented to the letter, the very right of the political establishment to supervise the religious life of the populace gave it huge social power, which could be utilized, when necessary, to counter the potentially destabilizing effects of domestic or foreign religions. To illustrate this, I shall briefly address the empire's relations with Buddhism, the single most powerful foreign religion that entered China and had a lasting effect on its history.

The complex story of Buddhism's multifarious adaptation to Chinese culture and China's adaptation to Buddhism has been told many times; here I focus exclusively on Buddhism's political interaction with the imperial establishment. By the fourth–fifth centuries CE, as the alien creed gained huge popularity among all social strata, it appeared to have the momentum to reshape China much as Christianity did the Roman Empire. This, however, is not what happened. While many emperors acted as devoted Buddhists, granted lavish gifts to monasteries and temples, and fervently performed Buddhist rites—one of them (Liang Emperor Wu, r. 502–549) even declared himself a monk for a short while—this did not change the basic pattern of relations between the throne and the Buddhist establishment (the *sangha*). The latter remained forever submissive and totally dependent on the emperors' goodwill. Emperors could patronize the *sangha*; could employ the monks as diplomats or personal aides; but they could also restrict the activity of the *sangha*, regulate the size and location of the monasteries, and even intervene in such matters as the ordination of monks and monastic discipline.[40] In a few cases, most notably in 841–845, the imperial state even outlawed Buddhism, suppressing or tremendously reducing the activities of the *sangha*.[41] What is remarkable is the ease with which the state dictated its rules of the game to the powerful religious establishment. The latter could resent the emperor but could not openly defy his will.

It is within the realm of religion that the Chinese emperors appear particularly powerful in comparison with their Occidental counterparts. Even in the "Caesaropapist" Byzantine empire, the emperor's intervention in substantial ecclesiastical matters, such as his support of iconoclasm in the eighth–ninth centuries, could cause considerable internal turmoil, if not outright rebellion.[42] In China this never happened. The emperor was simply far more "divine" than any religious establishment; even proud monks had to acquiesce in his sacredness. A single example suffices to illustrate this. In 402, a powerful dictator and would-be usurper, Huan Xuan (369–404), demanded that the monks perform obeisance to the emperor. Huan Xuan claimed that bowing to the ruler was due not just politically but religiously: as monks owed their very existence to the emperor's munificence, they should respect him as their father! Huan Xuan was eventually dissuaded from pressing the monks when his eminent opponent, Huiyuan (334–416), reminded him that since the monks ideologically did not cherish life at all and transcended normal human relations, the emperor's gift of life was of minor significance to them. Notably, Huiyuan dared not question the emperor's sacred role as the generator of universal life despite the obvious contradiction of this premise to the Buddhist worldview. Nobody—not even the venerated religious teacher—could openly contradict a claim based on the emperor's presumed sacredness; this issue was not open to religious counterclaims.[43]

Huan Xuan's attempt to subjugate the *sangha* to the throne is indicative of the way in which the abstract convention of the emperor's sacredness could be translated, under certain circumstances, into a powerful means of restraining the religious establishment. It is worth noting that the controversy took place under one of the weakest imperial regimes in China's long history (Eastern Jin, 318–420), and that for its participants it was clear that what was at issue was not the sacredness of the soon-to-be-replaced reigning monarch, Emperor An of Jin (r. 397–403 and 404–419 CE), who was a hapless puppet in Huan Xuan's hands, and who could by no stretch of the imagination be considered the true source of life for all human beings. What mattered was the institutional principle of the emperor's godlike position, and this principle was inviolable whoever occupied the throne.

This example prepares us to consider briefly other instances in which theoretical assertions of the emperor's superiority could be translated into practical steps aimed at strengthening the throne, increasing socio-political stability, or moderating the power of potentially threatening social groups. Let us turn to the broader socioeconomic role of the emperors. It is useful to recall in this context a sentence from the canonical *Book of Songs*: "Everywhere under Heaven is the Monarch's land, each of those who live on the land is the Monarch's servant."[44] At first glance, this statement seems a hollow slogan or wishful thinking: after all, as is well known, de facto private ownership of land existed through much of China's history, and the degree of the emperor's rule over different groups of subjects varied considerably in space and time.[45] Yet, once again, under certain circumstances activist emperors and courtiers could translate the abstract slogan into a reality and resolutely utilize their nominal power to regulate the society below.

Chinese history abounds in examples of bold initiatives undertaken by the throne, aimed at reshaping adverse social, economic, or cultural situations. Thus the imperial court could initiate far-reaching reforms of landownership, capping the size of individual plots of land or ordering massive reallocation of fields; it could create, redefine, or abolish hereditary social groups, from the aristocracy above to different types of outcasts below; it could profoundly reorganize rural and urban society, alter popular customs, change the subjects' surnames, establish new cults and abolish the old, and otherwise intervene in all imaginable spheres of life. Surely, not all of these initiatives were equally successful, but rather than analyzing each of them separately, let us consider for a moment the boldness of some of the policy makers, who used the power of the throne in a conscious attempt to reshape radically the entire society.

Consider the actions of Emperor Xiaowen (r. 471–499) of the Northern Wei dynasty (386–534), established by the Tuoba nomads. In the second half of his reign, the emperor launched a series of profound reforms in the economy, social life, and even the people's customs. The most important and the most successful of these reforms was the introduction of the "equal field" system, under which roughly equal (in terms of expected yield) plots of land were allocated to all peasant households; most of this land was alienable and redistributable according to the changing size of the household. In addition the emperor relocated the capital from the northern boundaries of the realm to the old Chinese heartland; imposed a series of radical measures aimed at "Sinicizing" his fellow tribesmen (even abolishing their polysyllabic names in favor of monosyllabic Chinese ones); and radically modified the composition of the high aristocracy. Not all of these measures were equally successful (some are believed to have directly contributed to the breakup of the Northern Wei a generation after the emperor's death); nor did they pass unopposed. Yet while our sources do narrate considerable resentment against some of the emperor's steps—from, among others, his closest kin—none of the opponents claimed that the emperor in principle had no right to abolish nomadic surnames, to outlaw steppe garments, or to intervene radically to alter landholding patterns.[46] All these were prerogatives of the throne, which were rarely utilized, but which could suddenly turn into a means of creating an entirely new sociopolitical, economic, and cultural order.

Few reforms in China's long history were as sweeping as those initiated by the Sinicized nomadic emperor Xiaowen. Many of the reforms undertaken by other emperors or, in their name, by powerful courtiers, were thwarted by a noncooperative bureaucracy or a noncompliant populace. Yet what matters for our discussion is the potential ability of the imperial court to initiate sweeping changes in any of the established practices. This suggests that the emperor's role as a universal regulator was not a hollow image: if utilized prudently and properly it could become—and at times it did become—a major force capable of reshaping society and addressing various political, social, or economic challenges. More often than not these reforms were pursued by officials with only the technical consent of the monarch; but without the sacral aura of the emperorship and without the consensus in favor of the absolute power of the throne, such steps would have been unfeasible and most probably even unthinkable.

"Checks and Balances" and Powerless Emperors

In the aftermath of the dramatic fall of the Ming dynasty (1368–1644) several eminent intellectuals, such as Gu Yanwu (1613–1682) and Huang Zongxi, identified the excessive centralization of power in the emperor's hands as one of the major maladies of the imperial system as a whole and of the Ming dynasty in particular. In the early twentieth century these ideas were translated by thinkers such as Liang Qichao (1873–1929) into a novel interpretation of Chinese history as a continuous descent into the abyss of dictatorship. Later, the idea of the ever-aggravating "despotism" in imperial China was further reinforced by Chinese, Japanese, and Western scholars, and, despite many reservations, it still recurs in many studies, particularly in China.[47] Yet despite this widespread view, in reality, as I shall demonstrate below, under most dynasties—in both the early and the late imperial period—the emperors' weakness rather than excessive authoritarianism was the rule. To understand this paradox, I shall now address how the imperial bureaucrats were able to neutralize most of the occupants of the dragon throne without making institutional adjustments in the system of emperorship.

As I have argued above, from the Warring States period on, Chinese thinkers were aware of the dangers of the monarch's ineptitude and of power abuse, and did their best to limit the negative impact of those factors by convincing the ruler to relegate his power to meritorious aides while preserving the semblance of omnipotence. The dissociation of the emperor from everyday government activities remained the latent desire of the imperial bureaucrats, who, as we shall see in the next chapter, were confident of their superior understanding of the realm's true needs and were ready to run the empire in the ruler's stead. This powerful bureaucratic stratum developed a variety of means aimed at reducing the monarch's whims: from openly dissuading him from being politically active, to remonstrating and protesting against his specific acts, to withdrawing essential information or sabotaging his decisions. An assertive and astute emperor could have overturned any opposition in court, but the majority of the rulers sought to avoid open confrontation, fearing both severe political disruption and the blackening of their image in the eyes of contemporaries and posterity. Thus the bureaucrats' power could serve as the most efficient antidote against monarchic excesses.[48]

Bureaucratic pressures aside, there were other reasons for the rulers to relegate their tasks to underlings. The sheer magnitude of the emperor's administrative and ceremonial tasks was simply too great to be managed by any save a few exceptionally gifted monarchs. Administratively, the monarch was supposed to make all the important decisions in any imaginable realm: from personnel matters to financial issues, from revision of death verdicts to the promotion of a minor deity, from military and diplomatic affairs to drafting examination questions. This concentration of tasks can be interpreted as a by-product of the emperors' insatiable quest for power, and this might at times have been the case, but it may also be seen as an astute bureaucratic device. Like Sir Humphrey Appleby from *Yes, Minister*, by overburdening the ruler the bureaucrats were effectively disempowering him. Whether or not the concentration of all administrative responsibilities in the ruler's hands was a bureaucratic ploy is debatable, but that this was the case with the emperors' ritual responsibilities is undeniable. The court ritualists persistently multiplied the emperor's ceremonial tasks so that by the late imperial period "even with the best of intentions, it was virtually impossible for an emperor to carry out all the prescribed rituals."[49] In this situation, relegation of power to the ministers and rubber-stamping their proposals was the default choice of the majority of the monarchs.

This observation requires reassessment of what is often identified as a milestone in the evolution of "imperial despotism": namely, the abolition of the office of chancellor (or "prime minister") by the Ming founder, Zhu Yuanzhang (1328–1398, r. 1368–1398). Huang Zongxi vehemently censured this step and many scholars echo him, claiming that "the elimination of the prime-minister in the early Ming significantly altered the character of the imperial state," allowing "fully developed despotism" to be exercised by either the emperors or their surrogates, such as "eunuch dictators."[50] In my eyes this conclusion is premature. Actually, attempts to abolish the position of chancellor and to concentrate all imaginable *real* power in the emperor's hands preceded Zhu Yuanzhang: they had been undertaken earlier, in the Sui, Tang, and Song dynasties.[51] Yet history proved time and again that turning an emperor into a full-time administrator was unsustainable in the long term, not least because it demanded almost superhuman abilities on the ruler's part, allowing him no respite. The Kangxi Emperor (r. 1662–1722), one of the most skilled and most active rulers in Chinese history, bitterly complained at the end of his life:

> Whereas the emperor's responsibilities are terribly heavy, there is no way he can evade them. How can this be compared with being an official? If an official wants to serve, then he serves; if he wants to stop, then he stops. When he grows old he resigns and returns home, to look after his sons and play with his grandsons; he still has the chance to relax and enjoy himself. Whereas the ruler in all his hardworking life finds no place to rest.[52]

Zhu Yuanzhang, to my knowledge, did not publicly express similar sentiments, but his work style, like that of the Kangxi Emperor, could be matched by only a few exceptionally able leaders. None of Zhu Yuanzhang's descendants was able to emulate his prowess; and the most meaningful bureaucratic result of his consolidation of executive tasks in the emperor's hands was a shift of power from the executive arm of the government to the emperor's secretaries and, worse, to his trusted eunuchs. Eventually, late Ming emperors, still acting within the institutional framework bequeathed by the dynastic founder, entered history as extraordinarily weak rulers. As early as "the mid-fifteenth century, the civil bureaucracy had made major inroads in defining the emperor's job," dramatically reducing the ruler's ability to influence policy making, and the emperors' real power had further deteriorated in the course of the dynasty's history.[53] Clearly, the institutional arrangements inherited from the founding emperor were of negligible importance in ensuring the ruler's actual power.

The decline of the rulers' individual prowess in the course of the dynasty's history, evidenced by the Ming example (and by the examples of other dynasties discussed below), has nothing to do with biological degradation of the founder's progeny, nor should it be related, *pace* traditional historians, to the supposed moral depravity of those who were born after generations of good life in the palace. Rather it appears to me as a built-in mechanism of dynastic life: the "deactivation" of the emperors was generated through the upbringing of future monarchs, who grew up without full understanding of the subtleties of administrative processes. Zhu Yuanzhang was well aware of this danger, warning his descendants that "a ruler born and bred deep within the palace, unfamiliar with the world," may well lack the necessary qualities to "extend imperial benevolence and authority throughout the realm."[54] This warning notwithstanding, Zhu Yuanzhang failed to prevent his descendants' eventual loss of power. This failure was not an accident; rather, it was yet another manifestation of the bureaucrats' long-term success in restraining the monarch.

At first glance, my claim that the emperors' deactivation was intrinsic to the process of their upbringing may sound surprising. After all, it is well known that almost every dynasty considered the education of an heir apparent, or even of each of the princes, to be a matter of high priority. The emperor-to-be was trained by the best literal minds of the empire; he was introduced to a plethora of historical documents from earlier dynasties and from the immediate past; he was given certain administrative or military assignments; and he was taught moral lessons, usually in the spirit of Confucius's teachings. It would appear that everything was done to prepare the most qualified candidate for the burdensome task of ruling "All-under-Heaven."[55]

But was it really "everything"? Not necessarily. The best training would be to entrust the ruler-to-be with a variety of real administrative and military tasks on a regular basis. In some cases this was done: especially in the early years of each dynasty, including the Ming, the emperors tended to trust their kin and progeny more than outsiders, assigning their sons and brothers important functions in military and civilian administration, or establishing them as rulers on the provincial level. Yet the general tendency of most dynasties was to discontinue active involvement of princes in the government, considering this a latent threat to political stability. It was all too likely that a powerful prince with substantial civilian and military backing would be encouraged by his entourage to act rebelliously: either to replace the designated heir apparent, or to make a preemptive strike against potential plotters from among his family, or even to depose his father and immediately ascend the throne. Well-known to any reader of dynastic histories was the example of Li Shimin (599–649), the illustrious Tang Taizong (r. 626–649), whose remarkable military and civilian career as a minor prince allowed him to amass sufficient backing to stage a coup against his brothers and force his father to abdicate.[56] It was expedient therefore to limit the potential monarch's involvement in everyday politics: the imperative to preserve dynastic stability far outweighed considerations of the future emperor's efficiency.

Lacking truly independent administrative experience, most of the new emperors were simply overwhelmed by the magnitude of their tasks and often opted to rely on their experienced courtiers rather than pursue an independent course. This choice was also a direct result of an heir apparent's training: his tutors, members of the same stratum that took a dim view of the emperor's activism, did their best to prepare the future ruler for the position of chief arbiter in court disputes but not that of an independent initiator of new policies. The emperor was made to believe that, as an embodiment of impartiality and fairness, he was expected not to initiate policies at all, but rather to approve or disapprove suggestions by his underlings. While an administratively astute ruler could thwart the efforts of his courtiers to turn him into a rubber stamp—either by utilizing his inner court servants, or by finding allies within the bureaucracy itself—few emperors possessed sufficient abilities and determination. For most, performing ceremonial tasks and rubber-stamping the proposals forwarded and approved by their trusted appointees was a much easier way of fulfilling their duties.

Manifold indicators suggest that the dynastic trajectory from assertive and charismatic emperors toward weaklings on the throne was not just an ex post facto historiographic construction, but rather a very real and pervasive tendency—one well reflected, for instance, in the gradual contraction of the geographic scope of the emperor's undertakings. While early dynastic leaders often personally led or accompanied their armies to the battlefield and crisscrossed the country on tours of inspection or for ritual purposes (e.g., for performing sacrifice at famous mountains), their successors were more often than not confined during most of their career to the precinct of the Forbidden City or to other palaces, emerging only under duress, as when rebellions or invasions impended. This pattern is observable in any major dynasty, including even those established by the nomadic conquerors (see below). The officials' antipathy to the emperors' departures from the capital was couched in terms of care for the ruler's security, of cutting the costs of imperial "tours of inspection," and of ritual considerations; but behind that smoke screen one can discern a desire for a passive and accommodating monarch, "whose body does not work, as he is the most respected," in Xunzi's words.[57] It is difficult to avoid the feeling that confining the emperor to his palace was an important step toward nullification of his personality.

The bureaucrats' persistent efforts to "deactivate" the monarch may explain the surprising ease with which they adapted themselves to child emperors. The rule of an infantile (or otherwise significantly impaired) sovereign was never welcomed, because it was feared that he would be manipulated by a ruthless regent, or, worse, by a potential usurper; in practice, however, the imperial administrative apparatus displayed a remarkable ability to run the empire under leaders whose regulatory role was a pure fiction. Insofar as regents acted prudently and did not alienate the officials, the court could maintain an atmosphere of business as usual, effectively distinguishing between the reigning emperor as a symbol of legitimacy and the real power-holder (a regent or a prime minister) as the center of administrative and political processes. In retrospect, the ease with which the empire survived lengthy periods (e.g., much of the second century CE) during which its supreme legislator, executive, military commander, judge, and pontiff was nothing but a nullity is a remarkable testimony to its vitality and also to its minimal need for imperial charisma.

The bureaucracy's adaptation to child monarchs suggests that, despite its repeatedly declared commitment to the idea of the sage monarch, the officialdom may actually have preferred a weaker monarch to a powerful activist. The emperor's individual input in political processes appears not to have been of great importance for the overall functioning of the political system over which he presided; insofar as he did not act in a disruptive or erratic way, the empire could be run in his name without his direct intervention. What the courtiers feared most was not a passive but an excessively active ruler; hence, despite the much-hailed ideal of the charismatic and sagacious True Monarch, in reality the empire was usually in no need of gifted sovereigns. Although weak emperors could become a liability at times of acute crisis, as discussed in the epilogue to this chapter, in general the officialdom preferred an inactive leader.

The above analysis calls into question the thesis with which I opened this section, according to which China's rule became increasingly more "despotic" as centuries passed. This conclusion appears to me to be built on a selective focus on several excessively powerful rulers from the late imperial period, and on misinterpretation of the increasing ritual gap between rulers and ministers as indicative of the overall disempowerment of the ministerial stratum.[58] In reality, however, neither the personal prowess of dynastic founders, nor institutional or ritual adjustments aimed at bolstering the emperor's power, could thwart the bureaucratic logic of the empire, which would sooner or later diminish the emperors' activism. To illustrate the pervasiveness of this process, I shall focus now on those rulers who came from the most charisma-oriented political culture—the steppe conquerors of China.

From Khan to Emperor: The Conquest Dynasties

Conquest dynasties provide the most interesting case study to test the functioning of the Chinese mode of emperorship in a highly different cultural setting. The nomadic and seminomadic conquerors of China represent a military-oriented political culture that differed in several crucial aspects from that of China proper. To make a rough generalization, it may be said that while the latter was predicated on stability, the former valued the ability of the ruler. The nomads shared the Chinese concept of Heaven's "Mandate," but in their view it rested with the ruling clan as a whole, each of whose members could lead the steppe dwellers insofar as he possessed sufficient charisma and martial skills. Moreover, Heaven (Tengri) did not bestow its mandate on every generation; only through military success could a leader demonstrate Heaven's ongoing support. The role of the leadership was therefore constantly contested: if the ruler failed to deliver victories, he could expect a coup and replacement by a more able candidate. The position of an heir was even more contestable: violent struggles among rival clansmen became such a persistent feature of nomadic life that Joseph Fletcher termed their succession system "bloody tanistry," that is, violent competition among potential heirs, resulting in the success of the fittest.[59] This system ensured the high quality of nomadic leaders, but it also introduced immanent instability in nomadic polities, which were repeatedly torn apart by bloody succession struggles among the closest kin.

Adoption of the Chinese model of emperorship became one of the most important steps taken by the nomadic regimes on their road toward eventual "Sinicization," or toward state formation in general, especially if the state was aimed at conquering parts of China.[60] Practically, it meant elevating the tribal leader to a new height: no longer would he be the primus inter pares, whose military skills determined his right to rule; rather, he would be a sacrosanct True Monarch, aloof from his subjects, whose position was unassailable in all but truly exceptional conditions. Similarly, according to the new rules of the game, the heir apparent was to be established through a regular procedure, diminishing the potential for violent succession clashes. This radically different pattern of rule was beneficial to the rulers and to political stability in general; but it also represented a cultural break with steppe heritage and potentially undermined the military prowess of the conquest leadership. Hence the adoption of Chinese imperial culture was usually a lengthy and gradual process, during which many steppe rulers tried to combine the posture of a Chinese emperor with that of a tribal *khaqan* or *khan*. Those who succeeded in blending the advantages of Chinese and nomadic traits of rulership were renowned as the most magnificent leaders in China's history, such as the great Qing emperors discussed below. However, this synthesis between the active/military and passive/civilian models of rulership was not sustainable for long. Gradually but inevitably, alien conquerors moved toward the Chinese model of a passive ruler.

A brief glimpse of two major alien dynasties, the Mongol Yuan (1271–1368) and the Manchu (Manju) Qing (1644–1912), illustrates this process. The leaders of each of these dynasties were well aware of the traps into which some of their predecessors had fallen, having become absorbed into the Chinese mode of life to the extent of losing martial prowess. The Mongols were particularly averse to the enticements of sedentary civilization; hence their full-scale adoption of the Chinese imperial system (even in its "reduced" form) took place only in 1271, a full sixty-five years after the establishment of the Great Mongol State by Chinggis Khan (ca. 1162–1227). Their early leaders were each renowned for military prowess, assertiveness, and activism; their succession system prior to 1271 retained traits of "warrior democracy," as the supreme leader had to be approved by the *qurltai* meeting of the tribal chiefs. Inevitably, succession struggles marred every reign after Chinggis Khan's death. It was partly the quest for internal stability that prompted Khubilai Khan (r. 1260–1294) to adopt the Chinese imperial title in 1271.[61]

Khubilai himself was a powerful and resolute leader, whose adoption of Chinese ways did not reduce his charisma; but his successors were progressively marginalized by their entourage. While the middle period of the Yuan dynasty is marred by bloody succession struggles that reflect the strong impact of the steppe heritage, court life moved gradually but irreversibly in the "Chinese" direction of decrease in the emperor's activism. The last emperor of the Yuan, Toghon Temür (r. 1333–1368), ended his lengthy tenure in a very "Chinese" way, as a hapless spectator of his empire's disintegration, unable to meaningfully influence the course of events.[62] It is noteworthy that Zhu Yuanzhang, who overthrew the Yuan, averred that the emperors' weakness rather than excessive power was one of the major maladies of the nomadic dynasty.[63] Thus, despite its relative brevity, the Yuan demonstrates the same pattern of marginalization of individual monarchs as is characteristic of Chinese dynasties.

The Qing dynasty exemplifies this pattern even better. Having crowned China's lengthy imperial age, this dynasty manifested, during its first century and a half, the best-ever blend of alien and Chinese, of the civilian (*wen*) and the martial (*wu*), of stability and efficiency. The first six Manchu emperors were renowned activists: they closely supervised and at

times personally led their armies, toured the country, and directly inter-
vened in policy making, if necessary through ruthless oppression of real
or imagined opposition. The imperial princes also participated in military
campaigns and in civil administration; and while the dynasty did not escape bitter succession struggles, those remained generally manageable,
while generating efficient rulers. The dynasty benefited in particular from
the combined civilian and military experience of its fifth monarch, the
Yongzheng Emperor (r. 1723–1735), arguably the most administratively
astute ruler in China's long history. Having ascended the throne as a mature statesman, this emperor had exceptional understanding of the functioning of the bureaucratic apparatus and was sufficiently self-confident
to impose his view on the opposition without sinking into senseless despotism. His reasonable leadership brought about, among other benefits,
a tremendous improvement in the dynasty's financial situation. The Yongzheng Emperor's father and his son, the Kangxi and Qianlong (r. 1736–
1795) Emperors, also proved to be particularly adept leaders, whose military and diplomatic skills contributed to the unprecedented expansion of
the Qing realm. Doubtlessly, the succession of capable monarchs was one
of the major reasons for Qing's overall success.[64]

The Qing model of assertive emperors adopted from the dynasty's
tribal past was one of its major assets, but it was not a lasting solution to
the gradual atrophy of imperial charisma. When we jump to the nineteenth century, the picture becomes dramatically different from the early
Qing reigns. Again, we see passive leaders, whose activities are largely
confined to the imperial capital in Beijing and the nearby summer capital
in Rehe (modern Chengde); leaders who appear to have been entirely unable to influence the adverse course of events that led to the ultimate
collapse of the empire. The familiar pattern of the Han, Tang, Song, Yuan,
and Ming dynasties (to mention only a few)—namely, a vigorous, if violent, beginning and an inglorious end—is exemplified in the Qing dynasty
as well.

These trajectories of rulership atrophy in the most charisma-oriented
dynasties in Chinese history suggest that the pattern of the monarchs'
declining ability to influence political processes can indeed be considered
one of the basic characteristics of the Chinese imperial system. The same
internal logic of the empire, which favored stability above all, was conducive not just to the concentration of all imaginable power in the hands of
an emperor as an institution, but also to systematic reduction of the impact of individual emperors on political processes. Invisible as they were,
Chinese "checks and balances" effectively reduced the danger of autocratic arbitrariness to a tolerable level. Yet, like every political choice, the
one made by Chinese statesmen had its price, both in terms of reduced
efficiency and in terms of persistent and sometimes debilitating tensions

at court. It is time now to assess the advantages and disadvantages of this choice.

Epilogue: The Price of Impotent Omnipotence

The Chinese concept of emperorship emerges from the above discussion as highly paradoxical from its very inception. As early as the Warring States period a palpable bifurcation existed between the thinkers' overall commitment to the principle of monarchism and their sober assessment that sagacious "True Monarchs" are a rarity, and that most rulers are prone to prove themselves to be mediocrities. This intrinsic tension between the ideal and the reality became even more pronounced in the aftermath of the imperial unification, when the First Emperor and his successors appropriated the stance of the True Monarch. Instead of unmasking the fallacy of this pretension and possibly damaging thereby the entire monarchic enterprise, thinkers and statesmen of the imperial era preferred to treat the emperors as if they were sagacious True Monarchs on the institutional level, while simultaneously realizing that the throne was more often than not occupied by erring and possibly inept human beings. This resulted in the major paradox of the empire: the monarchs theoretically enjoyed absolute and limitless power, but were actively discouraged from exercising it as individuals. Almost every emperor was both a sage and a mediocrity: a sage in the official parlance; a mediocrity in the hearts of his courtiers, and later in historical writings that mercilessly exposed the errors, transgressions, and general inadequacy of the throne's occupants. This coexistence of contradictory premises imbued the imperial institution with deep tensions that persisted throughout the two-odd millennia of imperial history.

How can we assess the results of this imperfect compromise between the image and the reality of imperial power? At times it clearly malfunctioned, giving rise to woeful abuses by vicious despots. An emperor who took his sagacity to be real, an ambitious ruler who mistrusted his aides, could utilize the huge power of the throne to impose his will on the entire empire—sometimes in the cruelest way. Among these despotic figures we find murderous psychopaths, who rarely reigned for long, as well as exceptionally perspicacious and gifted monarchs, whose activities may have benefited the realm, while extracting a huge human cost from their subjects. Such were, for example, the Ming founder, Zhu Yuanzhang, and the three "sage-monarchs" of the Qing: the Kangxi, Yongzheng, and Qianlong Emperors.

Despotism was a distinct possibility in China's imperial system, but it was not the rule; usually, the system of invisible "checks and balances" was effective enough in reining in the monarchs. Actually, most emperors appear in retrospect to have been overwhelmed by the magnitude of their power. Being responsible in principle for everything in All-under-Heaven—from rainfall to school curricula, from the submission of foreign rulers to the proper functioning of the dikes of the Yellow River—they were assigned a position more fitting to Almighty God than to a human being. Few were so ambitious or benighted as to believe that they could really shape the course of events in the subcelestial realm; for the majority it was more expedient to follow bureaucratic routine and enjoy enormous ritual prestige with little if any personal input into the empire's governance.

The tragedy of China's rulers was exacerbated owing to the inherent lack of clarity concerning the reasonable limits of the emperor's actions as an individual. As the embodiment of abstract principles of fairness and impartiality, the emperors found it difficult to act independently in almost any sphere of their public and private lives. Anxious to eliminate any gap between the emperor as, on the one hand, a sacrosanct institution and source of moral inspiration, and, on the other, a flesh-and-blood occupant of the dragon throne, the courtiers tried to limit any potential deviation of the emperor from the ritually prescribed activities. Even relatively innocent decisions, such as bestowing imperial favors on a monastery or promoting a certain concubine, could become a source of friction between the ruler and his entourage. When mishandled, such frictions could develop into debilitating confrontations and result in severe consequences for all the parties involved, including bloody purges or gloomy stalemates at court. Devastating controversies over such issues as the emperor's mourning obligations under Ming Shizong (r. 1521–1567), or over the naming of an heir apparent under Shizong's grandson, Shenzong (r. 1572–1620),[65] exemplify the imminent danger of collision between the monarch and his aides. The emperors, even those who were capricious and vindictive, can be seen, then, as victims of the system that denied them the right to individuality.[66]

In broader political terms, the nullification of the emperor's personality also had clear negative consequences, as it sharply contradicted the declared desideratum of a sagacious and perspicacious monarch on the throne. After all, even a "rubber-stamp" emperor had to make certain fateful decisions, most specifically in nominating chief executives and in resolving intrabureaucratic controversies. These tasks presupposed an intelligent monarch, who would not be duped or manipulated by unscrupulous aides. Yet as the system of submerging the ruler within highly ritualized bureaucratic routines directly led to his depersonalization, it curbed the emperor's abilities to perform effectively those tasks that demanded personal input. The consequences could be fateful: at times of crisis, when swift and resolute decision making was required, many emperors proved completely inadequate, fluctuating between competing court factions, acting erratically, and hastening their dynasty's demise. The notorious lack of effective leadership aggravated the crises—which should have been quite manageable—that led to the demise of the Northern Song, Ming, and Qing dynasties, among others.[67] The very collapse of the imperial enterprise in the early twentieth century can be related to the late Qing emperors' inability to exercise effective leadership during times of aggravating crisis.

Spectacular collapses naturally attract our attention; but let us look more closely at the interconnection between the mode of emperorship depicted in this chapter and the empire's longevity. Two observations immediately come to mind. First, the ultimate goal of the imperial architects—eliminating multiple loci of power and creating a unified system of decision making aimed at preventing internal disorder—was realized remarkably well. Although China did not avoid lengthy periods of turmoil and disintegration, those were less damaging and less frequent than in most other polities of comparable size and complexity. The unifying presence of the supreme monarch as an embodiment of the Great Unity of All-under-Heaven contributed toward political stability.

Second, the imperial system appears to have been quite manageable in the long term. Throughout millennia, the dragon throne was occupied by megalomaniacs and minors, by generals and peasant rebels, by nomadic warriors and refined literati, by elderly, infantile, and mentally or physically impaired monarchs, and even in one case (that of Wu Zetian, r. 684–705) by a woman.[68] That none of these, whatever temporary disruption they caused, inflicted lasting damage on the imperial enterprise is truly remarkable. It seems that despite its ostensible awkwardness, the Chinese variant of "checks and balances"—namely, distinguishing between the institutional and the individual power of the monarch—was well adapted to changing circumstances and could withstand most woeful crises, including (in the case of the Northern Qi dynasty, 550–577) a chain of mentally unstable monarchs,[69] without collapsing and disintegrating, and at times even without significantly impairing the normal life of the empire's subjects. This is an undeniable achievement, unparalleled in other ruler-centered polities.

Finally, the imposing figure of the emperor should also be considered as the most essential part of China's political identity. Many administrative aspects of the imperial polity, and even the ethnic and cultural composition of the ruling elite, changed over time, but the chain of monarchs, who were invariably presumed to be omnipotent leaders and had to be revered beyond anything in the mundane and supramundane realms, remained the single identifiable "Chinese" political feature throughout the millennia. Not incidentally, adoption of the imperial title was the most essential aspect of the "Sinicization" of China's conquerors; the native elite could compromise about anything else, but not about this most sacred symbol. It may not be excessive to say that the preservation of the monarchic order served no less than the preservation of the written language as a preeminent factor behind China's remarkable cultural—and not only political—longevity. "From the earliest generations, multiple states were extinguished in All-under-Heaven, but the Way of the ruler did not decline: this is because it benefits All-under-Heaven": the *Lüshi chunqiu* asseveration that serves as an epigraph to this chapter may also serve as the motto of Chinese imperial history.

CHAPTER 3

The Literati

> The heart of the ancient benevolent men . . . was neither to be delighted in things nor to feel sorry for themselves. At the loftiness of [imperial] temples and halls, they worried for their people, in the remoteness of rivers and lakes they worried for their ruler. Hence entering [the court], they worried; and leaving it, also worried: so when did they enjoy? It must be said: they were the first to worry the worries of All-under-Heaven, and the last to enjoy its joys. Oh! Without these persons, where could I find my place?
> —*Fan Zhongyan*

THE EPIGRAPH, taken from the "Inscription of the Yueyang Tower" by Fan Zhongyan (989–1052 CE), contains arguably the most famous lines by this leading man of letters of the Northern Song dynasty (960–1126).[1] Fan, one of the pivotal figures of the Northern Song intellectual revival, succinctly summarized certain basic features of the Chinese literati's self-image. Being dedicated to one's lofty ideals to the point of self-denial, being public-spirited and politically involved (worrying about the people and about the ruler), and having a sense of collective identity, a notion reflected in Fan's desire to "find his place" among his admirable predecessors—all these were normative characteristics of Chinese intellectuals. These proud men, the architects and guardians of the Chinese empire, are the focus of this chapter.

The stratum to which Fan Zhongyan belonged—*shi* in Chinese—was the major player in China's sociopolitical life. Defining the term *shi* is notoriously difficult: hence while it is usually translated into English as "literati," "scholar-officials," "gentlemen," in certain contexts it can be rendered also as "knights," "officers," "aristocrats," and the like. This semantic richness is not surprising given the fact that during approximately two and a half millennia the term *shi* was the most common designation of acting and aspiring elite members, and that during this period the composition of the elite and its nature underwent considerable changes. Yet these variations notwithstanding, we can speak of the *shi* as a well-defined group, primarily because of their distinct self-awareness and strong group identity. The *shi* were the core of China's educated elite, and it is justifiable, at least for heuristic convenience, to dub them "intellectuals," especially in light of a considerable semantic overlap between the Western term "intellectual" and the Chinese *shi*.[2]

The major peculiarity of Chinese intellectuals was their simultaneous hegemony in both cultural and political spheres. In neither realm was their position exclusive: through much of the imperial period Buddhist and Daoist monks possessed considerable cultural prestige, while politically speaking, the *shi* were only one segment of the ruling elite, and had to compete for power with military officers, the emperor's relatives, alien tribal leaders, and sometimes even eunuchs. Yet throughout most of the imperial millennia, the *shi* in their capacity as "scholar-officials" preserved their dominance in both intellectual and political realms, which turned them into an exceptionally powerful group. Their moral and intellectual prestige allowed them at times to defy the emperor and to counterbalance his whims, while their political power, in turn, further bolstered their moral and intellectual authority. They were furthermore a self-aware stratum whose distinctive consciousness was decisively elitist: the *shi* viewed themselves as moral guides of society, rulers and commoners alike. In addition, as the epigraph suggests, Chinese intellectuals developed a strong sense of mission: serving the ruler and the people was viewed not just as fulfilling individual career aspirations but as the route to moral self-realization. This combination of prestige, pride, and commitment to public service became the hallmark of *shi* identity throughout the imperial period.

In this chapter, I focus primarily on the upper segment of the *shi* stratum, which comprised most of the officials and leading thinkers, the men who actively sought careers in government and hoped to "order the generation." A broader lower segment of the *shi* encompassed the core of local elites, who shared the educational background and lifestyle conventions of the leading literati of their age; they will be the focus of the next chapter. I adopt this division primarily for the sake of heuristic clarity: in practice, the dividing line between the two segments was not always clear, and was not necessarily determined by one's examination degree or official rank. Rather, the distinction was more closely related to one's horizons and ambitions: those literati with whom I am dealing in this chapter were primarily those committed, in Fan Zhongyan's words, "to the ruler and to the people": those who transcended the parochial boundaries of their localities and aimed at "saving the world." Their activities determined the political and intellectual dynamics at the empire's core.

My discussion focuses on the intellectuals' voluntary attachment to the ruler's service as their single most significant choice. I shall try to elucidate both the advantages of this choice and its price. Having opted for a political career, leading intellectuals had to accept their position as the emperor's servitors, which was at odds with their self-proclaimed moral superiority over the throne; and the resultant tension between their roles as the leaders and the led generated persistent frustration and manifold tragedies. Yet bitterness aside, the voluntary attachment of the intellectuals to the throne had also greatly empowered the educated elite as a whole. For two-odd millennia, members of this stratum navigated the empire through many storms and challenges, contributing decisively toward the preservation of the imperial political structure, and of its cultural foundations, against all odds.[3]

The Rise of the Shi

The ascendancy of the *shi*, and the parallel transformation of the ruling elite from aristocratic to predominantly meritocratic, was the most consequential social development of the Warring States period. During the preceding Springs-and-Autumns period, the Chinese world was ruled by a hereditary aristocracy: a culturally and socially cohesive stratum, the members of which monopolized all high positions in the courts of regional states, and dominated the political, economic, military, and intellectual life of their polities. At that period, the *shi* were the lowest segment of the hereditary aristocracy, mostly minor siblings of powerful lineages, who made their living primarily as the aristocrats' retainers. Yet by the fifth century BCE, as aristocratic lineages were decimated in bloody internecine struggles, *shi* moved to fill in the void at the top of the ruling apparatus. Many rulers found it expedient to promote *shi*, who, lacking independent military and economic power, could not directly threaten their lords, while their administrative and military skills were often greater than those of hereditary nobles. By the fourth century BCE, the aristocrats were submerged within a new, broader, *shi*-based elite, and the term *shi* became thenceforth a common designation for acting and aspiring elite members.[4]

I shall leave aside the sociopolitical implications of the ascendancy of the *shi* and focus instead on its ideological consequences, specifically on the formation of *shi* self-consciousness and of their distinctive identity. This identity was decisively shaped by Confucius, the first known ideologically active member of the *shi* stratum, whose contribution to the evolving self-image of this group turned him into the most respected intellectual in China's history. Confucius redefined elite status as stemming chiefly from one's behavior rather than from one's pedigree. In particular, he reinterpreted the term "superior man" (*junzi*), which theretofore had been applied exclusively to high-ranking nobles, to refer primarily to one's moral qualities; thus morally upright *shi* merited designation as "superior men" and inclusion in the elite. Thenceforth *shi* was no longer a hereditary but an ethical category.[5]

The behavioral mode for the *shi* shaped by Confucius and his followers was patterned in many respects after that of hereditary aristocrats of the Springs-and-Autumns period, but there is one crucial difference. The *shi* were self-made men, for whom self-cultivation and learning were essential for both acquiring and perpetuating their elite status. This emphasis on individual merits remained a hallmark of the *shi* throughout history; even in the later periods, when this group's status was de facto defined by pedigree (especially in the third–ninth centuries CE), it was still conceived of as pertaining to behavioral patterns and to education rather than merely to birth. Back in the Warring States period, when social mobility was exceptionally high, the notion that merit should enable an individual to transcend social barriers became a common ideological conviction of competing thinkers. Many *shi* of that age prided themselves on their supposedly lowly background, claiming that they owed their status exclusively to personal abilities. Identifying themselves as "plain-clothed" (*bu yi*: literally, those who wear coarse linen rather than fine and expensive silk), these *shi* presented themselves as economically closer to the commoners than to high-ranking officials. This self-presentation, like anecdotes about erstwhile poverty and miserable conditions of eminent *shi*, should not be taken too literally; but it does indicate that potential openness to newcomers from the lower strata became part of the group's ethos from the Warring States period on.[6]

This openness to advancement from below did not mean, however, that the *shi* adopted an egalitarian outlook. To the contrary, they were immensely proud of their hard-won elite status and assumed a clear elitist stance. From Confucius on, the distinction between "superior men" and uncultivated commoners, the "petty men," became essential to the *shi* self-image. The distinction had social connotations, but it was primarily ethical. Confucius defines a petty man as selfish, narrow-minded, profit-seeking, servile, and unable to yield. A superior man, in distinction, is guided by dutifulness and righteousness; he aspires high but knows how to yield; he is steadfast and resolute, selfless and public-minded; he is benevolent, perspicacious, courageous, loyal, and filial.[7] Members of the elite frequently abused their rivals by categorizing them as "petty men": imposters who had attained high status unjustifiably, and who should be carefully distinguished from the true, morally upright *shi*. Self-identification as "superior men" became one of the perennial characteristics of *shi* identity.

Of the manifold positive attributes appropriated by the *shi* as they molded their identity, public-mindedness and commitment to the universal good appear to be singularly significant. Confucius and his followers actively promulgated the vision of a superior man who cultivates himself with the ultimate goal of "bringing peace to the hundred clans [all the people]."⁸ This concept of self-realization is intrinsically linked to *shi* involvement in government service, as discussed below; but its implications are much broader. In particular, their declared public-mindedness allowed the *shi* to assert themselves as moral and intellectual leaders of society, the only men able to cure its maladies. This attainment of moral and intellectual leadership by the *shi* was the second major by-product of their political ascendance.

The *shi* discourse of the Warring States period, which is reflected in a great variety of contemporaneous texts, unequivocally identifies the *shi* as exclusive possessors of the True Way (*Dao*)—the ultimate remedy for all social ills. While the precise content of the True Way was continuously debated by rival thinkers, and their practical recommendations varied considerably, there was a consensus among them that the Way rested with members of their stratum and not with the rulers. At least prior to the appearance of the future True Monarch, the *shi* were prone to claim intellectual autonomy from and superiority over the courts of regional lords.⁹

The attainment of intellectual autonomy and the subsequent intellectual hegemony of the *shi* is one of the most exciting developments of the Warring States period. Our sources indicate that prior to Confucius, ideological activity was concentrated exclusively in the courts—first in the Zhou royal court and then in the courts of regional lords.¹⁰ Soon after Confucius, however, this situation changed dramatically. Courts of the Warring States appear to have been devoid of any intellectual authority; the true source of such authority was thenceforth the *shi* Masters (*zi*), such as Confucius and his followers or major opponents. Ideological debates about the nature of the True Way were conducted within the *shi* stratum; the rulers were, of course, the primary addressees of these debates and potential employers of the Masters and of their disciples; but they had no power to determine ideological orthodoxy. Thus, amid profound administrative centralization and overall empowerment of the rulers, as discussed in the previous chapter, the field of intellectual activity became entirely independent of the power-holders. Rather than deferring to the rulers' wishes, the *shi* unequivocally claimed the right to teach the rulers and direct them toward morally and politically appropriate courses.

Our sources for the Warring States period—most of which were produced by the *shi* and for the *shi*—may somewhat exaggerate the degree of their intellectual dominance, but there is no doubt that the Masters decisively shaped the political and ethical discourse of their age. Contemporaneous texts routinely portray the rulers as deferential, seeking the advice of the *shi* about political matters and about matters of individual behavior, and we have no evidence whatsoever of external challenges to *shi* ideological dominance, either from the rulers or from other social groups. In the long term, the position of the *shi* as moral and intellectual guides of society would remain their single most important asset, which would preserve the indispensability of this stratum under a variety of imperial regimes.

By the end of the Warring States period, texts associated with the *shi* reflect an immense sense of pride on the part of the members of this stratum and their strong sense of collective identity. This feeling permeates most of the texts of competing thinkers, even those who, like Xunzi, were quite critical of the excessive boastfulness of fellow *shi*.[11] Sometimes the pride of members of this elite attained almost shameless proportions, as exemplified in the *Lüshi chunqiu*, a multiauthored text, composed by a group of *shi* on the very eve of the imperial unification:

> *Shi* are the men who, when acting in accord with [proper] patterns, do not escape the difficulties; when facing the troubles, forget the profits; they cast aside life to follow righteousness and consider death as returning home. If there are such men, the ruler of a state will not be able to befriend them, the Son of Heaven will not be able to make them servants. At best, stabilization of All-under-Heaven, or, second to it, stabilization of a single state must come from these men. Hence a ruler who wants to attain great achievements and fame cannot but devote himself to searching for these men. A worthy sovereign works hard looking for [proper] men and is at rest when maintaining affairs.[12]

This somewhat embarrassingly effusive panegyric epitomizes the enormous self-confidence of the *shi* at the end of the Warring States period. Pride, a feeling of moral superiority, the conviction that the *shi* possess the remedies to all political maladies—all these motifs recur in the *Lüshi chunqiu* and in many other contemporary texts. Of particular interest is the authors' haughty stance vis-à-vis the rulers, who are portrayed as being unable to make these proud *shi* their servants, or even to befriend them. Yet behind this veneer of haughtiness we can also discern the authors' anxiety to be employed; hence they urge the ruler "to devote himself to searching for these men." This curious contradiction (why should the ruler search for men whom he cannot turn into his servants?) is indicative of the deep and lasting tension between *shi* self-confidence and their political dependence on the rulers—the tension that was to inform the lives of Chinese intellectuals for millennia to come.

SHI IN THE MARKET OF TALENT

Voluntary attachment to government service became the single most important choice of the *shi* of the Warring States period, the choice that shaped the intellectuals' political role throughout Chinese history. Office holding attracted many *shi* because of its sheer advantages in terms of emoluments, prestige, and power: this was a way to "avoid the bitterness of tilling and sowing" and to persuade "the rulers to part with their gold, jade, silk, and brocade" for the sake of their aides.[13] Yet while seeking a career for its material benefits was common in the Warring States period and beyond, ideologically these selfish motives were discouraged. Instead, several leading thinkers promulgated the concept of government service as a means of moral self-realization. Their vision had a lasting impact on the lives of Chinese intellectuals.

Confucius appears, once again, as an initiator of the moral interpretation of political involvement. He wandered relentlessly throughout the Zhou world in search of appropriate appointment and seems to have been deeply frustrated by his failure to find an employer who would enable him "to revive the Zhou [dynasty] in the east."[14] A similar sequence of wanderings and frustration characterizes the life of one of Confucius's most eminent followers, Mengzi, who even averred that "service for a *shi* is like tilling for a peasant," meaning that a government career was the only appropriate mode of existence for an intellectual. The service, as Mengzi acknowledged, was important economically, but its true aim was moral. Mengzi explained that his mission was "to rectify the wrongs in the ruler's heart," thereby instilling morality first in the ruler and then through him in all of the subjects: "Just rectify the ruler and the state will be stabilized." In Mengzi's eyes this noble goal justified repeated attempts to find employment with the regional lords, whom he otherwise bitterly criticized as "criminals," "devourers of human flesh," and men with "the proclivity to kill humans."[15]

From the very beginning, the political commitment of the *shi* was accompanied by deep tension. These proud intellectuals, who considered themselves the ruler's guides and teachers, vied for the position of servants in the ruler-centered polity, which they themselves had designed. Balancing between their sense of moral superiority and political subjugation to the throne was a challenging task for lofty-minded *shi*. The solution, promulgated by Confucius and his followers, and adopted by many other *shi*, was to claim that they served not the ruler personally but rather the True Way; practically this meant that the ruler could—and should—be defied in the name of superior moral values. Thus, while these and other thinkers maintained that loyalty to the sovereign is one of the most important moral obligations of an intellectual, they interpreted this loyalty in such a way as to preserve their freedom of action.[16] Xunzi, the greatest synthesizer of political thought of the Warring States period, summarizes this stance in his essay "The Way of the Minister":

He who obeys the orders and benefits the ruler is called compliant; he who obeys the orders and does not benefit the ruler is called servile; he who contradicts the orders and benefits the ruler is called loyal; he who contradicts the orders and does not benefit the ruler is called a usurper.[17]

The minister should be loyal, but his loyalty does not preclude criticism: it is distinct from servility and flattery. An intellectual in the ruler's service may have an understanding of the ruler's interests superior to that of the sovereign himself; hence, if need be, he may disobey the ruler's commands. Xunzi's dictum, "Follow the Way, do not follow the ruler,"[18] remained the guiding premise for lofty-minded intellectuals throughout the ages. To be sure, this was not an assault on monarchy: the ruler was supposed to be the supreme beneficiary of ministerial action; but the minister knew better how to benefit the ruler and society as a whole. Thus, while remaining ostensibly loyal to the throne, the intellectual preserved considerable freedom of action, and, most importantly, his dignity and integrity, while dealing with the monarch. In contrast, servile sycophants and flatterers were despised as "petty men," from whom a true *shi* had to distinguish himself.

From the very beginning the desire of lofty *shi* to maintain their pride while remaining in the ruler's service was fraught with contradictions. Not every ruler was fond of critical-minded servants who routinely opted to admonish him and defy his orders in the name of the Way. It is not surprising, then, that the lives of many high-minded intellectuals, Confucius and Mengzi included, became an almost endless chain of appointments and resignations, or of unfulfilled appointments. In principle, this tension with the rulers could become detrimental to the intellectuals' political involvement; but during the Warring States period it did not damage the career aspirations of most *shi*. Even the most critical-minded individuals of that age could hope to find an appropriate patron. The reason for this odd situation was political: the world of the Warring States can be seen as a huge market of talent in which rival courts competed to attract the best of the *shi*, while the latter were free to cross boundaries in search of better appointments. Given the acute competition for gifted personnel, it was expedient for the ruler to tolerate the affronts of prestigious intellectuals in his service: punishing a critical-minded aide could backfire, causing a massive exodus of other *shi* from his court and inflicting a severe brain drain on the state. Unable to prevent free movement of the *shi* across boundaries, the rulers had little choice but to accept the haughty behavior of some of their subordinates.[19]

The multipolar world of the Warring States therefore ensured multiple employment opportunities for the *shi*, and this occupational autonomy was the true precondition for both their intellectual autonomy and their exceptional audacity when dealing with the throne. Indeed, the remarkably tolerant atmosphere of that age emboldened many of the *shi* to conceive of their relations with the rulers as reciprocal rather than hierarchical: relations resembling those between friends or even between a teacher and his disciple, rather than between a subject and the master. Feeling secure from prosecution, these *shi* were always ready to distinguish themselves from despicable flatterers by adopting an overtly critical tone when dealing with the rulers. For instance, Mengzi, who eventually became one of the most celebrated thinkers in the eyes of the imperial literati, was renowned for his outspokenness, bold criticism of contemporaneous sovereigns, frequent démarches, and even direct affronts to his employers. The following example illustrates his stance toward the monarchs:

> Mengzi said to King Xuan of Qi: "Suppose your subject had entrusted his wife and children to a friend, and traveled to Chu. When he returned, he discovered that his friend had let his wife and children suffer cold and hunger. What should be done about it?"
> —"Cast [the friend] away."
> —"When the Master of the *shi* is unable to rule the *shi* properly, what should be done about it?"
> —"Remove him."
> —"If there is no proper rule within the domain, what should be done about it?"
> The King turned to his attendants and changed the subject.[20]

Mengzi's message is clear: the dysfunctional king should be removed like any petty official. The discussion is not merely theoretical: the king understands well that Mengzi's parable is directed against him. Yet the king refrains from punishing his outspoken adviser, preferring to ignore an unpleasant criticism. We cannot assess the veracity of this and many similar anecdotes scattered through the texts of the Warring States period, nor do we know what the true limits of the ruler's tolerance were, but it is safe to say that the atmosphere of the courts of the Warring States was exceptionally conducive to the outspokenness of the *shi*.[21] This might have further bolstered the intellectuals' self-confidence and sense of superiority, as reflected in the *Lüshi chunqiu* statement cited earlier.

In the multipolar world, the willing attachment of the intellectuals to the ruler-centered political order appears, then, as a well-calculated gamble. Insofar as the demand for their skills outstripped the supply, the interstate market of talent ensured the *shi* a degree of immunity from prosecution, allowing them to maintain their high prestige under the ruler's patronage despite their obvious economic and political dependence on the rulers. It is ironic, therefore, that the *shi* were the staunchest proponents of the universal monarchy, which, when established, contributed decisively to the demise of the very political system that had allowed them to preserve their dignity in the ruler's service. In the age of the unified empire new rules of the game emerged, and these were markedly less advantageous to the *shi*.

Under the Imperial Monopoly

From a modern point of view, the Warring States period's ideological pluralism, and the esteem in which its intellectuals were held, appear extraordinarily attractive in comparison with the much chillier atmosphere in the imperial courts. Yet in an age when unity and stability were sought by all, pluralism was not a prized goal. While many thinkers of the late Warring States period appear fascinated with the intellectual flowering of their age, in many texts we also find an increasing concern with ideological divisiveness, and, most notably, with the unruliness and haughtiness of the *shi*. Some eminent thinkers began proposing curbs on *shi* activities. Thus a leading follower of Confucius, Xunzi, a staunch supporter of intellectual autonomy for the "superior men," was nonetheless among the first to call upon the future sage monarch to prohibit "illicit theories" and "illicit knowledge."[22] Xunzi's readiness to utilize the power of the state to quell his intellectual opponents remained somewhat qualified; but his erstwhile disciple and ideological rival, Han Feizi, was far more resolute:

> Accordingly, in the country of an enlightened ruler there are no texts written in books and on bamboo strips, but the law is the teaching; there are no "speeches" of the former kings, but officials are the teachers; there is no private wielding of swords, but beheading [enemies] is the valor.[23]

Han Feizi was the first known thinker to envision a total order in which the state controls everything, including ideology, while the intellectual elite becomes coterminous with officialdom. His proposal to "nationalize" learning by "turning officials into teachers" was indeed put forward shortly after the imperial unification. In 213 BCE, another of Xunzi's erstwhile disciples and the major architect of the unified empire, Li Si (d. 208 BCE), wary of ideological disputes at court, launched an overall assault against independent intellectuals. Having identified ideological pluralism, spurred by "private learning," with the political disorder of the past, Li Si explained why the unified empire should not tolerate intellectuals' autonomy and pluralism:

> Now that your Majesty has annexed All-under-Heaven, you have separated black and white and have fixed the single to be respected. But [adherents of] private learning continue to reject among themselves

the teaching of the Law. When they hear of orders, each discusses them according to his [private] learning; when entering [at court], negates them in heart; when exiting—discusses them in lanes and alleys. They oppose the sovereign to attain reputation, accept the unusual as lofty, and lead the multitudes to slander. If they are not banned, the sovereign's power will collapse above and cliques will be formed below. It is advantageous to prohibit them.[24]

Having identified two major maladies brought on by private learning—divisiveness and potential subversion—Li Si made his radical suggestion to eliminate copies of the semicanonical *Poems* and *Documents*, along with the *Speeches of the Hundred Schools*, from private collections, explicitly excluding, however, those in the possession of the court erudites (*boshi*). After enumerating the books to be burned and those to be spared, Li Si concluded, "And those who want to study laws and ordinances, let them take an official as a teacher!"[25]

Li Si's final recommendation, as well as his sparing of the erudites' collections, indicates the deep motives behind his drastic measures. The suppression of private learning was not primarily an ideological act—Li Si did not suggest any reprisals against his ideological opponents at court—but rather an institutional measure. Much like Han Feizi, Li Si considered the nationalization of learning to be the only way to establish proper relations between the *shi* and the finally solidified ruler-centered polity. The empire was in no need of an unruly stratum of scholars, whose very existence was intrinsically linked to the chaotic legacy of the past. They were to be either suppressed or incorporated into the officialdom. This might have become the grand finale of the process of centralization and abolition of independent loci of authority.

History was not kind to Li Si: he was executed by the notorious Second Emperor (r. 209–207 BCE), the empire he constructed collapsed shortly thereafter, and for generations of literati he became one of the most hated historical personages. Yet the project of redefining the nature of the intellectuals' relations with the throne in the age of political unity could not be abandoned altogether. While initially the weak Han dynasty tolerated a considerable degree of decentralization and did not strive to establish firm ideological control over its subjects, by the time of the active centralizer Han Emperor Wu (r. 141–87 BCE), the tide was reversed. Emperor Wu acted resolutely to put an end to the remnants of the market of talent that had been partly resurrected under the lenient rule of his predecessors. In 122 BCE he annihilated the rich principality of Huainan, whose ruler, Liu An (d. 122 BCE), patronized the last powerful "think tank" of independent scholars.[26] This was the end of an era. Soon enough, other autonomous loci of patronage for traveling thinkers, specifically those established by high ministers, were eliminated as well. With its monopoly on the avenues of advancement reasserted, the imperial court had greatly enhanced its power vis-à-vis the *shi*.

Among Emperor Wu's manifold innovations two are frequently singled out as most significant institutionally: the establishment of a rudimentary examination system, in which candidates recommended by various localities were examined in the capital before receiving official appointment, and the related establishment of the so-called imperial university, out of which a full-scale imperially sanctioned education system gradually evolved. Although it took more than a millennium before both systems matured under the Northern Song dynasty (960–1127), and although their immediate impact on the Han officialdom should not be exaggerated, both innovations do reflect a new ideological role for the throne. This role was well perceived by Dong Zhongshu (ca. 195–115 BCE), one of the major thinkers of the early imperial period. In his memorial to Emperor Wu, Dong Zhongshu proposed:

> Nowadays, the teachers have distinct Ways, the people—distinct theories, the Hundred Schools—distinct recipes; their directions and intentions are different. Hence the ruler has nothing to rely upon in ensuring unity and repeatedly alters laws and regulations; while the subordinates do not know what [laws] they should observe. I, your stupid servant, believe that whatever is not included within the Six Arts and Confucius's techniques, its ways should be severed, and they should not be allowed to present themselves altogether. When the perverse teachings are destroyed and quelled, it will be possible to unify governing principles, to clarify laws and measures; and the people will know what to follow.[27]

The rationale of Dong Zhongshu's proposal is strikingly similar to that of Li Si: the unified empire should tolerate no intellectual pluralism. Yet unlike Li Si, Dong Zhongshu did not envision complete integration of the educated elite into the officialdom; he was primarily concerned to prevent "perverse teachings" from entering into the latter. Hence the Han quest for ideological unity did not involve the drastic measures attributed to Li Si; instead of outlawing "private learning," the Han rulers simply limited the advancement opportunities of those who did not espouse the officially approved principles. This regulation proved efficient enough: most of the texts associated with the so-called Hundred Schools were relegated to the margins of intellectual discourse, while other texts, associated (justifiably or not) with Confucius and his "school," attained canonical status, so that their mastery became indispensable for an aspiring official and for an educated person in general.[28] The carrot policy worked better than the stick to instill a degree of ideological cohesiveness in the elite.

A once-popular narrative interpreted Emperor Wu's elevation of Confucianism as the ultimate "victory" of Confucian teaching over the Hundred Schools of the Warring States age; thenceforth, Confucianism supposedly became the state ideology. This account is somewhat simplistic, as is, in general, the supposition of a "victory" of one "school of thought" over the others; actually, imperial ideology remained quite syncretic, both before and after Emperor Wu. Yet the change in Confucius's status in the aftermath of Emperor Wu's reforms is undeniable: he was elevated far above all other preimperial thinkers; soon enough he was deified, and some Han sycophants even treated him as a semidemiurge, semiprophet who had envisioned the coming of the Han dynasty and prepared the institutional setting for the Han ruling house.[29] These latter excesses were of minor historical consequence; but the general elevation of Confucius and the incorporation of his teaching into the state-sponsored education system were of lasting importance.

Why did Emperor Wu decide to promote Confucius above other preimperial thinkers? Ostensibly, this was an odd selection: Emperor Wu's policy departed radically from what was—and is—usually identified as Confucius's legacy, and "Confucian" justifications for his centralization and expansion were very shaky.[30] Yet the endorsement of Confucius might have served another purpose: creating a new mode of coexistence between the emperor and the majority of the educated elite (to whom I shall henceforth refer as literati rather than *shi*). Confucius, once identified as "an ancestor" of the literati,[31] was the thinker who had decisively shaped the self-image of the "superior men," imbued them with a sense of mission, and contributed greatly toward their pride. By elevating this thinker and declaratively endorsing his legacy, Emperor Wu signaled to the intellectual elite that they would find his regime more accommodative toward them, not purely intimidating like the Qin. The court offered the literati a deal: absorbing them into officialdom while ostensibly allowing them to preserve their dignity. The offer was duly accepted. Emperor Wu might have benefited from his gamble: while many Han intellectuals lamented their diminishing status and noticed the resemblance of some of Emperor Wu's policies to those of the First Emperor, Emperor Wu was much more highly esteemed by subsequent historians and thinkers, and was never anathematized like his predecessor.[32]

A sympathetic account would interpret Emperor Wu's reforms as the beginning of a symbiosis between the court and the literati, a mutually beneficial coexistence between the possessors of cultural prestige and the holders of political power. A more critical view, by contrast, would lament the literati's loss of professional and intellectual autonomy in the wake of Emperor Wu's reforms, and the eventual subjugation of the literati to the throne. As is usual with such broad generalizations, each has its stronger and weaker points: the Chinese empire's long history provides abundant examples pro and contra each of these views. Undeniably, the literati's freedom of action had been considerably reduced under the imperial monopoly; and while large-scale persecutions were a rarity, they recurred sufficiently frequently, from Qin and Han to Ming and Qing, to suggest that the literati were never invulnerable in their position. Yet it would be unjust to let these gloomy events obscure a broader picture of the educated elite's ongoing cultural and intellectual hegemony, of the literati's dominance at the courts of most dynasties, of their persistent ability to offer critical advice to the throne, and of course of their enormous societal prestige. In what follows, by analyzing the limits of intellectual autonomy in the imperial age, and the relations between the literati and the throne, I shall show that despite ongoing persistent tensions with the emperors, the literati's position in the unified empire was prestigious enough to prevent the throne's unequivocal dominance.

IDEOLOGY AND POWER

Critics of the Chinese empire routinely lament the loss of intellectual vigor and élan of the Warring States period in the wake of the imperial unification and the subjugation of the literati to the imperial order. There is no doubt that they have a point. In a land where the emperor's regulatory functions were supposedly unlimited, it was only natural for the court to try to impose ideological uniformity on its subjects and to silence dissenting literati either through a stick policy, as in the case of Li Si, or with the help of the carrot, as exemplified by Emperor Wu's reforms. Having monopolized the routes of individual advancement, the court could deploy its power to define what kind of expertise and knowledge was required of an aspiring official, thereby directing the educational efforts of the vast majority of the literati toward desirable ends. In addition, coercive measures could further solidify ideological orthodoxy. Suppression of real or imagined dissenters, occasional proscriptions of a variety of literary, philosophical, and historical writings, and, most notoriously, cases of "literary inquisition," which peaked in the eighteenth century[33]—all those appear as a gloomy by-product of the imperial unification. It is in light of these events that manifold critics of the imperial order argue that behind the Confucian facade, imperial China appears largely to have realized Li Si's vision of the intellectuals' subjugation.[34]

This said, it is important to note immediately how *nontotalitarian* the imperial regime was. In general, traditional China was a far more pluralistic and intellectually tolerant society than, for instance, almost any traditional monotheistic culture. This quality is clearly evidenced in the ongoing court patronage—at times genuine, at times halfhearted—of Buddhism and Daoism as two major alternative traditions to the mainstream "Confucianism." More essentially, all of these (and many other) "isms" were in fact syncretic and highly heterogeneous traditions, within each of which a great variety of contradictory doctrines continued to coexist. This quality of Chinese ideologies hindered attempts to impose ideological uniformity, beyond the adoption of certain common symbols and rules of discourse. Although at times the court could intervene in debates over the proper interpretation of a canonical tradition or even of a Buddhist scripture, these interventions were rare and of limited influence on the intellectual life of the empire. Ideological debates, even if less pluralistic than in the Warring States period, continued throughout much of the imperial era.

Two additional factors impeded attempts to impose unity of thought on the literati and on society as a whole. The first was the relative monarchical indifference. Only exceptionally assertive monarchs, such as the Ming founder, Zhu Yuanzhang, actively tried to impose their vision on their subjects;[35] most other rulers were less interested in actively pursuing the path of ideological unification. At times, a ruler could endorse one of the competing traditions and try to advance its cause at the expense of other ideologies; but this situation was a rarity.[36] It was tacitly understood that an emperor's unequivocal commitment to a single doctrine would impair his impartiality, arouse unnecessary resentment, and endanger political stability. In any case, radical ideological innovations imposed by a reigning monarch rarely outlived him; for instance, Zhu Yuanzhang's attempt to ban the teachings of Mengzi or expurgate potentially subversive passages from this text was discontinued under his son, Zhu Di (the Yongle Emperor, r. 1402–1424), who restored Mengzi's position, trying thereby to mend his troublesome relations with the literati.[37] Suppression could work, but only temporarily.

The second, and arguably more important, factor behind the ongoing preservation of relative ideological pluralism under the unified empire was the aversion of most literati to the artificial imposition of ideological purity from above. To be sure, there were many zealots for ideological unity within the educated elite; suffice it to mention the illustrious Han Yu (768–824), who urged the court to suppress Buddhism and Daoism and "burn their books," since "unless their ways are blocked, our Way will not be implementable." Such radicalism was a rarity, however, and in the case of Han Yu these harsh phrases should be viewed as rhetorical exaggeration rather than a policy proposal.[38] Many literati, especially in the second imperial millennium, actively disseminated their ideological vision throughout society and hoped ultimately to attain unity of thought; yet it was tacitly understood that this task should be performed primarily from below, through educational efforts, and not through administrative means. Thus the court's rare attempts to impose ideological unity were frequently thwarted owing to the officials' minimal commitment to this goal.

This tendency of the literati to preserve at least relative autonomy in the ideological realm is most evident in the court's inability to rein in two major avenues of independent ideological activity: the printing industry and private academies. Both began developing in earnest at the beginning of the second millennium CE, in tandem with an increasingly palpable drive toward ideological uniformity, at least within the elite ranks. It is remarkable, then, that despite ongoing suspicion from the court and parts of the officialdom concerning the activities of academies and of publishing houses, and despite occasional efforts to curb these activities, both continued to prosper throughout the imperial period. The failure of the establishment to control these vehicles of ideological activism derived from multiple economic and administrative factors, but perhaps most significantly it reflected the basic reluctance of the scholar-officials to suppress the very kind of activities that were essential to the intellectual life of their stratum.[39]

It seems therefore that reducing the ideological atmosphere in the unified empire to a refined version of Li Si's quasi-totalitarian vision is grossly inaccurate. The ideological realm remained, rather, a field of constant negotiation, tension, and compromise between the court (which was staffed, at least partly, by the leading literati) and the bulk of the educated elite. The balance of power between the two differed considerably from one reign to another, but only a few rulers had a significant impact on the ideological course of the realm. The court's difficulty in imposing a uniform ideology on the literati is particularly evident in the complex history of the imperial examinations, a primary tool for selecting officials in the late imperial period. Despite its potential importance as a control mechanism, the examination system did not turn into an efficient means of imposing the court's vision of orthodoxy on the elite. Rather, it served as an arena of negotiation of the cultural and ideological modus vivendi between the court and the literati. As Benjamin Elman's seminal study shows, the court could dictate its rules in the short term, but long-term modifications were not possible without the elite's consent.[40]

To illustrate the complexity of intellectual dynamics in the late imperial period, I shall briefly focus on the Song dynasty (960–1279)—arguably the most intellectually vibrant period under the unified empire. Having reunified most of the country after a prolonged age of military disorder, the Song emperors opted to rely on the literati as their major political allies, displaying exceptional respect toward the men of letters and adopting a more cooperative attitude toward the intellectuals than was evident in most other dynasties. It was then that the examination system became a major and most prestigious avenue for entering the officialdom, and its sociocultural impact increased tremendously (see also chapter 4).[41] Yet this age of increasing affluence, flourishing intellectual life, and radical expansion of educational facilities was also marked by deep cleavages within the intellectual elite, prompted by the competing idealistic visions of the proper functioning of society and the state. As ideological contestation became increasingly acute by the late eleventh century, competing factions began resorting to state power to silence their opponents.[42] At one point, victorious supporters of the radical reformer Wang Anshi (1021–1086) tried to impose their uniform ideological vision on all future literati in a very "modern" way: they radically expanded the system of public education, planning to turn it into an exclusive avenue of advancement into officialdom; simultaneously, they imposed unprecedented ideological control over the curriculum. The opponents bitterly complained:

> Today, in all prefectures and counties, there are no entrance examinations which test the student's ability to write. The first thing the examiners look for is whether or not a candidate's essays refer to subjects currently tabooed. If the language of the candidate's essays touches on such tabooed subjects, then no matter how well he has written, they dare not pass him. It is tabooed to say: "in order to rest the people rest the military; to make wealth abundant, regulate expenses; eliminate the service requirements that are not urgent; incorruptably enter officialdom." All language like this [is tabooed].[43]

This account is an interesting testimony to the possible interdependence of public education and thought control; but for the present discussion what matters is that this attempt—like others before and after it—was short-lived, coming to an abrupt end when the reformers lost the emperor's support. Eventually, a long-term victory in the struggle among manifold intellectual currents of the Song dynasty was achieved by the so-called Neo-Confucians (or "The Learning of the True Way," *Daoxue*). Their initially marginal transcendent moralistic vision was disseminated not from above but from below, through the proselytizing zeal of their adherents, particularly through private academies, which gradually overshadowed the underfunded public education system. While the court's initial response to these activities ranged from indifference to enmity, and for a short while it even outlawed the "false learning" of the Neo-Confucians, the ultimate success was theirs. It came very slowly, taking generations, during which more and more sympathetic literati entered civil service and gained influence over the emperor. The triumph was complete in the thirteenth century when leading Neo-Confucian thinkers were enshrined in Confucius's temple, while their interpretation of canonical works was recognized in 1313 as a new orthodoxy and became an essential component of the modified examination system.[44]

This example of "victory from below," like Han Emperor Wu's decision to endorse Confucian learning fifteen centuries earlier, is indicative of the complex pattern of the elite's interaction with the throne in the ideological sphere. While any emperor at any given moment had the right to redefine the canon, to impose new examination rules, or to ban any ideological current, in practice intellectual life was guided primarily by the literati rather than by the throne. Through a variety of means the literati tried—quite successfully—to preserve their relative autonomy in the realm of ideology. This autonomy, in turn, allowed them to preserve their ideological hegemony as possessors of the True Way. Despite their nominal sagacity, only few emperors were able to redefine successfully the nature of ideological authority. The bifurcation between political and intellectual/moral authority, which was so much evident in the Warring States period, remained intact in the imperial age as well.

It is useful to recall here that the court's difficulty in controlling intellectual activities derived also from yet another source—the sheer volume of ideological production. The Chinese literati were addicted to writing, and the number of works they produced was huge, increasing over the centuries as the size of the literary elite grew and the market for books expanded accordingly. Printing enabled the wide dissemination of written works, and it was all but impossible for any censor to read them all; even occasional persecutions of publishers, authors, and the readers themselves, as in the case of the literary inquisitions, could not significantly influence this situation.[45] The court simply had to accustom itself to its inability to rein in the literati's production. This voluminous production created a vital sphere in which the intellectuals could preserve their dignity and pride. Its existence, in addition to the fateful decision of the Han and subsequent emperors to endorse the Confucian legacy, with its intrinsic respect for the intellectual, served as a powerful antidote to the overall subjugation of the educated elite by the throne. Having lost the advantages of the interstate market of talent, the imperial literati retained sufficient intellectual resources to prevent their debasement to the position of the ruler's servile yes-men. It is time now to investigate their relations with the throne under the new conditions.

BETWEEN THE RULER AND THE WAY

The above discussion suggests that the literati as a stratum were able at times to counterbalance the emperor's power; yet for an individual man of letters maintaining dignity vis-à-vis the throne in the unified empire was much more difficult. The change in the literati's position was already evident during Qin's persecution of private learning; but even the collapse of Qin and the relaxation of the intellectual atmosphere in the early decades of the Han dynasty did not necessarily improve their standing. Proud literati had to get used to repeated humiliations or even persecution should they anger their imperial patrons: some were forced to commit suicide; some were thrown into the pigpen to fight the pigs; others were relegated to the position of an entertainer, not different from "any singing girl or jester."[46] After Han Emperor Wu's ascendancy, the situation deteriorated further. Reportedly, when an aide reproached Emperor Wu for his repeated executions of the literati, the emperor laughingly dismissed the criticism:

> In every generation there are talented people. I am only concerned that one may not be able to recognize them. If one is able to recognize them, why should he be concerned that there won't be enough of them? The so-called 'talented people' are like useful tools. If they refuse to exercise their usefulness, they are no different from people without talent. What do I do with them if I do not execute them?[47]

The veracity of this anecdote is of minor importance; and Emperor Wu's attitude toward the literati was surely more complex than what is implied here. Yet it is symptomatic that a supposedly "Confucian" monarch is cited as humiliatingly equating intellectuals with dispensable "tools," in an indirect reference to the famous Confucian dictum "A superior man is not a tool."[48] This anecdote hints at the irreversible decline in the literati's position vis-à-vis the emperors. This decline is duly observable in every aspect of court life: from court rituals, which increasingly emphasized the ministers' inferiority and subservience, to the self-deprecating language routinely adopted by the ministers in their correspondence with the throne, to the proliferation of the lèse-majesté laws, to the introduction of humiliating corporal punishment for ministers in the late imperial period.[49] In this increasingly unfavorable situation regaining the high moral ground and preserving one's dignity was a challenge.

The depreciation of their status in the imperial court was extremely frustrating for the proud literati. Having remained committed to the idea of serving the throne, they had to accept an inferior position vis-à-vis the monarchs, whose moral and intellectual qualities the literati often held in low esteem. In their capacity as the ruler's servitors they owed him absolute obedience: but how to distinguish between this mandatory obedience and the groveling subservience of the despicable "petty men"? How to preserve one's proud stance as the ruler's guides—without jeopardizing the norms of ruler-minister relations? How to retain a critical attitude toward the throne, as appropriate to the "Men of the Way"—without endangering one's personal safety? So strong was the tension surrounding these questions that Liu Zehua went so far as to diagnose the imperial literati with "psychosis"—a kind of mental disorder stemming from their inability to maintain their double roles as moral guides of society, the emperor included, and as the rulers' "slaves."[50] Harsh as it is, this formulation encapsulates well the predicament of the imperial intellectuals who had to navigate between the Scylla of self-deprecating servility and the Charybdis of self-destructive haughtiness. Countless men of letters had to pay a high price for straying from the middle course.

To be sure, not all literati endorsed the critical stance at the expense of their hard-won careers. Many silently compromised their ideals, preferring not to alienate the ruler and their superiors; others developed the art of silent noncompliance with some of the monarch's decisions, while refraining from open criticism. Yet there were also those who were both conscientious and courageous enough to confront the sovereign. These men had two major options for demonstrating their moral superiority: either to shun service in protest against the restrictive and humiliating court atmosphere, or to remain in the court, while adopting an overtly critical attitude toward the emperor and toward insufficiently upright colleagues. Although both kinds of protesters were often perceived by the rulers and even by some of their colleagues as a nuisance, their radical stance had deep consequences for the balance of power between the ruler and his aides. The radicals' readiness to sacrifice their careers, and even their lives, reasserted the position of these individuals, and by extension of their stratum as a whole, as the ruler's moral superiors, and as exclusive possessors of the True Way. As such, the purists served the essential interest of the literati.

Let us begin with disengagement from public service, a complex phenomenon that gained prominence in the first imperial millennium, especially in the second–seventh centuries CE. Multiple philosophical, religious, or personal factors influenced individual recluses. Some, under the impact of Daoism and later of Buddhism, eschewed office in earnest, disengaging not just from political service but from the entire elite system of social and intellectual conventions. Others, on whose behavior I focus here, considered disengagement a temporary measure. As Confucius and Mengzi had done, they left service primarily to protest against the abusive and corrupt atmosphere at court, demonstrating thereby their moral purity. This protest could well be effective, since the upright monarch was expected to be able to attract the worthiest and most talented subjects into his service, and massive disengagement of supposedly gifted intellectuals could become a source of embarrassment for him. Hence not a few rulers in the tumultuous age from the end of the Han up to the establishment of the Tang dynasty invested considerable effort in bringing the worthy recluses back into service.[51]

The culture of reclusion was the most curious by-product of the mind-set according to which every gifted man was supposed to hold an office. It could proliferate only among a relatively well-defined group of men who were expected—owing to their pedigree, renown, or previous administrative experience—to pursue government careers. Having refused to serve, recluses demonstrated their integrity and became objects of admiration and emulation. While only a few literati shunned service in earnest, countless more expressed their admiration of reclusion, celebrating this ideal in poetry and painting, and through other means of artistic expression. Many rulers shared this admiration, and courted lofty recluses, pressing them to come and serve the throne. Curiously, for rulers and courtiers alike, the refusal to enter government service was the strongest manifestation of the recluse's fitness to serve.

Fascination with reclusion as the ultimate manifestation of one's integrity brought about manifold complex phenomena, from acting officials' adoption of the recluses' conventions to the fashion of "feigned disengagement": namely, pretending to shun the service only to enhance one's price in the ruler's eyes. The rulers had to distinguish carefully between the true recluse and the hypocrite who "hides his name in order to attract titles and salaries" and sees reclusion as a "shortcut to officialdom."[52] The first could risk his life should he stubbornly defy the ruler's summons; the latter would risk his reputation (and, occasionally, his life as well) should he respond too hastily. Numerous anecdotes feature rulers who tolerated the recluses' affronts but mercilessly punished feigned recluses for being insufficiently pure.[53]

The admiration of recluses by officeholders—and even by emperors—persisted until the very end of the imperial period, and culturally reclusion remained a highly respected ideal. Politically, however, reclusion as a means of protest lost its importance from the Tang dynasty on. As the social basis of the officialdom expanded, and examinations replaced recommendations as a primary means of selecting officials, fewer individuals could rely on their reputation's being so brilliant that their shunning office would attract the ruler's concern.[54] Thenceforth, the most audacious attacks on the rulers came not from those who eschewed service but rather from acting or aspiring members of the officialdom: from students in the imperial educational facilities to petty officials and high-ranking ministers. These men definitely wanted to serve, but they wanted to do it on their own terms: not as the ruler's tools, but as his mentors and moral superiors. Their struggle to reassert themselves against the throne fills the pages of dynastic histories: they became the true heroes of the literati.

A reader of Chinese historical records cannot but be impressed by the persistent willingness of officials or would-be officials to confront the emperor. Some voiced their criticisms as part of their role as "remonstrating officials," censors, or tutors, while others overstepped their bureaucratic responsibilities; some couched their criticism in conciliatory language, while others were more provocative; some employed celestial or terrestrial omens and portents to criticize the monarch, while others spoke on behalf of canonical wisdom or on behalf of "the people"—but each could expect his words to incite the emperor's wrath. Every dynasty has its list of martyrs; almost every reign has a much lengthier list of those who escaped execution but were incarcerated, dismissed, demoted, or otherwise humiliated or punished for their outspokenness. Nonetheless, punishments do not appear to have been effective; criticism of the throne lasted throughout the imperial millennia, and the critics' voices were not silenced even under the reign of the most ruthless monarchs.

What are the reasons for this recurring ministerial willingness to criticize the monarch and to pay the price? Surely, plenty of substantive issues prompted ministerial dissatisfaction, from the emperor's military or economic policies, to his excessive expenditures, to his ritual or religious policies, and the like. The emperor's personal misbehavior was another perennial issue for which ministers faulted the sovereign, since only a very few monarchs could satisfy the strict demands of their Confucian advisers. Yet beyond specific political and moral issues it is difficult to avoid the feeling that at least for some of the critics the main goal was to confront the emperor simply for the sake of confrontation, or, more precisely, in order to reassert their moral superiority over the ruler. Speaking on behalf of the True Way, these critics enjoyed huge popularity among the literati, impelling some rulers to complain that their opponents simply "fish for reputation and market uprightness."[55]

Radical critics of the throne played a dangerous game, but the risk may have been well calculated. To illustrate this, let us turn to the most famous case of radical remonstrance. In November 1565, a minor official, Hai Rui (d. 1587), submitted a scandalous memorandum to the Ming emperor Shizong (r. 1521–1566). The document went far beyond the limits of acceptable remonstrance, as it did not focus on a single fault of the monarch but rather condemned his behavior in its entirety. "The enumeration of [Shizong's] sins included his failure as a father, husband and ruler. The monarch was described as vain, cruel, selfish, suspicious and foolish. . . . The caustic tone of the memorial culminated with the sentence, 'It has already been some time since the people under Heaven started to regard Your Majesty as unworthy.'"[56] Although the screed ended with an optimistic promise that it was not too late for the aging monarch to rectify his ways and attain equality with the paragon rulers of the past, this did not soften its harshness.

The addressee of Hai Rui's memorandum, Ming Shizong, was one of the most ruthless, capricious, and autocratic-minded emperors of the Ming dynasty, who had brutally silenced oppositional voices in the past.[57] Not surprisingly, his first reaction was that the offender must be quickly seized and tried for the obvious lèse-majesté. Yet the enraged emperor was astounded to learn that Hai Rui was making no attempt to escape: rather, the remonstrator had already fully prepared himself for the inevitable death penalty, departed from his family, and even bought himself a coffin. At that moment Shizong realized that he was no longer acting as an individual in a circumscribed moment but rather was taking part in a historical spectacle watched not just by contemporaries (some of whom were not very happy with Hai Rui's eccentric purism in any case) but by posterity as well. The emperor hesitated: though he put Hai Rui in jail, he could not decide whether to punish his critic or to pardon him. The notoriously vindictive ruler, who did not hesitate to execute courtiers for minor offenses, was suddenly powerless before a petty official who sought martyrdom.

What emboldened Hai Rui and softened Shizong? I believe that the answer is the power of the literati's public opinion, as generated through what may be called the "literati-oriented discourse." This discourse, maintained through the huge corpus of historical, philosophical, and literary works, produced by the literati and for the literati, decisively shaped their mind-set; moreover, it had considerable impact on the emperors as well. The literati-oriented writings disclosed the hollowness of the emperor's sagacity, emphasized the perennial bifurcation between political and moral authority, and lauded courageous individuals who preserved their integrity and dignity vis-à-vis erratic rulers. The diachronic public opinion expressed in these works served as a major source of inspiration to the dissenters and empowered them in relation to the throne.

By boldly assaulting the emperor, the dissenters were acquiring the reputation of true "superior men," which promised lasting admiration not just from contemporaries but also from posterity. This support of the literati's public opinion was crucial for the dissenters in two ways. First, it could save them from execution: the emperor, fearful of being identified as an evil persecutor of superior men, might decide to exercise restraint. A prudent dissenter could anticipate that after an almost inevitable career setback, expulsion, incarceration, or even public flogging, he would still have a chance of being recalled when the ruler decided to mend his relations with the literati and display magnanimity, or when a new emperor ascended the throne. Second, even in the worst case, the admiration of the literati could turn execution into the dissenter's real triumph. It would ensure him such "commemorative immortality" as was due to a Confucian martyr; and in a highly history-oriented Chinese society, such immortality was no less significant for many literati than promises of Paradise have been for religious martyrs elsewhere.[58] The would-be martyrs' saying, "Even if I die, my name will linger for posterity," recurs too often in dynastic histories and other writings to be dismissed as purely a literary convention.

Paradoxically, then, a radical dissenter was in an advantageous situation when facing the throne insofar as his major goal was not to achieve substantial political change but to preserve his high reputation. Yet it would be grossly unfair of us to reduce the suicidal courage of Hai Rui and his ilk to the selfish desire to enshrine themselves in the Confucian pantheon. From a broader perspective it is clear that by boldly defying the emperor they served their stratum as a whole. By willingly facing martyrdom in the name of their moral principles, these men were reasserting the position of the literati as the exclusive bearers of the True Way, thereby denying the throne the position of moral leadership. Hai Rui could not predict whether or not he would be executed by Shizong; but he knew perfectly well that his memorandum would undermine the emperor's pretensions to sagacity, which Shizong took quite seriously. Other radical critics pursued similar goals. By dismantling the aura of the monarch's infallibility, they reconfirmed the position of the literati as the ruler's guides, and decisively altered the balance of power between the ruler and the officials in favor of the latter.

We are fully justified in hailing the literati's courage and their unwavering commitment to the True Way; but the story does not end here. The Way of the literati was the way of monarchism, of the ruler-centered polity, and as such it presupposed the utmost loyalty to the ruler—even when that ruler was one whom they bitterly criticized. Criticism and martyrdom were acceptable; but overall defiance of the ruler's power—definitely not. Hence, a few decades after the Hai Rui affair, when the dissenting members of the so-called Donglin faction were framed by the notorious eunuch Wei Zhongxian (d. 1627), they did their best to quell popular unrest in response to their arrest, even though they knew well that they were on their way to Beijing for sure execution. Their loyal death amid awful tortures, no less than their courageous enumeration of the crimes of Wei Zhongxian (and by implication of his patron, Ming Xizong [r. 1621–1627]), ensured their posthumous fame as paradigmatic "superior men."[59] Hai Rui's behavior may serve as another illustration of this norm. After months in prison, Hai was treated to an exceptionally good meal, which he ate calmly, believing that it marked the eve of his execution. Then, a warden congratulated him: the emperor was dead, and a new incumbent was expected to release Hai Rui and reemploy him. Having heard the news, Hai Rui broke into tears, crying bitterly until he vomited.[60]

One can cynically dismiss Hai Rui's weeping or even the Donglin members' martyrdom as a careful performance of their roles in the grand historical spectacle;[61] but I believe that these acts, even if somewhat melodramatic, do reflect something of the genuine feelings of the men involved. The Chinese literati—even the most critical-minded of them—remained firmly committed to the ruler-centered order. Even when Zhu Xi (1130–1200) and other so-called Neo-Confucians attempted to develop an alternative path to self-realization outside government service (see chapter 4), they never abandoned the expectation that a future enlightened ruler would employ them and allow them, finally, to implement their Way. This yearning for the True Monarch was shared by all major intellectuals, including Zhu Xi, who denied the sagacity of all rulers since the legendary sages of the remote past, or Huang Zongxi (1610–1695), who proclaimed that "the ruler is the one who does the greatest harm to All-under-Heaven."[62] It can be considered the essential common belief of China's intellectuals.

This understanding elucidates tragic dimensions of Chinese martyrdom. Unlike religious martyrs elsewhere, whose transcendental beliefs lead them to defy mundane authority, the Confucian martyrs acted out of a sense of deep commitment to the same monarchs whom they defied. Even after millennia of frustrations and tragedies, these clear-sighted critics of individual emperors remained unwaveringly committed to the monarchy as the only conceivable political system in which their moral vision could be realized. Hai Rui, weeping inconsolably over the death of an emperor whom he considered incompetent, epitomizes the intellectuals' bitter love for the throne. This immense and tragic tension between commitments to the Ruler and to the Way remained the single most important determinant of Chinese intellectuals' life until the very end of the imperial era.

Epilogue: Scholar-Officials and the Empire's Longevity

My discussion up to this point has focused on the complex interactions between the literati and the throne, which I analyzed primarily from the point of view of the lofty-minded intellectuals. We have seen that their voluntary attachment to the throne was a double-edged sword: it empowered their stratum as a whole by making it indispensable for the rulers, but it also generated frustration and bitterness for generations of literati. It is time now to analyze the broader implications of the intellectuals' political commitment for the functioning of the imperial order and for the empire's longevity.

The stratum of scholar-officials, which dominated the empire's political and intellectual scene for over two millennia, is peculiar to Chinese civilization. Bifurcation between spiritual and political authority is common in political cultures worldwide; but this was not the case in China. The same men who shaped the country's cultural values were also its political leaders, responsible for its well-being. Although not all the intellectuals were officials, and not all the officials intellectuals, the hegemonic position of those who combined these two roles remained characteristic of the empire's sociopolitical structure from its very inception. This combination of two sources of power in the hands of a single stratum became one of the important sources of the empire's stability.[63]

The intellectuals' political commitment had several positive impacts on the empire's functioning. First, it provided the realm with a pool of well-trained public servants, who in childhood had begun to acquire the skills necessary to run the civil administration. Even if their training seems to many of us today—as it seemed to many imperial literati as well—too bookish and scholastic, it nevertheless brought into government service a large number of truly capable men, many of whom displayed remarkable resourcefulness in dealing with a variety of domestic and foreign challenges. Despite its manifold deficiencies, the imperial system of training and selection of officials produced countless civil servants whose abilities and dedication to the common good cannot be denied. While it is difficult to systematically compare the performance of a Chinese magistrate with that of his counterpart elsewhere, it seems that on average the Chinese empire was run by more professional and committed servants than was the case in most other premodern polities.

Second, the predominance of the literati among the officials contributed to a certain extent to the manageability of court life. Despite their occasional divisiveness, factionalism, and internal cleavages, the literati were generally inclined to resolve these differences in a "civilized" way—through mutual impeachments and legal means, rather than through taking up arms, as was the case, for instance, with many generals and tribal leaders in the court's service. Although political divisions could be at times greatly damaging, and could even hasten dynastic collapse, as happened in the late years of the Northern Song and Ming dynasties, they rarely attained unmanageable proportions. On balance it seems that the cultural cohesiveness of the literati contributed toward bridging the differences rather than escalating them.[64]

Third, the literati played an important political role as a counterbalance to the excesses of monarchism. Their loyal criticism and willingness to remonstrate with the emperor served, even if inconclusively, to soften the monarch's abuses. Moreover, as a rule, their criticism was not politically disruptive, because it was couched in the language of ultimate loyalty to the throne. Even the most resentful and disgruntled literati were not prone to rebel—which made them incomparably more reliable servants than other members of the emperor's entourage, such as military officers or the emperor's kin. This, in turn, made the emperors more receptive to the remonstrance of their intellectual aides than to other sources of criticism. Eventually, the combination of professionalism, political predictability, and loyalty turned the literati into the default choice of most emperors in staffing their officialdom.

Aside from these direct benefits, the intellectuals' attachment to the imperial state and the formation of the "scholar-officials" stratum made another, deeper contribution to the empire's stability. The literati, with their common educational background and common values, served as the pillar of the realm's cultural unity, perpetuating it under a variety of challenging circumstances. Their determination to serve brought numerous literati to the courts of the most unlikely patrons: from peasant rebels to military adventurists to foreign conquerors. In these courts they often had to accept lowly positions, coexisting uneasily with outlaws, militarists, and alien tribesmen, and also incurred the derision of purists among their fellow literati, who refused to serve a "filthy" regime. Against these odds, the collaborationists pushed steadily for the accommodation of the newly established regime and its adaptation to the basic premises of Chinese political culture. It is due to their willingness to serve that the literati were able to contribute decisively toward the eventual "acculturation" of socially or ethnically "alien" regimes.

Finally, the literati, in their double role as bearers of the realm's cultural tradition and its political leaders, enormously enhanced the imperial regime's cultural prestige, and fortified the imperial political system's hegemony in the minds of its subjects throughout the millennia. The intellectuals were the empire's architects and custodians, and it was they who provided it with unparalleled cultural legitimacy. Even at times of crisis and disorder, when it seemed that the very foundations of the imperial polity had been irreversibly smashed, no alternatives to imperial rule were ever offered. Insofar as the stratum that determined right and wrong for the bulk of the population remained unwaveringly committed to the imperial political system, this system could withstand any domestic or foreign challenge, and could be resurrected after ages of the most woeful disorder and disintegration. It may be not a coincidence, then, that the end of the empire in the early twentieth century came shortly after the erstwhile intellectual consensus in its favor was shattered. Abandoned by its natural protectors, the empire fell with unbelievable ease, proving by the rapidity of its demise that throughout its history it had been primarily an intellectual rather than merely a sociopolitical construct, and that it owed its longevity overwhelmingly to the intellectuals, who designed it and ran it throughout the twenty-one centuries of its existence.

CHAPTER 4

Local Elite

> It is not difficult to govern: just do not offend grand families.
> Whatever grand families admire, all the state admires;
> whatever all the state admires, All-under-Heaven admires.
> Thus, moral influence can abundantly fill in all within the
> Four Seas.
> —*Mengzi*

MENGZI'S ASSERTION cited in the epigraph is a curious anachronism. It presupposes the existence of a socially and culturally powerful elite, on whose influence power-holders must depend to ensure smooth governance. This elite did indeed exist through the second third of the first millennium BCE, but by Mengzi's time (fourth century BCE) it was vanishing, submerged by the increasingly powerful bureaucratic Warring State. Yet retrograde as it looks, Mengzi's statement was also something of a prophecy: within a few centuries of his death the power of "grand families" would be duly resurrected, and they would play a crucial role in sociopolitical dynamics until the very end of the imperial age and beyond.

In this and the subsequent chapter, my narrative shifts from the imperial core to localities, and from the upper to the middle and lower levels of China's sociopolitical pyramid. Away from the capital, in China, as in many other premodern polities, powerful local elites that wielded considerable social, economic, cultural, and at times political power in their communities served as an intermediary between the imperial state and the general populace. As such, the elites counterbalanced the power of the officialdom, and at times significant tension ensued between them and the imperial bureaucrats. Yet despite this tension and occasional conflicts of interest, the imperial officials and local elites gradually achieved a remarkable degree of cooperation and even complementarity. Through a variety of means, from co-optation and moral suasion to intimidation and occasional oppression, the bureaucracy succeeded in maintaining a tense but reasonably efficient modus vivendi with holders of local societal power. In what looks in retrospect like one of its major achievements, the imperial state turned local elites from potential competitors into its agents and reliable guardians of the imperial order. This success came at a price, and tensions between local elites and the officialdom persisted throughout the imperial millennia; but the overall contribution of the former to the imperial polity's perpetuation, especially in the late imperial period, is undeniable.[1]

Of the manifold means by which local elites were co-opted, the imperial examinations are justifiably singled out as the most important, especially for the second imperial millennium. It was once common to identify local elites—which are frequently dubbed "gentry" in Western scholarship—with degree holders from the imperial examinations. Recent studies have shown that this identification is imprecise: in different times and localities wealth, pedigree, military power, or religious and technical expertise were far more important than an examination degree in ensuring local power and prestige.[2] Yet this chapter will focus primarily on those members of local elites who were connected to the government apparatus—either through the examination system; or, earlier, through the recommendations system; or otherwise, for instance, through family ties. These wealthy and well-educated landowners provided the broad pool of talent from among whom the high-level literati discussed in the previous chapter were drawn; they were the core of local elites in much of China proper throughout most of the imperial period; and their lifestyle and values were emulated by other elite members. This core group of local elites decisively shaped state-elite interactions throughout imperial history.

In what follows, I shall first outline historical changes in the character of local elites and in their relations with the preimperial, the early imperial, and the late imperial state. I shall show that the process of establishing viable relations between these elites and the bureaucracy was a lengthy and painful one, and that it took more than a full millennium for the empire to learn how to harness local elites to its cause. Even then, as we shall see, tension between holders of social and of administrative power remained highly visible, and cycles of cooperation and contest between them shaped much of the political dynamics of the imperial age.

FROM ARISTOCRATIC TO BUREAUCRATIC STATE

In a once-influential study, Karl Wittfogel depicted China as perennially ruled by the omnipotent agro-managerial bureaucracy.[3] The accuracy of Wittfogel's assessment for the entire imperial period is debatable, and in any case it is clear that he was completely wrong with regard to the formative period of Chinese civilization. Only in the Warring States period did an assertive and intrusive state that resembles Wittfogel's model come into existence; while initially, most notably during the aristocratic Springs-and-Autumns period (771–453 BCE), the political structure was very loose. The polity of that age was but a hierarchical network of settlements run by hereditary nobles under minimal control from the central government. The nobles—an early version of local elites—did not just mediate between the regional lord and the local populace but to a considerable degree served as independent power-holders in their localities. Gradually they came to possess exclusive command over the material and human resources of their allotments, gained autonomy from the lord's control, and contributed thereby to the systemic crisis of that age, mentioned in chapters 1 and 2. The first experience of the Chinese political system with powerful local elites ended therefore in disaster; and this legacy instigated lasting aversion to further devolution of state power to local potentates. For several centuries to come the trend was toward ever more efficient centralized bureaucratic control over society and abolition of the aristocratic elite's power.

The reforms of the fifth–fourth centuries BCE brought into existence the Warring State, which represents a radically different model of rule. The statesmen's desire to rein in forces of disintegration brought about a process of centralization and the penetration of the increasingly assertive and powerful bureaucracy deep into all social strata. The new state no longer tolerated independent loci of power and left nobody outside its direct control. It managed the economic lives of its subjects, registered them and tightly supervised their movements, and routinely mobilized them for a variety of labor and military tasks. It penetrated the entire society much as did the modern European state, which reached, in Eric Hobsbawm's words, "down to the humblest inhabitant of the least of its villages."[4] The government apparatus itself became increasingly centralized and much more tightly controlled, eliminating in the process any semblance of the autonomy local potentates had once enjoyed. With the absorption of the bulk of former aristocratic elites into the state bureaucracy, no powerful independent group remained to mediate between the officials and the lower strata.

Of all the competing Warring States, nowhere was the bureaucratic revolution as thorough and successful as in the state of Qin, which ultimately established the first unified imperial dynasty on China's soil. The bureaucratic logic of Qin seems to have worked in the direction of complete absorption of any elite group—from the ruler's kin to village elders—into the expanding state apparatus, or at least into the state-maintained hierarchy of status. One of the most important reforms underlying the rise of Qin was the replacement of the system of hereditary aristocratic ranks with a new one in which ranks were granted for merit and, with minor exceptions, were not fully inheritable. The state had thenceforth the exclusive right to determine the individual's status, with its accompanying sumptuary and legal privileges; practically this meant that there was no space for autonomous elite groups. It is doubtful that

Qin succeeded fully in unifying the individual's rank, wealth, and societal power, but the very desire of its leaders to craft this uniform hierarchy is indicative of their remarkable assertiveness and their strong aversion toward autonomous loci of authority. From the currently available textual and epigraphic data, it seems that Qin moved most decisively toward creating a "total power" state of the kind depicted by Wittfogel.[5]

We still lack sufficient details about the sociopolitical structure of most other rival Warring States, but it seems that their development trajectory did not differ considerably from that of Qin, even though the process by which the hereditary aristocracy was replaced by the new elite might have been less sweeping. In none of these states do we know of an independent socioeconomic elite that could meaningfully have counterbalanced government power. The absence of a land market and strict control of the state apparatus over nascent industry and commerce hindered independent accumulation of wealth by individuals outside the state-mandated sociopolitical hierarchy; the vast majority of rich persons in the Warring States period were those whom the state allowed to amass riches. Thus while members of the *shi* stratum, discussed in the previous chapter, were intellectually and occupationally autonomous of individual power-holders, economically speaking they remained dependent on the ruler and his apparatus. Lacking independent sources of wealth, preimperial *shi*, in sharp distinction from their imperial-period descendants, had no visible role in local communities. There only a minor elite existed, represented by village elders; but even these were increasingly incorporated—in Qin, but possibly elsewhere as well—into the expanding state apparatus.[6]

It is highly significant that during the formative age of Chinese political thought and political culture, no powerful independent elite existed on Chinese soil. It explains why—aside from a few incidental remarks, such as that cited in the epigraph—preimperial thinkers did not address the issue of state relations with the "grand families," and did not provide the empire builders with either theoretical elaboration regarding the elite's social role or practical means of maintaining proper relations between the officialdom and local elites. This inadvertent negligence may explain why the reemergence of powerful local elites in the aftermath of the imperial unification came to power-holders as a surprise, and why many centuries elapsed before a truly viable mode of state-elite relations was elaborated by the imperial literati.

THE RISE AND FALL OF THE IMPERIAL ARISTOCRACY

The First Emperor of Qin, who unified the Chinese world in 221 BCE, inherited what may have been the single most effective and powerful bureaucratic mechanism in Chinese history prior to Mao Zedong's era. In the wake of unification, he had duly attempted to expand Qin regulations and its sociopolitical system to the entire newly unified realm; and as recently unearthed materials from some of the remotest Qin localities suggest, the emperor may have been reasonably successful in his endeavor (see also chapter 1). However, maintenance of direct control of the state bureaucracy over the entire population was an enormously costly enterprise. Supporting the huge army of officials, clerks, scribes, postmen, and runners required for continuous flow of information throughout the vast realm—and all these, in addition to a plethora of military and civilian projects, strained the empire's resources, contributing directly to the swift collapse of Qin in the wake of popular uprisings. The Han dynasty, established in the aftermath of the bloody civil war of 209–202 BCE, learned the lesson. Maintenance of direct control over the localities was possible but not feasible in the long run. A degree of relaxation was necessary.

Modification of Qin practices was a lengthy process, the details of which are still not very clear. The Han had inherited much of the administrative structure and legal system of Qin, but it seems that its early leaders were reluctant to utilize fully the power of their state. Relaxation of control over the populace, cessation of large-scale military and civilian projects, and proliferation of a laissez-faire economy: all these brought much-needed respite to the population.[7] A side impact of this policy was the reemergence of local elites as powerful economic, social, and political actors.

The reappearance of independent elites in the early Han period may have been directly related to the laissez-faire policy that the Han leaders adopted as a deliberate alternative to Qin rule. In particular, the Han permitted private entrepreneurs to replace the state in the lucrative fields of iron and salt production; allowed private minting of coins; and turned a blind eye to powerful families' land accumulation. This last development was particularly consequential in the age when the nascent land market was being formed, as it allowed formation of large estates, the size of which was no longer related to the owner's position within the state hierarchy. Gradually, a new social group came into existence: the so-called magnates (*haojie*), large landowners or entrepreneurs who became economic and social leaders in their localities. Initially, these magnates may have remained largely outside the Han administrative system, the upper echelons of which were staffed by the associates of the dynastic founder, Liu Bang, and by their progeny. It is possible, though, that magnates gained access to the lower levels of the administrative pyramid. In the course of a few generations, they became a formidable force for local officials to reckon with.[8]

The renewed centralization and territorial expansion under Han Emperor Wu (r. 141–87 BCE) soon brought him into conflict with local magnates, whose wealth he coveted. Many of Emperor Wu's initial steps were overtly coercive, such as reprisals against tax evaders, expropriation of individuals' property based on trumped-up charges, and intimidation of magnates by the so-called cruel officials. More significant were other steps, aimed at reducing the magnates' economic space, such as reintroduction of the salt and iron monopolies, and other, less successful attempts to expand the economic activity of the state apparatus.[9] Yet parallel to his assault on local magnates, Emperor Wu offered them a carrot: as mentioned in the previous chapter, he was the first to experiment with a system of recommendations cum examinations, which, for members of local elites, opened avenues of advancement into the central government. Thenceforth, members of the magnate families who adopted state-approved behavioral norms, such as Confucianism-inspired "filiality and incorruptibility," or those who learned to master the state-approved texts (the so-called Confucian classics) could expect promotion into intermediary or even high levels of the bureaucracy. This was the modest and yet historically significant beginning of the millennia-old alliance between the state and the local elites. Emperor Wu's decision that local elites should not be eliminated but rather should be co-opted and utilized as the auxiliaries of the state apparatus remained the basic policy guideline throughout the Han period and beyond.

Han Emperor Wu's initiative met with immediate success: many of the magnates and their kin responded enthusiastically, and an increasing number of them began entering government service. However, as the government learned shortly after Emperor Wu's death, this incorporation of local elites into the imperial bureaucracy was a mixed blessing. The newly recruited officials who came from the local magnate families emerged as firm opponents of state economic activism, and supporters of a reversal from the more Qin-like policies of Emperor Wu to a noninterventionist looser model of "benevolent government," which was associated in their eyes with the early Zhou dynasty.[10] The clash of views became evident as early as 81 BCE, during the fascinating court debates over the fate of the iron and salt monopolies, when recently promoted provincial literati presented a united front against the government's assertive economic policies, causing a reduction in the scope of monopolies.[11] Thus the more these literati came to dominate the court, the less supportive it became of aggressive centralization and expansion à la Emperor Wu.

The increasing power of local elites and of their representatives in the government became obvious during the reign of the idealistic reformer and usurper of the Han throne, Wang Mang (r. 9–23 CE). When Wang

Mang tried to emulate Emperor Wu's assertive policies, he failed miserably, amid the magnate families' strong resentment and dissident officials' widespread sabotage. The strongest opposition was directed against his attempt to abolish the land market and restrict the size of latifundia, which, if implemented, would directly interfere with the magnates' interests.[12] It became increasingly evident that the state apparatus was no longer representative of the court's interest vis-à-vis the elites but, rather, leaned to the latter's side. Thenceforth, only a few exceptionally powerful and determined leaders were able to turn the tide and utilize the government against elite interests; for the majority this was no longer an option.

The series of rebellions and civil wars that brought about the fall of Wang Mang provided yet another indication of the local elites' increasing prominence. Among manifold rebellious and loyalist groups, the most notable were magnate-led militias, the appearance of which signaled the emergence of local elites as not just an economic power but also as an important military force. The restoration of the Han dynasty in 25 CE became possible only because of the founder's reliance on these militias, which further strengthened the throne's dependence on the magnates. The throne reciprocated by gradually abandoning economic activism, such as the state monopolies, and also by letting the manorial economy proliferate. Administratively, the state became less assertive as well; the tight control over the population eased, mass conscription was discontinued, and the interventionism of the Qin and early Han officialdom was replaced by much looser ways. This in turn increased the officials' dependence on cooperation with the local magnates below.[13]

As time went on, the balance of power between the court and the local elites tilted decisively in the latter's favor. Since members of the elite firmly dominated the officialdom, they could utilize their position to promote their families' economic interests. In particular, the grossly unfair Han taxation system benefited huge manorial estates rather than small peasant households. Overburdened by government taxes, peasants preferred to transfer their land to a local magnate and become his tenants, which was demeaning in terms of status but beneficial in terms of livelihood. In time, the center of economic and social gravity had shifted from the imperial government to the magnates' estates.[14] While many eminent statesmen and thinkers recognized this development as dangerous and proposed curbing the estates' size, the officialdom in general was clearly unconcerned. By the end of the Han dynasty, as dynastic power disintegrated in the wake of popular rebellions and military mutinies, local magnates in their huge estates with armies of devoted tenants remained the single most important sociopolitical force to be reckoned with.

The last years of the Later Han dynasty (25–220 CE) witnessed another development that marked the triumph of local elites. A new system for entering the officialdom emerged, in which the individual's status was to be determined according to what was termed "local rank." This rank was fixed according to one's reputation in his locality, which in practice reflected the opinion of local elite families. This meant that powerful lineages created webs of mutual recommendations, effectively preventing outsiders from joining the national elite.[15] Practically, this brought about a reemergence of hereditary aristocracy, which combined wealth, status, and power, and which completely overshadowed the throne. Meritocratic principles of government were not abandoned but were significantly compromised; and the throne proved unable to regain the initiative and curb the aristocrats' privileges. Especially under the Jin (265–420) and its successor dynasties, which ruled southern China during the age of Fragmentation (318–589 CE), the power of the throne reached its nadir. This age is widely renowned for its cultural florescence, but politically speaking, it was marked by a systemic crisis on a par with that of the Springs-and-Autumns period.[16]

The progressive weakening of the imperial state from the early Han to the Southern Dynasties demonstrated the dangers of excessive reliance on local elites. Although the court retained its symbolic power, it failed to restrain the elites, because these held the rope at both ends, dominating local society as well as the officialdom. It may be not incidental, then, that the resurrection of the throne's power came from the northern dynasties, established by nomadic and seminomadic conquerors, who brought in a new, tribal, aristocracy, superimposing it on the native, Chinese, one. The ability of some of the northern emperors to maneuver between these two constituencies allowed one of them, Emperor Xiaowen (r. 471–499), to introduce the "equal field" system," surely the most significant reform of the early imperial period (see chapter 2). A century later, another nomadic regime initiated military reforms (the establishment of the so-called territorial militia [fubing]), which provided the throne with a powerful and loyal military force.[17] Finally, in the aftermath of the imperial reunification of 589, the Sui (581–618) monarchs discontinued the "local ranks" system, and the throne regained its position as the ultimate source of status and power for members of the elite. The combination of these three developments marked the resurrection of the centralized state after centuries of its devolution.

The Tang dynasty (618–907), which crowned China's aristocratic age, was incomparably stronger, domestically and internationally, than any of its predecessors since the Han dynasty. This success derived in no small measure from the Tang emperors' ability to co-opt the aristocratic elite without ceding the power of the throne, as happened under the Later

Han and its successors. The complex system of selection and promotion adopted by the Tang was tailored so as to benefit the aristocrats, but it did not allow them to monopolize power, and it perpetuated the court's role as the ultimate source of societal prestige.[18] Simultaneously, insofar as the Tang rulers preserved the "equal field" and "territorial militia" systems, they were able to prevent devolution of economic and military power to the aristocrats. It may have seemed that finally, after eight centuries of imperial rule, the court and the aristocratic elite had found a sustainable modus vivendi. This was not the case, however.

In the course of the Tang dynasty, a curious development ensued. Having secured preferential access to political power, members of aristocratic clans gradually shifted their centers of gravity to the imperial capitals in Luoyang and Chang'an, becoming increasingly dissociated from their local power base. As these clans—or, more precisely, the segments of these clans that relocated to the capital—turned into a national superelite based in the empire's center, new elites began emerging in the provinces. These new elites failed to replace established aristocrats at the higher echelons of power, but they compensated themselves with employment opportunities under the regional courts that proliferated in the second half of the Tang dynasty in the aftermath of An Lushan's rebellion (755–762) (see chapter 1). From the point of view of the dynasty, this was a highly negative development. The court, addicted to its venerable symbiotic relations with the old aristocracy, failed to absorb the newly emerging elites, who in turn were much less inclined to safeguard the dynasty's interests than were the aristocratic clans. The lack of support from new elites weakened the court's control over the localities, strengthened its rivals from among provincial military potentates, and eventually hastened the dynasty's demise.[19]

We may summarize the first millennium of imperial history as a lengthy age of trial and error during which the empire's leaders sought ways to accommodate themselves to the power of local elites. Measures that were effective in the short term proved unsustainable in the long term. Elimination of independent elites in the context of absolute bureaucratization of the society, as attempted by the Qin, was financially burdensome; relaxation of control, as in the early Han, meant progressive weakening of the state; while careless co-optation of the elite in the aftermath of Han Emperor Wu's reforms resulted in the elite's incorporation of the officialdom rather than the reverse, and, in the long term, resurrection of the politically inefficient aristocratic mode of rule and dramatic devolution of the state's power to the aristocrats. The Tang model surely was the most successful of all, but the court's alliance with the old aristocracy prevented its timely incorporation of the newly emerging elites and was responsible for the partial withering away of the Tang state in the late ninth century.

For the aristocratic clans their alliance with the Tang dynasty proved to be equally disastrous in the long term. Having focused too intently on preserving power in the imperial center, most of these clans abandoned their local power base, and did not survive the dynasty's fall. With the collapse of the Tang in the early tenth century, the old aristocracy vanished as well, paving the way for the rise of new elites.[20] It was up to these newcomers to redefine elite-throne relations; and their ultimate success contributed decisively toward much greater political stability in China during the second imperial millennium.

THE SONG DYNASTY: FROM "NEW POLICIES" TO ELITE VOLUNTARISM

The Tang–Song transition is widely recognized as a crucial divide between the early and late imperial periods in Chinese history; and changes in the composition and functioning of the elite are considered to be among the primary features of this divide. When the Tang dynasty collapsed amid great domestic turmoil and its old aristocracy perished, its demise opened the way for different groups—from military strongmen to wealthy landowners, from rich merchants to refined but impoverished literati—to compete for status and power. In this open situation, the decision of the founding Song emperors to rely overwhelmingly on the literati as primary allies of the throne appears singularly consequential. Not only did the emperors appoint men of letters to the highest and most prestigious positions, but they significantly modified the examination system so as to enhance its openness and fairness, turning it into the primary vehicle for advancement into the officialdom.[21] Although the examination system still witnessed ups and downs well into the early fifteenth century, it was under the Song that it gained for the first time its importance for defining elite status.

The examination system became the single most important factor shaping social dynamics in late imperial China. Contrary to a widespread misconception, its primary importance was not necessarily in enhancing social mobility: actually, wealth, particularly landownership, remained throughout the second imperial millennium the sine qua non for acquiring elite status. Yet, as many merchants knew perfectly well, wealth alone was insufficient to sustain one's status, let alone to perpetuate it for generations. It is in this regard that examinations became exceptionally significant. While only a tiny percentage of those who entered the examination competition could realistically expect to proceed to the top of the ladder and attain official positions, even a low degree, or, at times, even student status, drew huge prestige and manifold economic and legal privileges. Most importantly, even a minor examination success allowed an individual to join the broad body of literati, who were all understood to be *potential* officials. This would grant him direct access to local magistrates, protect him from unwelcome litigation and from abuse by members of the notoriously corrupt clerical subbureaucracy, and allow him to serve as a mediator between his community and the magistrate. Hence sitting for examinations became the default choice for acting and aspiring elite members.

In addition to its social impact, the examination system had far-reaching political and cultural consequences. The relative fairness of the examinations beginning in the Song dynasty meant that any elite male (and, nominally, any male except for members of several social groups that were discriminated against) could expect that he or his offspring would earn the right to join the officialdom. This expectation attached the entire body of elite members to the state in a much stronger way than had been possible in the aristocratic age. Moreover, the proliferation of the examinations culture in the life of local elites meant that thenceforth their identity as the literati was much stronger than before. The examinations ensured a certain degree of cultural and ideological cohesiveness (although not necessarily uniformity) among members of the elite throughout the imperial realm, and strengthened their feeling of belonging to the "national" (i.e., empire-wide) elite body. Local elites became a more important political factor than they had previously been, and a more stabilizing and unifying force as well—in both cultural and sociopolitical terms.[22]

The profound impact of the examination system became fully visible as early as the first century of Song rule. As robust economic growth increased the number of wealthy individuals, while proliferation of printing technology decreased the costs of learning, a great many more men than at any time in the past turned toward examinations, with the number of candidates swelling from dozens to hundreds of thousands during the dynasty's life span. A parallel expansion in educational facilities brought about further dissemination of the so-called Confucian ideas and values associated with the examinations. All these developments led to the formation of a new type of local elite: broader, more ideologically cohesive, more dependent on the throne to validate its status, but also more politically active than its predecessors.[23]

The renovation of the elite and its deep political involvement may explain some of the ideological vitality of the Song period, particularly its first half, the Northern Song (960–1127), which, at least in terms of political thought, brought about a much larger volume of innovative work than any preceding or subsequent dynasty. In particular, thinkers and statesmen of that period tackled anew a variety of questions related to state-society relations and to the roles of local elites in the imperial order. This topic did not figure prominently in the political discourse of the Warring States period, when independent elites did not play a significant societal role, nor was it systematically discussed by early imperial think-ers. Hence views of the Song statesmen and thinkers and their proposals for developing state-elite relations were of profound consequence for the future development trajectory of imperial China.[24] In what follows I shall focus on two of the most important approaches, namely, the radical statism of the great reformer Wang Anshi (1021–1086), and a distinct "community-oriented" (or, more precisely, elite-oriented) ideology asso-ciated with the so-called Neo-Confucian thinkers, most significantly Zhu Xi (1130–1200). The ultimate failure of the former resulted, even if not immediately, in the ascendancy of the latter approach, which informed the rest of the empire's history. In particular, Zhu Xi's promulgation of what Peter Bol defines as the literati's "voluntarism"[25]—inspiring community-oriented voluntary action undertaken by morally motivated members of the educated elite—became, arguably, the single most impor-tant contribution of Neo-Confucianism to Chinese political culture.

Wang Anshi's ideology was a curious blend of moral idealism and pragmatism, of the quest for social justice through redistribution of wealth and an equally powerful desire to increase state revenues through tapping the burgeoning economy. His "New Policies," launched in 1068, shaped sociopolitical dynamics in China for almost sixty years, becoming the most audacious political experiment in imperial history. Wang initi-ated a complete overhaul of the state administration in order to enable it to deal adequately with new demographic pressures and the impact of commercialization; and he hoped that the reinvigorated state apparatus would also promote social fairness through reallocating resources from the wealthy to the needy. Wang's program brought about a radical expan-sion in the government bureaucracy and a parallel unprecedented surge in bureaucratic activism in all spheres of life. This was by far the boldest departure ever from prevalent practices, the hallmark of Northern Song innovativeness.[26]

Among Wang Anshi's numerous innovations, several were directly aimed at reducing what he considered the disruptive role of local elites in socioeconomic life. The single most controversial of his steps was the in-troduction of the so-called Green Sprouts policy, which turned the state into a competitor with local elites as a source for rural credit. Normally, on the eve of planting or harvest, peasants had to borrow seeds or food from local magnates, and exorbitant interest rates sucked many of them into perennial indebtedness and eventual loss of property. Wang Anshi hoped to reverse the situation through loans distributed by officials at a tolerable interest rate of 20 percent. He explicitly stated that this inter-vention would not just help the peasants; it would also destroy the hated "engrossers" (*jianbing*), powerful elite members who benefited from the peasants' plight, and whom Wang viewed with an enmity that a modern observer likened to class hatred in the early years of the People's Republic of China.[27] This was the state's boldest intervention into the rural economy since the cessation of the "equal field" system three centuries earlier, and it threatened to undermine the very foundation of the elite's local economic dominance.

Other measures undertaken by Wang Anshi were similarly detrimental to elite power. Thus to enhance local security he initiated the formation of a new village-level mutual responsibility system, based on the *baojia*, a unit of five or ten households, headed on a rotating basis by a sequence of wealthy local landowners. From its initial modest goals of facilitating mutual control by the neighbors and providing militia training, the *baojia* soon evolved into a low-level administrative unit—one that could potentially facilitate the penetration of the state authorities into local communities, to the marked disadvantage of local elites.[28] Other actions advanced by Wang Anshi, such as state intervention into commercial activities and his planned educational reform (for which see chapter 3 above), also angered many of the literati.

Why did Wang Anshi, who himself came from an elite family, opt for a radical antielite stance? Several answers suggest themselves. First, many of Wang's policies may have been more detrimental to large northern landowners than they were to people like himself who came from the more commercialized southern areas. Second, on a more idealistic level, Wang, like many other "elite-bashers" from among the officialdom, perceived himself to be representing the "public" (*gong*) rather than narrow "private" (*si*) interest; thus his readiness to harm his own social stratum could have been considered a manifestation of his moral superiority and selflessness. Third, and most significantly, Wang was ideologically disinclined to accept the existence of an independent elite stratum. Rather, as argued by Peter Bol, he envisioned a new order in which all the literati—that is, all those who deserved elite status—would be ultimately employed by the state.[29] Should this happen, China would revert to the Warring States–Qin situation in which there was no place for independent elite groups. However, this ideal, even if Wang had wholeheartedly pursued it, was unattainable under the socioeconomic conditions of his age; and, in any case, it was not shared by the majority of the literati.

Wang's excessive activism engendered bitter opposition, which grew exponentially as his policies progressed. Some of his opponents, such as the eminent historian and thinker Sima Guang (1019–1086), were averse in principle to his assault on the wealthy, arguing that this stratum was essential to society's well-being.[30] Others disliked Wang's arrogance and his attempts to impose ideological uniformity on the literati; yet others opposed some of his economic or administrative measures. Their specific arguments varied considerably; but most of the reformer's adversaries were unified by intense dissatisfaction with Wang's infringement on the interests of their stratum. Wang Anshi's policies generated deep political schism among the literati.

Amid bitter struggle between the opposing factions, the "New Policies" were twice discontinued and resumed again, peaking once more in the reign of Emperor Huizong (r. 1101–1125).[31] That emperor's patronage, however, proved disastrous in the long term: when Huizong's intemperate foreign policy caused a major military debacle and the loss of the Central Plain to the invading Jurchens, this fiasco was blamed on the emperor's fascination with Wang Anshi–inspired activism, which was thenceforth branded as political heresy. As the battered Southern Song dynasty (1127–1279) tried to restore its fortunes in a bitter competition first with the Jurchens and later with the Mongols, its leaders were no longer prone to renew the assertive state policies that Wang Anshi had promoted.[32]

The cessation of state activism in the Southern Song dynasty reflected not just disappointment with Wang Anshi's perceived failure, but also a deeper change in the literati's behavior, dubbed by researchers a "localist turn." This turn came as a result of growing frustration with the political sphere, viewed as corrupt, fragmented, and unable to realize high moral goals, and, more significantly, because of the increasing difficulty even the most brilliant men of letters faced in their efforts to attain office. As the number of examination candidates soared, ambitious literati's chances of earning the highest degree markedly decreased, prompting many to look for alternative ways to secure their social position. New generations of literati sought primarily to enhance their standing and prestige in local society, while political activism was largely discontinued. This localist turn was duly mirrored in the realm of political thought. In the Southern Song, gone was the quest for increased centralization and deeper penetration of the state into society; to the contrary, leading thinkers sought to improve the sociopolitical situation through elite activism from below rather than through invigoration of the state apparatus.[33] This change is apparent in the approaches of the single most important thinker of the late imperial period, Zhu Xi.

Zhu Xi shared some of Wang Anshi's goals, such as caring for the weaker members of the society, disciplining the elite, and enhancing social order; significantly, though, Zhu Xi, who never attained high position, was much less concerned with the problem of state revenues. Yet what critically distinguishes Zhu Xi from his predecessor is his radically different recipe for attaining his objectives: rather than advancing the position that the state should remold local society, he believed that social problems should be resolved through voluntary action from below undertaken by morally upright and public-spirited literati. Having successfully synthesized the ideas of his predecessors, Zhu Xi and his associates promulgated several initiatives that mirrored those of Wang Anshi but were not imposed from above. Thus privately established academies were to augment or replace the dilapidated state education system as a locus for the moral and ideological instruction of the literati; in place of the hated "Green Sprouts" loans, charitable granaries run by prominent elite members would provide support for the needy; and the "community compact," a voluntary association of the literati (or of all the villagers), would increase mutual moral supervision, superseding the state-imposed *baojia* mutual surveillance system.[34]

Communal self-support had existed long before Zhu Xi; for centuries it was actively promulgated by Buddhist monasteries and lay associations; and it was also a part of the expanding repertoire of lineage-oriented activities that had been proliferating among the elite since Northern Song days.[35] Other thinkers before Zhu Xi similarly sought ways to strengthen communal solidarity and buttress internal hierarchy, to promote philanthropy and establish educational facilities. Zhu Xi's major innovation was his successful synthesis of local activism with the notion of moral self-cultivation and self-realization of the elite member. Zhu Xi allowed the "superior man" to realize the True Way not only in the political realm, by acquiring office, but in his immediate vicinity, on the community level. In the Neo-Confucian interpretation, the mission of "ordering the world" could be accomplished not only from the top of the sociopolitical pyramid downward, but also from the base, the local communities, upward—which meant radical empowerment of local elites, provided these elites were led by upright literati.

Zhu Xi's linkage between the moral realization of the "superior men" and local voluntarism came, as noted above, at the crucial juncture when more and more literati realized that official careers might elude them forever owing to ever-fiercer competition. By redirecting their public-spiritedness from government service to quasi-government communal activities, Zhu Xi not only found an outlet for the literati's sense of mission but also helped to redefine the nature of elite membership. If philanthropic activities were a manifestation of one's moral superiority, then their role in perpetuating one's elite status became as crucial as acquiring education and maintaining the conventional lifestyle of the literati. This encouraged generations of elite members to take care of their communities, and even to perform tasks that may have been economically disadvantageous for at least some of them, such as revising the tax rolls in their county to ensure fairer distribution of the tax burden.[36] This latter example of extraordinary public spirit was a rarity, to be sure, but many other communal activities of the literati were not. The state thenceforth could relegate much of its social burden to its willing aides, for whom the very right to serve the community was instrumental in preserving their prestige and status. Zhu Xi provided the throne with reliable, unpaid servants, thereby contributing decisively to the ongoing success of the imperial enterprise.

TENSE SYMBIOSIS: THE ELITE AND THE STATE IN LATE IMPERIAL CHINA

As is well known, shortly after Zhu Xi's death he was lionized as the greatest imperial Confucian, while Wang Anshi was relegated to the margins of history, to be rediscovered only in the twentieth century. But does this mean that Zhu Xi's vision of the symbiosis between the state and the elite was thenceforth uncritically accepted? In the past, not a few scholars have answered affirmatively, arguing that in practical terms elite members safeguarded the imperial autocracy, while the state protected the interests of rich landowners. Others have proposed a radically different view: they averred that the elite's relations with the state were characterized by persistent struggle, or even a "zero-sum game," and that elites were guardians of community interests against the intrusive state apparatus. Nowadays, most scholars tend to synthesize both views: the relations between the elite and the state were marked by mutual dependency and cooperation, but also by competition and tensions.[37] And yet, as we shall see, the general tendency was toward increased mutual reliance and dependence—even though not necessarily for the idealistic reasons envisioned by Zhu Xi.

Cooperation between the imperial state and local elites had solid institutional, social, and ideological foundations. Institutionally speaking, reliance on local elites was the officials' default choice owing to the peculiar structure of the imperial bureaucracy. Throughout most of the late imperial period, the cream of the bureaucracy, the civil servants (most of whom were degree holders), numbered no more than thirty thousand men. This contingent was simply too thinly spread over the vast reaches of the empire to effectively deal with the variety of local challenges. A county magistrate, who represented the emperor and the civil service on the lowest administrative level, was in charge of more than one hundred thousand people, and was supposed to deal with multiple administrative, fiscal, educational, and judicial tasks, which, if performed thoroughly, would absorb all his spare time. Moreover, customarily he was not supposed to serve in his native province nor to occupy his office for more than three years, which meant that he was usually a newcomer in a strange area, the colloquial language of which he could not understand,

and the local conditions of which he rarely could learn in advance. From the very beginning, the magistrate was put in an almost impossible situation.[38]

To deal effectively with his everyday tasks, the magistrate had to rely on the clerical subbureaucracy, which was probably the weakest link of the imperial system. Originally, clerks, who stayed "outside the stream" (*liu wai*) of prestigious offices, were minor partners of civil servants; but in the wake of the Song reforms their position greatly deteriorated. Denied the right to participate in the examinations, most of the clerks could no longer hope to advance into the civil service, which made their position singularly unprestigious. Civil service employees normally viewed their clerical underlings as avaricious and selfish "petty men," prone to abuse their power; this stereotype provided moral justification for the clerks' lowly position. As so frequently happens, the negative stereotype turned into a self-fulfilling prophecy, as chronically underfunded clerks routinely had to extort funds from the local population through a variety of illegal means. This state of affairs perpetuated and aggravated the alienation between proud members of the regular bureaucracy and their clerical staff, which made effective cooperation between the two highly improbable.[39]

In this situation, the officials could not fulfill their responsibilities without reliance on members of local society. It is against this background that the social proximity between the elites and the officials became particularly important. The elite members were natural allies of the magistrate. Having a similar educational background, speaking the uniform "officials' language" ("Mandarin"), and having the right to access the magistrate directly, they were the obvious choice when magistrates needed advice or allies in times of need. The elite members, many of whom were either related to officials or themselves potential officeholders, were also close to the magistrate culturally and ideologically; and many of them were genuinely imbued with public-mindedness and willingness to serve the community. It was only natural that officials utilized this spirit and mobilized the elites to perform a variety of administrative, economic, and even judicial tasks on the local level, alleviating the pressure on the officialdom.

Local elites were ideal intermediaries between the state and the local society: they acted as voluntary aides to the magistrate, performing their tasks out of sheer commitment to their lofty moral goals, or—according to a more cynical interpretation—out of the need to preserve their exalted status in the local community. They were instrumental in such fields as education, welfare, public works, local security, moral instruction to the community, and resolution of local conflicts. They could run a local school, a Confucian temple, a charitable granary; gather the villagers for periodic ritual performances and instruct them to behave morally; control their neighbors and kin; train a local militia unit; and initiate construction or maintenance of roads, bridges, dams, irrigation ditches, and other public facilities in their localities. Although the practical involvement of the elites in these and other matters differed considerably over time and space, their overall contribution to local prosperity, social order, and cultural life is undeniable. The bureaucracy came to appreciate it, knowing that efficient cooperation with the elites in a variety of educational and philanthropic projects could bring about remarkable benefits to society.

From the elites' point of view, cooperation with the magistrate was also the default strategy. Not only could it safeguard them from potentially abusive treatment by the state apparatus, but it also brought about many important social advantages. As many researchers have noted, the social power of the elite in their communities derived not only from their economic affluence and cultural prestige but also from their role as mediators between the state and the commoners.[40] Smooth relations with officials were an important asset, which could, if properly applied, protect the villagers from litigation and from excessive taxation, help them to attain government support in the wake of natural disasters, and benefit them in a variety of other ways. For a local elite member, ties with the magistrate were, therefore, instrumental for preserving his elite status.

In addition to institutional and social factors, ideology also played a role in cementing the magistrate's ties with the local elites. This topic has been partly addressed in the previous section and will be discussed again in the next; here I shall focus on a single ideological incentive for increased reliance on the elites: namely, the persistent desire of Chinese thinkers and statesmen to attain political order through minimal coercion. The ideal of spontaneous moral transformation of the people (*jiaohua*), as exemplified in this chapter's epigraph, supported the endorsement of semiautonomous communities run by morally upright local leaders. Moreover, the notion of an autonomous social unit was embedded in the Confucian view of the family as the basic social cell, in which harmony and internal hierarchy coexisted "naturally" and were not imposed from outside. With the renewed proliferation of lineage organizations since the Song dynasty, the lineage rather than the nuclear family was widely considered to be the ideal self-governing unit, one that enjoyed a considerable degree of autonomy. Not a few thinkers and statesmen considered it appropriate to expand the autonomy of the lineage to a broader community, such as a village or, rarely, the whole canton (*xiang*, a subcounty unit that usually comprised a township and several villages around it). Insofar as these communities were headed by respectable local literati, their autonomy and cohesion were deemed conducive to the preservation of the sociopolitical order and not threatening to state authority.[41]

While all the factors described above encouraged the officials to deepen their cooperation with and reliance upon the local elites, there were equally compelling reasons to be less enthusiastic about this cooperation and to view the elites' power in general with deep suspicion. Most fundamentally, there was a persistent conflict of economic interests between the elites and the state apparatus. While the officials were normatively inclined to increase state revenues—most specifically through ensuring that nobody avoided taxation, that all the arable land was properly registered, and that most peasants possessed enough land to pay their taxes—from the elites' point of view this represented a threat to their fundamental economic interests. As officials knew very well, many elite members routinely utilized their amicable ties with the magistrates to avoid full taxation of their assets; or, worse, bullied weaker members of the community, grabbing their lands and turning them into bond servants. These "local bullies and evil gentry" were disruptive both to the state's fiscal needs and to the very social order that the officials had to preserve; and their actions undermined the foundations of the normally amicable ties between the elites and the magistrates.

Writings by officials, and by many conscientious elite members, provide a reader with an almost endless repertoire of tricks used by unscrupulous local elites to empower themselves economically: from underreporting the acreage of their landholdings to false registrations of private fields as charitable estates; from utilizing community granaries for commercial needs to impoverishing the peasants through exorbitant interest rates on the all-important loans; from violent seizing of neighbors' plots to socially abusive behavior. These men could utilize lineage solidarity for such disruptive goals as persistent litigations, tax resistance, or assaults on neighboring communities. Even seemingly innocent irrigation projects could hide malicious motives, enabling the local strongmen to appropriate an unfairly large portion of the much-needed water, or to build dams to expand their arable lands at the expense of increasing flood danger further downstream.[42]

The persistent problem of local bullies meant that the elite could not be entirely entrusted with local affairs, but should be closely watched and disciplined when necessary. It was for this reason that, *pace* Zhu Xi, many officials viewed the elites' voluntary actions from below with deep suspicion. However, discarding the elites' support and subduing them was not a viable option either. At times, individual magistrates, such as Hai Rui (d. 1587), whom we encountered in the previous chapter, could courageously assault local bullies; but such activism could backfire and in any case was unsustainable in the long term. First, local elites often had sufficient connections within the officialdom to arrange the impeachment or at least the replacement of an excessively interventionist magistrate (as in the case of Hai Rui, among others).[43] Second, a confrontational attitude on the magistrate's part would tremendously hinder his abilities to utilize the elites for successful performance of his manifold tasks. Third, and most significantly, the social and cultural proximity between the officials and local elites made prolonged action of the former against the latter highly unlikely. Some of the emperors were well aware of possible connivance between the bureaucrats and elite members, and launched periodic campaigns against it (more on this below). Nonetheless, such campaigns could only discipline the elites and the officials for the time being, without altering the fundamental workings of the bureaucracy, which prescribed the utilization of the elites' power rather than its suppression.

To understand the imperial government's fundamental incapability of adopting a harsh course against the elites' power, we should turn to the activities of one of the most resolute monarchs ever, the Ming founder Zhu Yuanzhang. A former rebel, who rose from the very bottom of society (after his parents died during an epidemic, he spent some time as a Buddhist novice and a wandering monk), Zhu Yuanzhang was exceptionally attentive to the plight of the commoners and also deeply suspicious of the literary elite, especially the members of his bureaucracy. Having come to power after the Yuan dynasty government's prolonged period of deterioration and decades of civil war, Zhu Yuanzhang was determined to restore political order through harsh measures, if needed. He declared:

> Formerly, when I was among the people, I saw that many of the provincial and county officials did not pity the people. Everywhere there was corruption and lust, debauchery and neglect of affairs and the people were miserable. I saw these things and I conceived a great hatred for the officials in my heart. Therefore, now there are severe laws to stamp out this sort of thing and those officials who are avaricious and who harm the people are punished without mercy.[44]

Zhu Yuanzhang's distrust of the literati and his conviction that only strict disciplinary measures would prevent their abuses brought about some of the bloodiest repressive campaigns in Chinese history against corrupt and allegedly subversive officials. Amid these reprisals, many powerful elite families were targeted as well: countless estates were confiscated and their land redistributed to petty landholders. Zhu Yuanzhang also acted resolutely to reimpose imperial order in the localities. He created a variety of subcounty administrative units, initiated a series of population and land surveys, adjusted taxation, and vehemently punished alleged corruption. All these measures were intended to reinvigorate the imperial state after decades of malfunctioning, and to lay the foundation for a lasting and perfect sociopolitical and moral order. They were also intended to put an end to abuses perpetrated by the elites, abuses that had plagued Yuan society.[45]

It is tempting to view Zhu Yuanzhang, as many scholars have done, as a precursor to Mao Zedong: a rebel-turned-emperor, who remained the champion of the masses, detested the upper strata, and aimed at destroying the elites' power.[46] It is certainly true that Zhu's attitude toward the elites was much harsher than that of most other emperors; and his oppressive measures may have contributed directly to the massive personnel changes among the elites in the early Ming dynasty.[47] This is only one side of the story, though. Zhu Yuanzhang never tried to build a regime in which the imperial state would eliminate the elites' power altogether. He shared the belief of most contemporaneous statesmen in the advantages of small government and sought to reduce administrative costs by minimizing the number of officials on the payroll. Thus, instead of increasing the size of the bureaucracy, he preferred to see the newly created subcounty units run by local wealthy landowners, village elders, and other community leaders, who were largely independent of the magistrates and could even supervise and punish the magistrates and the clerks. Community heads had a broad variety of tasks: from supervising taxation to providing local security, maintaining community schools and community granaries, dealing with local crimes, and, most importantly, providing moral leadership, encouraging good behavior, and shaming miscreants, whose names were to be published on purpose-built kiosks in the villages. The system is so much at odds with bureaucratic activism, and appears so indebted to Zhu Xi's vision, that Peter Bol plainly interpreted it as a codification of the Neo-Confucian program.[48]

Zhu Yuanzhang's village policies underwent many twists and turns, but their general trend remained consistent: he favored community autonomy and tried to insulate communities from the intrusive state apparatus. Thus while in the short term his policies may have undermined the power of elite members, they also created extraordinarily favorable conditions for the reemergence of new powerful elites soon after Zhu Yuanzhang's death. The intrinsic weakness of the regular bureaucracy left a sociopolitical vacuum at the lower administrative levels, which was duly filled in by new generations of local elites. The Ming dynasty gradually but irreversibly transformed itself from the elites' nightmare into their paradise. In particular, tax exemptions granted to degree holders and to imperial students proved exceptionally favorable to the restoration of the elite's economic power, as many peasants consigned their lands to local elite members to escape corvée obligations. By the sixteenth century the renewed power of the elites and their unruliness became the major cause of the dynasty's decline, with officials powerless to do anything but complain bitterly about the machinations of the elites and about troublemaking degree holders.[49] The regime that began with an attempt to reinvigorate the imperial state ended with much weaker centralized control than ever before.

Zhu Yuanzhang's reforms may be judged a misguided attempt to preserve a powerful state amid overall bureaucratic budget and personnel cuts; but they may be read differently, as a reassertion of the increasingly symbiotic relations between the state and the bearers of societal power in local communities. The resemblance of these reforms to Zhu Xi's policies is not incidental: voluntary action from below and state activism from above were increasingly viewed as mutually supportive rather than mutually exclusive. Thus, in the second half of the Ming dynasty, when the system established by the founder lost its vitality, it was the turn of petty officials and elite members to respond by reinvigorating voluntary activities, such as community compacts, the *baojia* system, and the like, which, in turn, closely resembled Zhu Yuanzhang's initiatives.[50] From this perspective, Zhu Yuanzhang's efforts can be seen as a costly experiment in disciplining local elites rather than a real attempt to replace them altogether.

The Qing dynasty provides yet another example of the local elites' resilience. The Manchu practice of relying on the military aristocracy— the bannermen—diluted the erstwhile power of Chinese local elites within the officialdom, allowing the Qing emperors to launch repeated assaults on the elites' privileges and malpractices. The renewed power of the state apparatus was fully utilized by Yongzheng Emperor (see chapter 2), whose overhaul of the financial system enabled the formation of a much more vigorous and activist state than what had existed ever since Wang Anshi's experiments.[51] Yet under Yongzheng's lenient son, the Qianlong Emperor (r. 1736–1795), assaults on the elites' power were discontinued, and the momentum of state activism was lost. By the nineteenth century the power of local elites was as strong as ever.[52]

In late imperial China, the onetime bifurcation between statism and elite-oriented political activities, observable under Wang Anshi, had all but disappeared. Despite ongoing elite malpractices and complaints against "evil gentry," cooperation rather than openly expressed conflict was the norm. Late imperial thinkers and practitioners could advocate strengthening the elite at the expense of the clerical subbureaucracy, as Gu Yanwu (1613–1682) proposed; or they could seek potential new avenues for state activism, as advocated by the model statesman Chen Hongmou (1696–1771); but all agreed on the need to improve cooperation between the bureaucracy and the elites, their differences concerning details rather than essentials.[53] Despite certain obvious disadvantages, the imperial state opted to rely on the elites, because it could no longer survive without their cooperation. The symbiosis between the holders of political and of societal power had been reconfirmed once and for all.

The Three Bonds: Ideology of the State-Elite Convergence

The discussion above elucidates the persistent difficulty facing the state in establishing a modus vivendi with local elites: overreliance on their support meant giving free rein to the elites' abuses, while oppression was too costly and required fundamental adjustment of the administrative system, a course that was ruled out after Wang Anshi's debacle. This lack of institutional remedy for the state's addiction to the elites' support explains in turn the importance of ideological factors for ensuring smooth cooperation between the elites and the imperial state. Above I have briefly addressed how the Neo-Confucian idea of voluntary action from below contributed to the strengthening of the elites' ties with the throne; now I want to explore the impact of another ideological construct on the relations between the state and the elites: the notion of congruence between patriarchal and monarchical authority, and the related idea that strengthening the family means strengthening the state, and vice versa.

The concept of the fundamental unity between the family and the state is so deeply rooted in Chinese imperial ideology that it is often viewed as a perennial feature of Chinese political culture. This was not always the case, though. In particular, during the aristocratic Springs-and-Autumns period, as powerful noble lineages routinely challenged the ruler's authority, it was tacitly understood that lineage cohesiveness might be detrimental rather than conducive to sociopolitical stability.[54] It was only after the replacement of the hereditary aristocracy with the *shi* stratum, and the parallel demise of powerful lineages, that family values were interpreted as supportive of political order, as exemplified in this saying by a disciple of Confucius: "Few are those who, being filial and fraternal, are still inclined to disobey superiors."[55] To be sure, there were dissenting voices, such as that of the great thinker Han Feizi, who cynically observed that "a filial son is the one who turns his back to the enemy";[56] but the overwhelming majority of known thinkers accepted the idea that the patriarch's authority and the monarch's were compatible and should be upheld in tandem.

The belief in the essential unity between the family and the state, and between filial piety and loyalty to the sovereign, had been strengthening since the beginning of the imperial era. Even the resurrection of large patrilineal families in the Han dynasty and thereafter did not bring about state attempts to suppress kinship solidarity. To the contrary, the authorities promulgated the concept of filiality—and, by extension, commitment to one's kin—as one of the primary requirements for an aspiring official. It was also under the Han dynasty that the idea of congruence between the monarch and the patriarch crystallized in the concept of the Three Bonds (*san gang*)—the relations between the ruler and his subjects, the father and his sons, and the husband and his wife (wives). The Three Bonds were interpreted as manifestations of the uniform hierarchical principle of human relations, the unshakable foundation of human morality and of sociopolitical order. Eminent imperial thinkers from Dong Zhongshu (ca. 195–115 BCE) to Zhu Xi provided metaphysical and religious underpinnings for the Three Bonds, elevating them to the position of supreme sociopolitical truth. Indeed, the supremacy of the Three Bonds in guiding human relations was not questioned until the very end of the imperial period.[57]

In the course of imperial history, the concept of the Three Bonds became the core of the value system of elites and commoners alike, the heart of what Liu Kwang-Ching defines as socioethical orthodoxy. Its power transcended the philosophical and religious beliefs of individual statesmen and literati. Their metaphysical or religious precepts could be contested, the authority of the canonical works questioned; but fundamental adherence to the Three Bonds remained unshakable. These core beliefs about the ruler and the family were disseminated throughout society through a variety of means: from legal codes to ritual regulations, from school textbooks to popular novels, from Daoist and Buddhist rites to works by leading philosophers. The Three Bonds became the unifying framework that held the imperial sociopolitical order intact.[58]

The proliferation of the Three Bonds ideology, and specifically the equation between filial piety and loyalty, are particularly interesting in the context of their contribution to the throne's relations with the elites, especially in the late imperial period, when lineage cohesiveness became essential to the perpetuation of the elites' power in many parts of China. The lineage patriarchs were the primary beneficiaries of the promulgation of family morality; and the state's efforts to strengthen rather than weaken kinship values were essential to convince the lineage heads of the perennial congruence of their interests with those of the imperial regime.[59] The state's commitment to the promotion of family-oriented ideology appears to be one of the most significant features of Chinese imperial polity.

The empire mobilized a substantial portion of its formidable resources to strengthen the patrilineal family. Thus unfilial behavior and crimes against kin fell under the unpardonable "ten abominations," the heinous nature of which matched that of crimes against the throne. The state recognized the lineage as a legal entity, both for punitive purposes, upholding the shared communal responsibility of lineage members, and also in positive terms, granting lineage heads judicial power over their kin, including, occasionally, the right to execute an erring lineage member.[60] It furthermore distributed manifold positive incentives to strengthen kinship organization: from granting corvée exemptions to members of "communal families," who did not divide property for several generations, to conceding tax exemptions for charitable estates and other forms of common lineage property.[61] Filial sons were granted particularly preferential treatment, and at times (most notably during the Han dynasty, but also at later periods) a reputation for filiality could lead to one's nomination for an official position. The Ministry of Rites additionally encouraged filial sons and chaste widows through granting them various insignia and partial tax exemptions; in the late imperial period the commendation took the highly visible form of towering commemorative arches, some of which remain visible in the Chinese landscape even today, despite massive destruction during the twentieth-century upheavals.[62] Through all these means, the imperial state positioned itself as the primary guardian of the patriarchs' interests—and they, in turn, had to guard the interests of the throne.

The commitment of the empire to the promotion of family values is often considered almost a natural by-product of its underlying Confucian ideology. Yet "natural" as it may seem to modern observers, this commitment was not free of problems. By recognizing the patriarch's power, the state yielded some of its rights to penetrate the society to its bottom; by generously disseminating tax exemptions to the filial and the chaste, it gave up some of its income; by meticulously checking claims of filiality and chastity, it added another burdensome task to its bureaucracy. Even such an innocent regulation as the recognition of an official's right to mourn his parents could become extremely burdensome, as it usually required approving mourning leave for the most important public servants.[63] The imperial leaders agreed to bear this burden because it proved politically expedient. Insofar as society retained its belief in the essential unity of the Three Bonds, and specifically in the identity of filial piety and loyalty to the throne, it was expected that the state's commitment to family values would be reciprocated with the parallel commitment of the elites to strengthening the emperor's authority. This expectation was well founded, as can be seen from the following example.

At the very end of his reign, Zhu Yuanzhang finalized his endless experiments with communal self-rule by issuing the *Placard of the People's Instructions*, which summarized his policy innovations. The document contained, among other material, "Six Injunctions"—the core of his message to the subjects, which had to be read in every village throughout the empire every five days:

> Be filial to your parents, respect superiors, maintain harmony with neighbors, instruct and discipline sons and grandsons, live and work in peace and contentment, do not commit wrongful acts.[64]

It is most remarkable that the "Six Injunctions" do not address state concerns at all: they call for neither loyalty to the emperor nor obedience to the magistrate; actually they mention no political obligations whatsoever. This is not an occasional omission: in later versions of these admonitions, the so-called Sacred Edict (more precisely, "The Sage's [e.g., Emperor's] Edict") promulgated by the Qing emperors, the structure remained the same: while the Qing rulers added brief references to the need to pay taxes and observe the law, the bulk of their injunctions reflected the emperors' concern with the interests of the local community and its internal harmony rather than with its relation to state power.[65] This concern of the state with the community's internal order was duly reciprocated by the community leaders, who committed themselves to safeguarding the interests of the throne. Thus, in the sixteenth century, as the Ming literati revived the community compact ceremony, they introduced the theretofore unknown ritual of "Five Bows and Three Kowtows" commonly performed by all the participants before the wooden tablet bearing Zhu Yuanzhang's maxims.[66] The initiative to display the utmost loyalty to the throne came from below, as a natural complement to the community-oriented initiative that came from above. The ideological unity between the state and the elites had been reconfirmed.

Epilogue: Stability and Stagnation

The imperial state benefited enormously—economically, politically, and culturally—from its persistent cooperation with and co-optation of the local elites. The most immediate advantage stemming from this cooperation was the tremendous cut in administrative costs. Throughout much of the imperial period, and most notably in the second millennium CE, the imperial state successfully relegated to the elites many of its tasks related to welfare, public works, education, local security, and ideological indoctrination; at times it also heaped much of its judicial and tax-collecting burden on the shoulders of its willing aides. It is well known how costly these functions are for the modern state; in light of this we can appreciate how substantially elite voluntarism mitigated the workload of the imperial administration. Although the scope of this voluntarism and the degree of its social impact differed in time and space, we are justified in asserting that a significant portion of the Chinese population benefited from elite philanthropy—a much greater portion than would have been possible had all the socioeconomic and cultural tasks undertaken by the elite been performed exclusively by the state apparatus.

No less remarkable were the political benefits the empire reaped from the co-optation of the elites. The throne developed a variety of means to attach the elites to its cause. Coercion and intimidation were, to be sure, perennially available tools, and at times, such as the beginnings of the Ming and Qing dynasties, state terror against local elites was an important means of curbing their unruliness; yet in general the carrot policy was more effective than that of the stick. The single most important asset of the imperial state in co-opting the elites was its possession of symbolic capital. An individual could attain high status in his community through a variety of means; but this status was generally unsustainable unless approved and confirmed by the imperial authority, either through examinations or otherwise. Hence most of the local elites were dependent on and firmly attached to the throne, acting as the guardians of the dynasty's interests and protecting it against its enemies. On the whole, therefore, the elites played a stabilizing role in the political realm.[67]

State-elite cooperation also had far-reaching ideological and cultural consequences, which further contributed to overall stability and the empire's longevity. In particular, the examination system, initiated primarily as a means of attracting elite members to government service, became an exceptionally powerful means of imposing common values and cultural patterns on society at large. Aside from enhancing the legitimacy of the political system, the imperial examinations helped spread the culture of the literati throughout the proprietary classes, enhancing the cultural cohesiveness of the upper strata to the extent that "the late imperial gentry elite was arguably the most unified (though not uniform) elite in the world."[68] This cultural unity at the elite level contributed to the successful integration of the empire's heterogeneous population and further strengthened the hegemonic position of the imperial political ideology.

In addition to these economic, political, and cultural benefits, the empire's sophisticated means of co-opting the elites may have contributed to the imperial bureaucracy's vitality. As noted above, devolution of state power to the elites did not result in the bureaucracy's atrophy. Insofar as officials were aware of the need to control the elites' activities, especially those connected to fiscal matters, they remained vigilant and did not allow elite voluntarism to become a full-scale substitute for government policies. On the contrary, officials tended to monitor and coordinate a variety of elite-run welfare, public works, and educational projects; and when successful cooperation was attained, the results were often remarkable.[69] The specific forms of cooperation varied considerably from one locality to another, requiring a high degree of flexibility and adaptability on the part of the government bureaucrats. This in turn enhanced the general flexibility of the imperial administrative system, preventing its ossification in bureaucratic routine.

The above observations leave no doubt that successful co-optation of local elites became one of the major pillars of the empire's longevity. Yet it is important to note the manifold negative aspects of this co-optation. Reliance on the elites decreased the state's ability to penetrate local society and to tap its resources. Whether this penetration would have been harmful or beneficial to the lower strata is debatable, as we cannot determine which kind of exploitation was worse: that by officials or that by local bullies. Yet from the point of view of the imperial center, the negative effects of power devolution are undeniable. Having become addicted to cooperation with the elite, the imperial officialdom was gradually but irreversibly losing its ability to dictate to society its rules of the game, especially in terms of ensuring the state's fiscal interests. Combating the vested interests of rich landowners, who happened to belong to the same stratum as the officials themselves, was difficult—if not impossible—save under an exceptionally assertive and determined government. The perennial cycle of the government's aggravating impoverishment under any lengthy dynasty is clearly related to the elite's ability to shield its wealth by minimizing transfers to the state's coffers.

The negative impact of the elite's power on the dynastic cycle is obvious. As noted by Ray Huang, the moment of a dynasty's establishment was the only time in its history when "basic tax laws were proclaimed by dynastic founders and enforced with the sword. An aggressive fiscal policy had a greater chance of success during a dynastic turnover than at any other time. Once conditions were stable, the population would resist change."[70] This generally correct observation can be slightly modified. At its establishment, the new dynastic regime was not greatly obliged to preserve the vested interests of local elites, aside from those associated with its immediate supporters. Yet as time passed and the elites were successfully incorporated into the officialdom, the likelihood diminished that the government would vigorously pursue tax reforms at the expense of rich landowners. No less than popular resistance, it was the power of local elites, whose representatives permeated the bureaucracy and whose collaboration was crucial for any magistrate's success, that thwarted attempts to reallocate wealth once the dynastic power was stabilized. The difficulty, not to say inability, almost any lengthy dynasty confronted in the effort to initiate substantial reforms may explain the positive role played by mass popular uprisings, discussed in the next chapter. Without violent shattering of local elites and of their symbiosis with the officials, considerable reallocation of wealth might have been simply impossible.

Moving from the individual dynasty as an analytical unit toward even broader generalization, we may address now the much-debated issue of the elites' negative impact on China's path to modernity. Nowadays we no longer subscribe to the once-popular branding of late imperial elites as obstinate and parochial; nor do we consider the term "stagnation" to be justifiable with regard to late imperial China; even the very supposition that there was a uniform path toward a singularly acceptable "modernity" is no longer considered valid.[71] This said, we cannot ignore the fact that beginning in the nineteenth century and through much of the twentieth, the Chinese empire and the Republic that inherited it (1912–1949) fared badly in dealing with domestic (primarily demographic) and external (primarily Western and Japanese) challenges. In particular, its notorious inability to mobilize sufficient material and human resources for industrialization and warfare was the primary factor that led first the Qing empire and then the Chinese Republic through generations of "national humiliation."

I believe that this sad state of affairs has much to do with the power of the elites—although not necessarily in the same ways as was perceived decades ago by Western and many Chinese observers. The problem was neither ideological backwardness nor the supposed parochialism of the elites, but, rather, more essentially, the very structure of the late imperial state. Having opted to maximize stability through relegation of many of the state's tasks to the elites, the empire's architects, particularly the architects of the late imperial state, had yielded the possibility of restoring the assertive state typical of the Warring States period. As has been discussed, under the Warring States and the short-lived Qin dynasty China acted in a very "modern" way, as bureaucracy penetrated the entire society and the entire population was successfully mobilized for "agriculture and warfare"—two pillars of the state's prosperity, as defined by the great Qin reformer Shang Yang (d. 338 BCE). Not incidentally, during that period local elites played no role in the social fabric and possibly did not exist as such.

From its second inception under the Han dynasty, the empire opted for a less efficient but also much less costly mode of administration: minimization of government activism and relegation of power to local elites. This system was contested at times, especially when a plethora of new domestic and external challenges required that the central government be financially and administratively strengthened, as was the case under Han Emperor Wu, and again, much later, during the Northern Song dynasty. Yet the system of governmental minimalism was repeatedly resurrected, and it peaked under Zhu Yuanzhang, whose experiments with maintaining only a skeletal administration and relegating much power to local communities has been mentioned above. These arrangements, reaffirmed under the Qing dynasty, laid the foundations for the late imperial order as a whole, and in the long term they strengthened the state's addiction to the elite's support.[72]

China did not become stagnant in the aftermath of Zhu Yuanzhang; to the contrary, many important adjustments and modifications to his model were made both under the Ming and, more successfully, under the Qing dynasty. Yet while these adjustments were sufficient to deal with malfunctions in certain fields, they were inadequate to tackle the nineteenth-century crisis. The combination of external and domestic challenges required a complete systemic overhaul, possibly a reversion to the Warring States model, but on a much larger scale. For the elites such a reversion would have meant political annihilation; and it is not surprising, then, that while some elite members audaciously proposed profound renovation of the state, the majority procrastinated, having found no feasible way to preserve their and their family's status under the new conditions. That the imperial leaders found it difficult to propose substantial reform in these circumstances comes as no surprise.

In the final analysis, the fate of local elites in the late imperial period resembles the fate of the Tang aristocracy. Back then, the symbiosis between the dynasty and the aristocrats was so strong that the collapse of the former marked the demise of the latter. Similarly, late imperial elites failed to navigate successfully in the wake of dynastic collapse. In the past they had learned how to survive powerful uprisings that decimated the elite families but never targeted the economic, administrative, and ideological foundations of elite power in general. Now, the situation differed. Having lost their major asset—intimate ties with the imperial officials—the elites remained powerless. Being identified, justifiably or not, as part of the despicable ancien régime, they were shattered by the Republican Revolution of 1911, and then eliminated by the most powerful and thorough political upheaval that China has ever encountered: the Communist Revolution. They had outlived the empire that cherished them by slightly more than one generation.

CHAPTER 5

The People

> The ruler is a boat; commoners are the water. The water can
> carry the boat; the water can capsize the boat.
> —*Xunzi*

THE WORDS OF XUNZI (ca. 310–230 BCE) cited in the epigraph proved to
be prophetic. Prior to his age, China witnessed no popular uprisings that
left an imprint in historical texts, but shortly after his death a huge rebellion toppled the first imperial dynasty, Qin (221–207 BCE). Since then
mass uprisings have recurred repeatedly in Chinese history, bringing an
end to several major dynasties and severely crippling others. The scope,
frequency, ferocity, and political impact of these uprisings dwarf any
comparable insurrections elsewhere in the premodern world.

Twenty-two centuries after Xunzi, British interpreter and intelligence
officer Thomas Meadows, who lived in China during the early stages of
the Taiping uprising (1850–1864)—arguably the single most devastating
civil war in human history—wrote *The Chinese and their Rebellions*.
Meadows, an astute and sympathetic commentator on China's past and
present, made several interesting observations. First, he averred that "*of
all the nations that attained a certain degree of civilization, the Chinese
are the least revolutionary and the most rebellious.*" Second, he argued
that Chinese government is not despotic but autocratic; this autocracy is,
however, qualified by the right to rebel: "The Chinese people have no
right of legislation, they have no right of self-taxation, they have not the
power of voting out their rulers or of limiting or stopping supplies. They
have therefore the right of rebellion. Rebellion is in China the old, often
exercised, legitimate, and constitutional means of stopping arbitrary and
vicious legislation and administration." Third, rebellion, in Meadows's
eyes, was "a chief element of a national stability . . . the storm that clears
and invigorates a political atmosphere." Meadows concluded that the
doctrine of righteous rebellion constitutes one of the three major pillars
(together with the principles of moral government and of meritocracy) of
"the unequalled duration and constant increase of the Chinese people, as
one and the same nation."[1]

Meadows's observations, even if somewhat outdated and naive for a
modern reader, shall serve as a departure point for my discussion in this

chapter. In particular, I want to explore the reasons for the recurrence of large-scale popular uprisings throughout imperial history. Further, how does the idea of rebellion correlate with fundamental principles of Chinese political culture, such as monarchism and intellectual elitism? And why did the rebellions serve—at least in Meadows's eyes, but surely not only in his—to support rather than disrupt the empire's longevity? These questions will be related to the broader issue of the political role of the "people," here referring primarily, although not exclusively, to the lower strata, in the Chinese imperial enterprise.

In answering these questions, I intend to focus on ideological and social factors that both legitimated rebellions and also enabled their accommodation within the imperial enterprise. This perspective inevitably leads me to reject the dichotomous division of imperial society into "rebels and their enemies," to paraphrase Philip Kuhn's famous book title, or into supporters of "orthodoxy" and of "heterodoxy."[2] This does not mean, of course, that I intend to ignore the rebellions' disruptiveness, or to downplay their clearly pronounced class overtones, especially the bitter struggle of the have-nots against the elites.[3] Yet I shall try to show that, while terribly destructive in the short term, the rebellions remained firmly rooted in the imperial political tradition. To a certain extent they can even be seen as a by-product of this tradition, or, more precisely, of intrinsic tensions between the ostensible respect for the commoners in Chinese political culture and their exclusion from political processes, and between hierarchic and egalitarian mind-sets. There was sufficient overlap between the rebels' ideology and the establishment worldview, and between the social composition of the rebel leadership and of their opponents, to support both the rebellions' legitimacy and their eventual co-optation into the imperial order.

Finally, for the sake of clarity I must emphasize that I distinguish popular uprisings from other instances of collective violence and massive insubordination against the imperial authority, such as military mutinies (e.g., An Lushan's rebellion, 755–762) or dynastic rebellions (e.g., the insurrection of the Prince of Yan, the future Yongle Emperor [r. 1402–1424] in 1400–1402); and I distinguish them also from related small-scale phenomena such as localized mass protests or banditry. The large-scale popular rebellions are, first, "popular"—that is, they attract large segments of the population, particularly, but by no means exclusively, the have-nots; and, second, they are "rebellions"—they usually aim at replacing the reigning dynasty, rather than protesting against specific misdeeds of local officials or just trying to reallocate wealth through violent means. Popular rebellions differed considerably from one another in terms of their internal organization, in the importance of underlying religious factors, in the nature of their leadership, and, most significantly, in the degree of their success. Yet differences aside, they share many important similarities that allow us to discuss them as a well-defined political phenomenon that occupies a prominent place in Chinese history.

"The People as the Root" and the Right to Rebel

At first glance, China seems an unlikely candidate for the title of the world's "most rebellious nation." Traditional China is popularly imagined as a paternalistic society, in which the commoners were objects of the monarch's and the elite's munificence but not political players in their own right—a society in which strictly hierarchical and monarchical political culture should have precluded political activities from below. While it is not my intention to contest these observations, I would like to show that Chinese political culture was nonetheless flexible enough to accommodate the ideas that legitimated—at least to a certain extent—mass action by the lower strata. In particular, the concept of the people as the "foundation" or the "root" of the polity (*min ben*), and that of righteous rebellion, both of which were deeply ingrained in traditional political thought, became particularly conducive to the legitimating of popular uprisings throughout the millennia.

Let us begin with the concept of the people as the polity's "root." Even a cursory reading of political texts from the earliest stages of Chinese political thought brings to light abundant pronouncements in favor of "the people" as the raison d'être of the polity, whose well-being should be of primary concern to the rulers and the ultimate goal of political action. More surprising, in light of the paternalistic image of Chinese political culture, are manifold pronouncements that identify the people also as a legitimate and important political player in their own right. In particular, the people's level of satisfaction with the ruler is considered crucial for determining the ruler's legitimacy and his very survival on the throne. While these views should not be interpreted—as is sometimes erroneously done—as proximate to Western notions of "popular sovereignty" or "democracy" (more on this below), they could at times serve as justification for popular political action and eventually endowed popular rebellions with a certain degree of legitimacy. At the very least, these ideas served as an important corrective to the prevalent paternalistic view of the lower strata.[4]

Some of the aspects of what may be dubbed "people-oriented thought," such as the ubiquitous insistence on the ruler's duty to provide the people with a decent livelihood and personal security, may be considered a common feature of political thought worldwide, and I shall not focus on them here. Instead, I want to explore the notion of the "people" as kingmakers:

as the ultimate source of the ruler's authority and as important political
actors, whose attitudes might directly influence the survival of a ruler or
a dynasty. This view is evident in the earliest Chinese political documents—the Western Zhou–period texts from the canonical *Book of Documents*, many of which deal with the Zhou replacement of the Shang
dynasty. Among these earliest-known justifications for dynastic overthrow, the sentiments of the "people" figure prominently. The documents'
authors insist that while only the supreme deity, Heaven, can decide
whether to replace an erring ruler, its decision is directly influenced by the
people's sentiments and is reflected in the people's action. A text attributed to one of the Zhou dynastic founders says: "Heaven sees through
the people's seeing, Heaven hears through the people's hearing," and
"Heaven inevitably follows the people's desires."[5] These citations succinctly summarize the gist of many other early Zhou texts.

As is common in political parlance, the precise referent of the term
"people" in these and other texts varies considerably—it may refer either
to all the ruler's subjects, or only to the commoners, or even to the entire
population, the ruler and the ruled alike. It is possible, as I have argued
elsewhere, that early pronouncements about the importance of "the people" reflect the clan-oriented mentality of the Zhou founders, and the
term "people" refers exclusively to the Zhou clansmen;[6] but this is of
minor importance for the present discussion. From the Warring States
period on, these pronouncements were interpreted as referring to the
lower strata in general, and generations of Chinese statesmen absorbed
the tenet informing some of the earliest and most revered political texts:
"the people" stood at the center of political activities, and there was a
direct link between the people and the supreme deity, Heaven.

We know very little about the actual role of "the people" (insofar as
the term refers to the lower strata) in the overthrow of the Shang or in
early Zhou political life; but for the subsequent Springs-and-Autumns
period we have ample evidence of political activism on the part of the
lower strata. The so-called capital-dwellers (*guo ren*)—a relatively broad
stratum that comprised the lower nobility and commoners (but not
slaves)—became extraordinarily active in the political lives of major polities. Strategically located in the immediate vicinity of the ruler, capital-
dwellers became important power brokers during domestic feuds, when
their intervention could determine the outcome of any major conflict.
The rulers and the nobles duly recognized the political importance
of armed commoners, and in times of emergency they even assembled
capital-dwellers and performed a covenant ceremony with them—the
closest Chinese analogue to the popular assemblies of the Greek world.[7]

It was during the Springs-and-Autumns period, probably under the
impact of capital-dwellers' activism, that the idea that "the people are the

root of the polity" became an intrinsic part of political discourse; and it remained so in the political thought of the subsequent Warring States period. Although by then new sociopolitical developments had nullified the erstwhile importance of capital-dwellers, and "popular assemblies" were discontinued as well, the importance of the lower strata in political life and political thought had only increased. Two powerful developments required the ruling elites to remain concerned with the people's mood. First, the advent of new armies based on mass conscription rendered the problem of the conscripts' morale and willingness to fight exceptionally acute; and many thinkers argued that proper martial spirit would not materialize unless the government satisfactorily addressed the people's economic concerns. The second problem was that of migration: in the aftermath of the "iron revolution" of the fifth–fourth centuries BCE, massive efforts to turn virgin soil into farmland brought about acute shortages of labor in many states, the rulers of which had to lure immigrants from abroad and prevent emigration of the native population. This, too, prompted many thinkers to propose a variety of "people-oriented" policies aimed at improving the lot of the population and attracting immigrants from afar. Practical political recommendations varied considerably; but all thinkers—from "people-lovers," like Mengzi, to "people-bashers," like Shang Yang (d. 338 BCE)—were unified in their insistence that the people's compliance was critical for the very survival of the state.[8]

The consensus among rival thinkers with regard to the people's political importance is truly remarkable, especially when considered against the immense variety of concrete proposals as to how to deal with the lower strata. Some, like Mengzi, advocated "benevolent government"; others, like Shang Yang, opted for oppression; some called for "enlightening" the people, while others recommended preserving their "simplicity"; yet all agreed that addressing the people's needs and taking their sentiments into consideration were crucial for political success. Xunzi's adage cited in this chapter's epigraph epitomizes this consensus: unless the people's needs are properly addressed, they will capsize the ruler's boat.[9]

This respect for the people's political role, and repeated calls for the leaders to "attain the people's heart," may convey the misconception that preimperial Chinese political thought contained the seeds of democracy. It did not, though. In what appears at first glance as a paradox, not a single thinker from among those who advocated "listening to the people" ever proposed any institutional arrangements that would allow the people to voice their opinions on government affairs. Even the modest tradition of popular assemblies from the Springs-and-Autumns period had been all but forgotten, never becoming a full-fledged participatory mechanism. The rulers were urged to address the people's sentiments without being provided with any institutional means of learning what these were!

This apparent lapse of the Warring States–period thinkers is not incidental, of course. It reflects deeply ingrained intellectual elitism, which made the "superior men" disdainful of unmediated political views voiced by the morally and intellectually impaired "petty men." Thus Confucius claimed, "When the Way prevails in the country, the commoners do not debate [politics]"; while Mengzi explained: "Some toil with their hearts, some toil with their force. Heart-toilers rule men; force-toilers are ruled by men. . . . This is the common propriety of All-under-Heaven."[10] It seems, then, that thinkers preferred to speak on the people's behalf and in their stead. Hence, during the imperial millennia, while the rulers were repeatedly reminded of the importance of listening to the people, any practical means of ascertaining "public opinion"—from collecting popular songs to the complaint system—invariably reinforced the position of the educated elite as representatives of popular sentiments.[11] This shrewd appropriation by the intellectuals of what Tu Wei-ming aptly defines as "the most generalisable social relevance (the sentiments of the people)"[12] may have been too important an asset to be yielded to the uneducated masses. It was in the best interests of these self-proclaimed champions of the people to keep the commoners excluded from political processes.

The paradoxical coexistence of declared respect for the people's sentiments and practical exclusion of the lower strata from political processes inadvertently contributed to the proliferation of what may be called the "protest culture" in China, including the most powerful manifestation of protest—rebellion. A variety of protest activities—from absconding from one's village or fleeing from the battlefield, to assaulting tax collectors or openly rebelling against the authorities—were the only meaningful outlet through which the commoners could make their sentiments known to the power-holders. These activities were unlawful, to be sure, and their participants faced grave consequences. Yet insofar as "the people" were unanimously treated as the polity's "root," and insofar as their mood was considered the primary determinant of the regime's legitimacy, widespread protest activities were indicative in the eyes of elites and commoners alike of Heaven's disapproval of local power-holders, or, worse, of the ruling house. Thus protest, and even rebellion, while illegal, were legitimated, politically speaking, by the very fact of their occurrence.

An additional, more direct source of the rebels' legitimacy was the concept of "righteous rebellion," yet another paradox in Chinese political thought. In China's rigidly monarchistic political culture, violent insubordination was not supposed to be an option for the subjects; and yet the right to overthrow a vicious tyrant was firmly incorporated into the theory of monarchism, as noted in chapter 2. Associated with the paradigmatic overthrow of the Shang by the Zhou dynasty, the single most important event in early Chinese history, the concept of righteous rebellion became an inalienable part of China's political tradition. It provided future rebels with an ideal ideological justification for their action.

Insofar as it was a highly sensitive topic, the concept of righteous rebellion was never elaborated analytically with the degree of sophistication applied to most other issues in traditional Chinese political thought. Hence, while precedent clearly dictated that a heinous monster on the throne should be replaced by a virtuous contender, it was never entirely clear what conditions justified such an act.[13] Among the few theoretical discussions on this issue, three are particularly interesting. Mengzi proposed the most sweeping justification for the overthrow of a vicious ruler. He argued that any ruler who violated the norms of "benevolence and righteousness" should be dethroned, and even executed like "an ordinary fellow."[14] This was the broadest interpretation of the right to rebel, which could allow almost any self-righteous contender to defy the dynasty's legitimacy. At the opposite extreme, Han Feizi proposed the suppression of all discussion of past rebellions, because such discussion was intrinsically subversive.[15] The third approach, more moderate and sophisticated, was put forward by Han Feizi's erstwhile teacher, Xunzi. Xunzi denied the legitimacy of rebellion as such, but averred that when the ruler is unable to ensure fundamental sociopolitical order, his authority is no longer legitimate and replacing him is justifiable.[16] As we shall see below, Xunzi's observation foreshadowed the dynamics of future rebellions: it was not the dynasty's cruelty but rather its loss of authority that turned rebellion into legitimate action.

Neither Mengzi nor Xunzi wrote "for the masses"; their views concerning legitimate rebellion were aimed at warning the rulers rather than providing future mutineers with ideological justifications. However, the concept of "righteous rebellion" eventually proliferated throughout society and became a powerful weapon in the hands of insurrectionaries. Countless rebel movements of varying ideological affiliations routinely claimed Heaven's support, and the adjective "Heavenly" or "approved by Heaven" (*tian*) became the most common element of the rebel leaders' self-appellations. Thus these leaders clearly appealed to the common denominator of Chinese political culture: the belief in the justifiability of insurrection against an unrighteous regime. It appears, in sum, that Meadows's observation was quite accurate: the right to rebel was indeed ingrained in the Chinese political tradition—and it was the only "right" through which the oppressed and the dispossessed could gain some leverage vis-à-vis the ruling elites.

The Question of Equality

One of the persistent features of popular uprisings in Chinese history is the rebels' adoption of strongly egalitarian slogans.[17] Calls such as "Level the noble and the base, equalize the rich and the poor!" were voiced repeatedly, suggesting the rebels' assault on two pillars of political order: social and economic hierarchy. These slogans had clear practical implications: by assaulting the elites and ennobling their own followers, the rebel leaders were "leveling the noble and the base"; while by violently reallocating wealth, and, infrequently, by reforming taxation and landownership patterns, they tried to "equalize the rich and the poor." These slogans and practices were of particular interest to modern Chinese and Soviet scholars engaged in the analysis of class consciousness among the so-called peasant rebels; and lively debates ensued as to whether or not this egalitarian outlook was subversive of the extant ("feudal") sociopolitical order.[18] Other observers identify these assaults on the socioeconomic hierarchy as a manifestation of the rebels' perceived "heterodoxy."[19] Countering this view, I shall try to demonstrate that, like the idea of rebellion itself, the rebels' egalitarianism was rooted in the mainstream political tradition, and this connection legitimated some of the rebels' radical slogans and practices.

The existence of egalitarian trends within the establishment ideology is ostensibly at odds with the established image of Chinese political culture. After all, it is well known that mainstream Chinese thought was highly elitist, built around the dichotomy between "superior" and "petty" men (see chapter 3), and that strict maintenance of the sociopolitical and economic hierarchy was considered essential for the society's survival (see the discussion of the Three Bonds, in chapter 4). Egalitarian trends, when observed in the writings of preimperial thinkers, are often termed "heterodoxy" and are associated with ideological rivals of Confucius, such as Mozi and Laozi.[20] But this perspective does not take into account certain ideological traits even within the so-called Confucian school that moderated the thinkers' staunch elitism. The first and most important of these was the broad belief that human beings are fundamentally equal in terms of their potential. According to this view, status distinctions reflected differences in the realization of one's potential, but they were neither inborn nor immutable. This view was put forward with great clarity by one of the staunchest supporters of social hierarchy, Xunzi:

A petty man can become the superior man, but he is indisposed to become a superior man; a superior man can become the petty man, but he is indisposed to become a petty man.[21]

Xunzi's message is clear: if he were disposed to become a superior man, the petty man could transcend his original status. There is nothing absolute in social barriers; actually, social mobility is no less important for the society's functioning than is observation of strict hierarchy. Xunzi clarifies:

> Although a man is the descendant of kings, lords, *shi*, and nobles, if he does not observe the norms of ritual and propriety, he must be relegated to the status of a commoner; although he is a descendant of a commoner, if he accumulates learning of the texts, rectifies his behavior, and is able to observe the norms of ritual and propriety—then he must be elevated to the rank of high ministers, *shi*, and nobles.[22]

I have purposely selected Xunzi's citations to illustrate the pervasiveness of preimperial thinkers' belief in the changeability of one's status. Xunzi was renowned for his exceptionally rigid insistence on the need to observe social gradations; yet even this strict elitist was unequivocally committed to the idea of social mobility, which rendered status distinctions among human beings relative and reversible rather than absolute. The idea that "neither should the officials be perpetually esteemed, nor the people forever base,"[23] reflects the fundamental consensus of the Warring States period and is mirrored in contemporaneous social praxis. In that extraordinarily dynamic age, an ambitious commoner had indeed multiple avenues of upward social mobility, most notably due to military merit or economic success. Intellectuals, alternatively, emphasized the importance of learning as the best means of climbing the social ladder; as mentioned in chapter 3, many of them took pride in their supposedly base social origins and presented themselves as entirely self-made men. It would not be an exaggeration to say that the desirability of social mobility became part of the "genetic code" of Chinese political culture from the Warring States period on.

It is with this understanding in mind that we shall now address the rebels' slogan "Level the noble and the base." With the imperial unification and subsequent stabilization of society, lowly commoners' opportunities for social advancement began disappearing. Thereafter, rebellions appear to have provided an alternative route for satisfying the ambitions of those from the bottom of society. The desire to invert the social pyramid and elevate "the base" is vividly evident already in the first known popular uprising. Chen She (d. 208 BCE), who initiated the revolt against the Qin, reportedly tried to entice his fellow soldiers to rebel by appealing to their ambitions: "We shall die but shall attain great Name. Kings, lords, generals, and chancellors—are they sown?"[24] Chen She implied that many kings and lords are self-made, and it is clear that this hope to ascend the social ladder, rather than pure hatred of Qin or (nonexistent in his case) economic slogans, was the prime mover of his uprising—and many others.

The rebels' attempt to overhaul the sociopolitical hierarchy of their day was manifested primarily in two types of action: excessive violence against officials and elite members, on the one hand, and lavish distribution of elevated positions and noble titles to their followers, on the other. At times, attempts were made to enhance social mobility institutionally: thus the Taiping leaders introduced a new type of civil service examinations, which allowed an incomparably higher proportion of candidates to succeed than was possible in the normal imperial system.[25] It is significant, however, that no rebel regime ever attempted to abolish social distinctions in general. The rebels tried to reshuffle the sociopolitical pyramid by opening new avenues for upward and downward mobility—but they did not intend to dismantle it altogether and to "level the noble and the base" literally.[26] Therefore, their goals (although not their means) remained well within the framework of traditional rules of the game. Massive elevation of have-nots was ideologically legitimate, and elite members had a moral right to collaborate with rebel leaders, even if those leaders came from the very bottom of society. Such cooperation might have been unthinkable in more rigidly pedigree-based societies; yet in China, with the pervasive belief that "the people would not remain base forever," it was entirely acceptable.

Turning to the second aspect of egalitarian thought, demands for economic equality, we stand on shakier ground with regard to its acceptability to the elite. Clearly, mainstream Chinese thought favored a strict economic hierarchy, which ideally should match the sociopolitical one. The very ritual system that regulated the life of the elites during much of the preimperial period, and became the cornerstone of Confucian thought, was based on gradations of sumptuary privileges. Everybody's consumption in life and death had to reflect his social rank; equality was unacceptable. Yet, this said, strong indignation was voiced against excessive inequality as well. In texts of the Warring States period we find a few surprising statements in favor of equal distribution of wealth—at least insofar as concerns distribution of wealth within the lower strata. These statements are scattered even through mainstream texts, such as the *Analects* of Confucius and the *Mengzi*;[27] they are asserted more strongly in the writings of such thinkers as Mozi, who spoke of an ideal state of affairs in which the people would "work for each other" and share surplus commodities.[28] The egalitarian vision is most vivid in a short passage incorporated into a Confucian canonical compendium, *Records of Rites* (*Liji*):

When the Great Way was implemented, All-under-Heaven belonged to all. The people selected the worthy and the able; their words were trustworthy, and they cultivated amicability. Thus men were not attached to their parents only, nor did they treat as children only their own sons. The old were provided for until their natural death; the able-bodied were employed, the young were provided for growing up. They pitied widows, orphans, childless, disabled and sick, nourishing each of them. Males had their allotment; females had their homes. They detested throwing away extra commodities, but nor did they hoard these for themselves alone; they detested not utilizing their labor, but nor did they work for themselves alone. Hence scheming was blocked and did not rise; robbers, bandits, and rebellious criminals did not act. Hence the outer doors remained open and were not shut. This is called the Great Uniformity (*Da tong*).[29]

This short passage became the major source of inspiration for a variety of utopian-minded thinkers both from within the establishment and from the rebel ranks; the concept of *Da tong* was associated with such diverse personalities as the Khitan emperor Yelü Deguang (r. 928–947), the Taiping rebels, the major late imperial reformer Kang Youwei (1858–1927), and the twentieth-century revolutionaries, including Sun Yatsen (1866–1925) and Mao Zedong (1893–1976).[30] The very fact that this section survived in the Confucian canon indicates much broader tolerance of egalitarian ideals by establishment thinkers than we would intuitively assume.

Ideas of economic equality never became mainstream establishment ideology, but they had a deep and persistent impact on both the leaders and the led. As mentioned in chapters 2 and 4, as early as the Han dynasty (and most notably during Wang Mang's interregnum) attempts were made to limit inequality by capping the size of large landholdings; later, the desire for economic fairness underlay the introduction of the "equal field" system in the late fifth century. Opposition to excessive inequality permeates the political thought of many establishment literati, who repeatedly expressed their indignation over the economic polarization in which "the rich amass fields in thousands while the poor have not enough land to stick the point of an awl." Wang Anshi's hatred of "engrossers," mentioned in chapter 4, reflects a similar sentiment. This clear dissatisfaction among the proprietary classes with excessive gaps between the rich and the poor explains why the radical egalitarianism of certain rebel groups was not considered outright heretical and did not preclude cooperation of elite members with the rebels. Radical as they were, slogans in favor of equalization of wealth remained within the framework of legitimate political discourse.

The partial overlap between rebel and the establishment ideologies discussed in this and the previous section had a complex impact on the rebels' cause. First, it provided a degree of ideological justification for the rebels, which served their cause well and facilitated massive mobilization to their ranks. Second, it rendered rebellion less "revolutionary," to borrow Meadows's distinction—that is, radical as they were, the rebels' slogans did not put them outside the pale of acceptable rules of the political game. This brings us to the third observation: the semilegitimacy of the rebellion was also an essential precondition for its eventual co-optation into the existing sociopolitical order. In what follows, by analyzing the trajectories of some of the rebellions, we shall see how these ideological factors influenced actual political processes.

AGENTS OF DISORDER

A reader of Chinese historical and literary sources cannot but be overawed by the almost apocalyptic dimensions of mass rebellions. The reasons for their exceptional destructiveness will be addressed later; here I want to focus only on the exorbitant cost of rebellions for their instigators and leaders. While a few of the rebel leaders succeeded either in establishing a dynasty or at least in attaining a prestigious position in exchange for timely surrender, countless more were exterminated: the lucky ones perished in battle; the less fortunate ones were seized, tortured, and executed with unspeakable cruelty, often together with their kin, followers, and even neighbors. What, then, prompted charismatic men and women to defy the government against all odds? Who were the "agents of disorder" who repeatedly triggered unrest under any major dynasty? In analyzing the social and ideological background of the would-be rebels, we shall move one step further away from the simplistic "government-rebels" dichotomy.

Two groups can readily be identified as perennial "agents of disorder." The most obvious was the so-called bandits. "Banditry" is a pejorative term that was liberally used in imperial historiography to denote a great variety of the dynasty's enemies, from alien tribesmen and rebels to ordinary brigands. In practice, however, it was not at all easy to draw a clear dividing line between the bandits and respected members of local society. Only some of the bandits were professional outlaws, usually members of purely criminal gangs numbering from a dozen to a few hundred men and women who engaged in extortion, smuggling, robbery, and similar illegal activities. Many others were only part-time bandits: peasants who engaged in robbery during the slack agricultural season and then returned to peaceful life; members of officially sanctioned militias or lineage self-defense groups, who expanded their activities from purely defensive to predatory, intimidating neighboring villages; and even constables and professional soldiers who turned to banditry as an additional source of income. To further complicate matters, professional bandits could be employed by magistrates as auxiliary military forces whenever a greater danger (from rebels, foreign invaders, or particularly powerful gangs) was imminent. Thus it was not always easy to distinguish outlaws from those who were supposed to suppress them.[31]

Banditry was not only a social but also a cultural phenomenon; some of the brigands observed Robin Hood–like codes of chivalry and enjoyed prestige and close ties with local populations. The bandits' popularity was particularly disruptive from the establishment's point of view, because it legitimated an alternative sociopolitical "career ladder" to that maintained by the imperial authorities. Economically and socially, gangs attracted landless peasants and other people at the margins of the rural economy; and their military expertise turned them into latent challengers of the extant order. While as a rule "bandits" refrained from openly rebellious activities, under an ambitious leader they could turn from brigandage to politically motivated antigovernment actions. A large and well-organized gang always had the potential to become politically threatening and not just socially and economically disruptive, and if the authorities procrastinated in dealing with this potential threat, they could pay a high price for their laxity.

The second major threat to order came from religious organizations, variously labeled as "heterodox sects," "popular religious movements," "millenarian rebels," and the like. Elite writings routinely depict the sectarians in highly negative terms, and it was once fashionable to uncritically accept this propaganda and view the sects as intrinsically politically subversive, and as socially and morally disruptive. Now this view has been superseded by a more balanced approach, which holds that the sectarian label was applied—at times unjustifiably—to a great variety of groups, which were in most cases loosely organized, protean in nature, and quite often indistinguishable from lay associations that existed on the sidelines of such approved religions as Buddhism and Daoism. In terms of their social composition, the sects were heterogeneous as well, at times attracting considerable elite membership; their ideology—as judged from their "precious scriptures"—was not fundamentally defiant of the state and of prevalent social norms; and they were often engaged in a variety of philanthropic activities quite similar to those initiated by local elites. All this suggests the fallacy of a simplistic "orthodox-heterodox" dichotomy with regard to most of the sects. Nonetheless, the latent challenge represented by some of the sects to the dynastic peace was real, and it was intrinsically linked to certain social and ideological peculiarities of the sects.[32]

Several factors distinguish rebellious sects from other religious or lay congregations that coexisted peacefully with the establishment; of these the sectarians' millenarian inclinations seem singularly important. Eschatological beliefs were proliferating in religious Daoism by the end of the Han dynasty, and were later reinforced by Buddhist and, possibly, Manichean beliefs. From its inception in China, the millenarian tradition was strongly associated with potential rebelliousness. The expected cosmic cataclysm, sectarians believed, would be accompanied by the violent collapse of the extant political order: and this very tenet was conducive to antidynastic activities. Most significantly, these beliefs were intrinsically linked with expectations of the coming of a redeemer, who was variously identified as Maitreya, the Buddha of the Future, or the Daoist Messiah, Li Hong, or another divine personality. The redeemer would allow the adepts to survive the coming apocalypse and, as the chosen "seed people" (*zhong min*), to establish the future "New Jerusalem."[33] Thus the redeemer was perceived as a future ruler—an identification that put his supporters on a course of inevitable collision with the authorities.

Millenarian beliefs were not inevitably conducive to immediate rebellion, insofar as the expectation of the end of the *kalpa* (i.e., the end of this world) could be directed into the remote future. However, in periods of crisis, a charismatic sectarian leader could argue that the end was imminent and that the pious should prepare themselves for the coming clash. These calls would invigorate his followers and direct them into immediate action against the dynasty. The energetic leader would then turn a sect into a much more coherent community, distinguished by community-oriented social ethics and moral codes, and engaged in active proselytizing. The resultant expansion and strengthening of the congregation would enhance the likelihood that the authorities would spot its activities and persecute it. The fear of persecution would in turn hasten the sectarians' action against the dynasty.[34]

The potential of millenarian sects to become politically subversive was well known to the imperial authorities and made them strongly intolerant of any kind of sectarian activities. The precise content of the sectarians' ideology and their allegedly "immoral" behavior (e.g., licensing a much stronger public role for women than was acceptable in the Confucianized society) mattered little: at times the sectarian label could be attached to what appear to have been ideologically "orthodox" groups.[35] Far more important factors impelling persecution were the sect's proselytizing activism and, most notably, its size. A vigilant official would notice an increase in the number of sectarians, and would act promptly and mercilessly. This inevitability of persecution created, in turn, an impetus for rebellion. The sectarian leaders, fearing execution as "heterodox bandits," would opt to act rebelliously as a kind of preventive action. Thus the reciprocal fear polarizing the sectarians and the establishment was the prime mover of inevitable conflict, pushing many sect leaders to the extreme. To a certain extent, the officials' fear of sectarian uprising became a self-fulfilling prophecy.

Bandits and sectarians were the two most immediate threats to dynastic peace; but there was yet another "agent of disorder." The third potentially threatening group came from the ranks of those who were supposed to protect the dynasty rather than assault it. These were members of subelites, or minor elites, such as holders of lower examination degrees, clerks, petty military officers, merchants, monks, and the like—all of whom normally were connected to the political establishment, benefited from these connections, and had a stake in the present order. While some of these men might be engaged in illicit activities (including banditry and sectarianism), they usually did not cross the line from criminal or disruptive behavior to political revolt. However, having decided—or having been forced—to cross this line, the elite or subelite rebels became the dynasty's most formidable enemy.

There were many reasons that pushed elite members from the camp of the dynasty's protectors to that of its foes. Some were fueled by personal ambitions; some were wronged or implicated in criminal cases that left them no room for accommodation within the existing political framework; others were driven to rebellion by adverse political circumstances, as when, during times of political turmoil, imprudent local officials mistook their self-defense forces for rebels in disguise and decided to persecute the alleged ringleaders. Having joined the ranks of the rebels, these elite and subelite men could critically endanger the dynasty, because they were better positioned than ordinary brigands or sectarians to apprehend and take advantage of the government's vulnerability. Moreover, the very fact that a significant segment of those who were supposed to protect the dynasty began joining the rebels' camp was in itself the clearest indication of the dynasty's aggravating weakness. Hence elite members became the most dangerous agent of disorder. However, as we shall see later, these very men who contributed decisively to the old dynasty's collapse were also instrumental in restoring political order in the rebellion's aftermath.

The existence of "agents of disorder"—individuals and groups who were under certain circumstances willing to defy the ruling dynasty—was the single most important precondition for the outburst of rebellion. However, as we have seen, most of these "agents of disorder" were normally not prone to rebel, unless pushed to that decision by the government's action. Indeed, the complaint that "officials force the people to rebel" was frequently voiced by the rebels themselves and by not a few historians.[36] It is time now to explore how the rebellions started, and how their dynamic was related to the (mal)functioning of the imperial state.

To Rebel Is Justified

In the year 209 BCE, shortly after the death of the First Emperor of Qin, a group of conscripts headed to their garrison. They failed to arrive on time owing to heavy rains that made the roads impassable, and faced execution for the delay. One of the squad leaders, Chen She, turned to his fellows: "As things stand, we face death whether we stay or run away, while if we start a revolt we would likewise face death. Since we must die in any case, would it not be better to die fighting for [establishing a new] dynasty?"[37] Shortly thereafter, Chen started the rebellion that ended Qin rule.

This story, immortalized in Sima Qian's *Historical Records (Shiji)*— the single best-known historical text in traditional China—offered important lessons for the imperial literati. For most of them the message was clear: a harsh and oppressive regime (and Qin was identified as such) will face popular indignation and ultimately will be ousted. This view may strike a chord in the hearts of many modern readers, hateful of tyrannies; and it can be supported by stories of other "evil rulers," such as Sui Emperor Yang (r. 605–617), who similarly brought about their own demise through their excessive cruelty.[38] Yet even if "politically correct," this conclusion proves somewhat premature when we seek to identify a broader pattern of popular uprisings in Chinese history. Politics played an important role in facilitating or preventing uprisings—but the connection between the regime's harshness and the occurrence of uprisings is much less self-evident than the Chen She anecdote suggests.

Of the many factors that facilitated uprisings, the economic one appears to be singularly important. Insofar as the majority of China's peasants lived only slightly above subsistence level, any major natural or manmade disaster could threaten their survival. A sustained crisis would push many peasant households into perennial indebtedness and eventual loss of their land, causing them to join the army of landless vagabonds, tinder to fuel any future unrest. These desperate men and women were the first to join gangs, urban or rural rioters, and also the rebels' armies. This economic background to most unrest and many rebellions was clear to the majority of dynastic leaders, who invested considerable effort in preventing the degradation of the peasant economy and in minimizing the phenomenon of propertyless peasants.[39]

Unfortunately for China's rulers, there was no long-term remedy to counter the gradual swelling of the ranks of landless peasants. Most fundamentally, population increases during periods of relative peace and orderly rule would decrease the land/man ratio below the subsistence level. Other factors, such as ecological deterioration due to the growing population's overexploitation of soil and water, landgrabs by local elites, and increasing tax burdens, would also accelerate the transformation of landowning peasants into agricultural laborers, or, worse, into vagabonds and bandits.[40] The pace and scope of these processes differed considerably from one dynasty to another, but their persistence from Han to Qing is undeniable, and so is their negative impact on the dynasties' survivability.

The economic degradation of peasant households was singularly important in fueling the unrest, but it did not necessarily bring about the immediate outbreak of massive uprisings. Even under tough conditions, the imperial regime could act prudently and preserve relative stability. Insofar as the government was able to respond adequately to economic crises (e.g., through a variety of assistance measures to the most hard-hit areas); insofar as its bureaucracy and military forces maintained adequate vigilance against potential disturbances; insofar as it commanded the allegiance of the absolute majority of local elites—it could prevent major rebellions. Under these conditions, economic hardships would spur local disturbances, such as food riots, rent and tax resistance, or sporadic attacks against local officials, clerks, wealthy merchants, and local bullies, but not a rebellion.[41] Elizabeth Perry notes that most protesters in traditional (and modern) China preferred to "play by the rules,"[42] limiting the scope of their protests and steering clear of large-scale uprising. This allowed the court, in turn, to keep the situation under control through a combination of suppression and conciliatory moves, including punishment of guilty officials and reform of abusive practices, when appropriate. Insofar as these "rules of the game" were maintained, the crisis—even under the most adverse economic conditions—remained politically manageable.

The major factor underlying the protesters' willingness to "play by the rules" was the dynasty's awesomeness. For most political actors—from vagabonds to disgruntled literati—it was clear that a direct challenge to the emperor would be suicidal. The dynasty possessed—at least nominally—almost limitless military and administrative resources to deal with those who threatened its existence. Although regular military forces were only thinly spread throughout the country's interior, a magistrate could still count on a local garrison, on police forces, and on the militia run by the local elite to deal with any calamity. In case of emergency, he could mobilize an ad hoc militia, ask for support from neighboring magistrates, or, in the worst case, request the intervention of regular troops from elsewhere. The combined power of these forces normally sufficed to deter potential rebels. So long as the dynasty's awesomeness was not shattered by domestic or foreign debacles, it could expect that protests and collective violence would remain a localized phenomenon.

This said, in certain conditions the would-be rebels had a chance. The imperial bureaucracy was often sluggish and inefficient; local military forces, uncoordinated, understaffed, and underpaid, lacked martial spirit; and the future rebels or their sympathizers could penetrate the lower levels of the administrative and military machine, gaining precious intelligence, and launching surprise attacks on government strongholds. Most importantly, the would-be rebels knew that a few successes would turn them into an attractive alternative for the latent opposition, the myriads of have-nots, who would then join their ranks and give them a decisive numerical advantage over the government forces. More often than not the rebellion started more or less accidentally, when one of the "agents of disorder" was pushed into a corner and challenged the local authorities; but if this challenge proved successful, then the rebellion would spread dramatically.[43]

Significantly, from the known trajectories of most rebellions—including those meticulously studied by Susan Naquin—it is clear that the government's oppressiveness was of little significance as a cause of rebellion. Belying traditional complaints that officials "forced the people to rebel," the government's major problem was not its excessive use of force but rather its meekness and ineptitude. To be sure, Zhu Yuanzhang and the early Qing emperors were immeasurably harsher and crueler than their successors; but it was only under those latter weaklings on the throne that huge rebellions shattered the Ming and Qing dynasties. Weakness, not brutality, was the most unforgivable mistake of the dynastic leaders. Should the dynasty fail to suppress a criminal gang, should it allow sectarians to score a few victories, should it let rioters escape punishment— all these laxities would be interpreted as ominous signs of its decay and would change the balance of power. In that case even the government's victories, unless decisive, would matter little; yet should the bandits, rioters, or sectarians inflict a major defeat on the government forces, the road to mass rebellion would be open. It was usually after such initial successes that a group of ordinary outlaws would proclaim their political aspirations to replace the dynasty. This would mark a new stage in the rebellion: the moment it outgrew the scope of a localized disturbance and turned into a dynasty-threatening calamity.

One of the most remarkable features of many rebellions is the amazing speed with which they spread after an initial success. Time and again we read of "dozens of thousands" and even "hundreds of thousands" of rebels flocking to a new leader, "gathering like clouds," "responding to him like an echo," and "following him like a shadow." Why, then, did these insurrections spread like wildfire? Again, the immediate answer would be economic factors. For the masses of desperate men and women who had lost all their property and faced starvation, joining the rebellion brought amazing opportunities to benefit—even if for a short while—from the dolce vita of the proprietary classes. Looting of granaries, pawnshops, and the houses of rich landlords was the rebels' modus operandi, and it surely attracted the dispossessed multitudes. Second, in the case of millenarian rebellions, some might have been attracted by the sects' promises of salvation. Finally, not a few rank and file were simply coerced to join the rebels.[44]

Yet, economic and religious factors aside, I believe that political factors were of primary importance in igniting rebellion. It was no coincidence that a rebellion spread only after an initial failure on the part of government forces. The rebels' victories, especially successful occupation of prefectural seats, or, better, of provincial capitals, signaled to many wavering fence-sitters that the dynasty was approaching its end. The moment the government's awesomeness expired, it could no longer deter its foes or command the allegiance of its erstwhile supporters. The most desperate have-nots would be the first to swell the rebels' ranks; but they would be followed by many others, for whom the collapse of the old order meant not just redistribution of material wealth, but also redistribution of power and prestige. Long before "The Internationale" was introduced to China, countless men would eagerly adopt its promise—"We have been nought, we shall be all!" The moment the dynasty appeared doomed, it was prudent to join the ranks of its foes. Not for ideological but for purely personal reasons many of those who joined the rebellion would say, anticipating the slogan of the Great Proletarian Cultural Revolution (1966–1976), "To rebel is justified!"

GOING TO THE EXTREME

The transformation of riots, brigandage, and minor forms of resistance into full-scale uprisings was accompanied by woeful disintegration of the sociopolitical order. One of the immediate indicators of and causes for this disintegration was the comprehensive militarization of the society. Unable to contain the rebellion, the government had to rely on a broad variety of ad hoc paramilitary forces, from the elite-run militias to criminal gangs and alien tribesmen who were enlisted as the dynasty's protectors; and these largely unreliable and unruly forces wreaked havoc in local society. Worse, even the government's regular forces could become undependable in the wake of prolonged military crisis, with generals more interested in promotions and riches than in crushing the rebellion. Similar disintegration was endemic in the rebel camp as well. A common pattern was an increasing degree of autonomy on the part of regional rebel leaders, some of whom vied for recognition from their nominal superiors as new regional potentates, while others sought complete independence as the first step toward becoming full contenders for the rule in All-under-Heaven. Thus a rebellion triggered a war of all against all, in which competing armies, gangs, self-defense forces, and various militias could depopulate whole provinces. It is not surprising, therefore, that in the aftermath of rebellion, population registers would decrease by millions and even by tens of millions of subjects.

One of the most prominent features of rebellions was their extremely violent nature. To be sure, violence was endemic during any period of war and dynastic replacement, but it is difficult to avoid the impression that during popular uprisings it was exceptionally ferocious. Entering a life-or-death contest with the government, the rebels pitied neither their foes nor their own kin. This was particularly true of millenarian insurrections. For instance, the allegedly Daoism-inspired rebels led by Sun En (399–402) routinely eliminated those who refused to join their camp, including children and infants; and their ruthlessness extended even to their own progeny. The story is told that when the rebels were on move and unable to take their children with them, they would toss them into the water, saying: "We congratulate you on the first ascending to the Hall of Immortals! We shall follow you shortly."[45] Similar fanaticism characterized many other sectarian uprisings, culminating with the apocalyptic carnage wrought by the Christianity-inspired Taipings.

It is tempting to attribute exceptional brutality to "religious fanatics," but this would be a gross oversimplification. Those rebellions in which the religious factor was less important present us with similarly hair-raising stories of massacres. Let us look briefly at Huang Chao's revolt (874–884), which delivered a nearly mortal blow to the illustrious Tang dynasty. Dynastic histories and a series of independent accounts uniformly attribute to Huang Chao, the self-styled "General [who brings] Equality," an almost pathological hatred of the Tang regime and a desire to "clean out" its supporters. After occupying the Tang capital, Chang'an, in early 881, his army embarked on a systematic campaign of terror against local elite families, seizing their possessions, violating their daughters, expropriating their mansions, decapitating officials, and butchering all the members of the imperial lineage. When the rebel armies recaptured Chang'an for the second time, Huang reportedly ordered the killing of eighty thousand inhabitants to "wash the city" with their blood. These events are interpreted by some Chinese scholars as examples of "class struggle," which may be the case;[46] but Huang Chao's victims were not exclusively the wealthy and the powerful. The laconic dynastic history narrates:

At this time, the people [near] the imperial capital barricaded the valleys to protect themselves. [Since farmers] were thus unable to cultivate the lands, the price for a peck of rice rose to thirty thousand cash. . . . There were those who seized the barricaded people and sold them to the bandits [i.e., Huang's army], who used them as food. Each of such people brought several hundred thousand cash.

Elsewhere the story continues:

. . . The people were for the most part starving and on the verge of dying by the city walls and ditches. When the bandits captured them, they used them as food. Daily, several thousands of them were thus arranged together, while a hundred great pestles ground their skin and bones in the mortars. [The bandits] would eat them completely.[47]

It is possible, of course, that some of these gruesome scenes were invented by the literati historians who hated Huang Chao, but it is difficult to reject them all as pure invention. The pattern of extreme violence in accounts of the rebellions is too persistent to be merely propagandistic; and while exaggerations are inevitable, the evidence of the rebels' exceptional brutality is simply overwhelming. The elites were the rebels' primary victims: officials, members of the imperial clan, eunuchs, ordinary literati, wealthy merchants, rich landowners—all were targeted both for their political identification with the ruling dynasty and for their wealth. However, as in Huang Chao's case, many commoners were annihilated as well, particularly in the cities whose populations refused to surrender to the rebels.[48] What accounts for this apparent addiction to violence?

The ferocity of the rebellions had multiple sources. On the most immediate level, it reflected a common pattern of brutality in Chinese wars, in which extermination of the noncombatant population was permissible, although by no means laudable. It was mirrored by the violence of government forces, which repeatedly massacred actual or imagined rebel supporters, and executed ringleaders in particularly cruel ways, such as by slow slicing. It was furthermore instrumental in cementing the unity of the rebels and preventing new recruits from absconding: once they had committed murders, they could no longer reasonably expect the government's pardon.[49] Yet beyond these immediate explanations, I believe that the rebels' violence is directly related to what may be described as the culture of rebellion. In saying this, I do not intend to address anew such issues as the cultural aspects of violence, or the relations between martial (*wu*) and civilian (*wen*) values in Chinese culture,[50] but rather to focus on a specific "rebel culture" in which violence was essential for the rebellion's legitimacy. This issue was analyzed and aptly presented by the most sophisticated rebel in China's history, Mao Zedong. In his 1927

Report on an Investigation of the Peasant Movement in Hunan, having approvingly depicted the peasants' brutal treatment of their foes, Mao concluded:

> Without using the greatest force, the peasants cannot possibly over-throw the deep-rooted authority of the landlords which has lasted for thousands of years. The rural areas need a mighty revolutionary up-surge, for it alone can rouse the people in their millions to become a powerful force. All the actions mentioned here which have been la-beled as "going too far" flow from the power of the peasants. . . . It was highly necessary for such things to be done. . . . It was necessary to overthrow the whole authority of the gentry, to strike them to the ground and keep them there. . . . To put it bluntly, it is necessary to create terror for a while in every rural area, or otherwise it would be impossible to . . . overthrow the authority of the gentry. Proper limits have to be exceeded in order to right a wrong, or else the wrong can-not be righted.[51]

Mao's *Report,* arguably one of his greatest literary masterpieces, was written amid complex political polemics within the revolutionary camp, and it does not pretend to be a scholarly analysis of the history of "peas-ant rebellions."[52] Nonetheless, I think Mao grasped well an essential rea-son for the rebels' ferocity: the association of extreme violence with "righting the wrongs." One can easily identify a powerful undercurrent in Chinese culture of stories that exalt and laud those who fought resolutely for the sake of justice or to avenge themselves and their friends. These intrepid fighters, such as assassin-retainers or "knights-errant," never hesitated to draw a sword or a dagger to settle accounts with the power-ful and the wealthy, and for centuries they remained extraordinarily pop-ular figures for members of all social strata.[53] The popularity of these personages testifies to the existence of a strong antihierarchical current within Chinese culture, and to the tradition of associating extreme vio-lence and defiance of established sociopolitical order with the utmost righteousness. This worldview is most powerfully depicted in a great lit-erary masterpiece, *Water Margin* (fifteenth–sixteenth centuries), a novel dedicated to a group of rebels who defied the Song dynasty and strove "to implement the Way in Heaven's stead" (*ti Tian xing Dao*).

Water Margin is a complex work, which developed over a few centu-ries, and which may have incorporated popular narratives about the rebel heroes, while modifying these in accordance with the complex philosophical and ideological agenda of the literati who served as its authors and redactors. It is by no means blindly laudatory of rebellions and insurrections—in fact, the novel reveals their ultimate vanity.[54] Nor do the authors necessarily condone their protagonists' excessive resort to violence: at times they seem disgusted with the bloodthirstiness of such men as Li Kui, whose proclivity to kill indiscriminately is only partly whitewashed by his identification as the reincarnation of the "Murderous Star." However, the novel clearly sympathizes with the rebels, whose righteousness is contrasted with the corruption and machinations of the imperial court; and it largely countenances violent means of righting wrongs. Even Li Kui, whose darker traits are fully exposed in the narrative, is also clearly admired for his righteousness, his straightforwardness, his strongly pronounced antihierarchical mind-set, and, most noteworthy, his rebellious spirit. The reader's sympathies are clearly with his call to "slaughter our way into the Eastern Capital and seize the friggin throne,"[55] and his readiness to rebel even at the very last moment of his life. In the final analysis, it appears that his atrocious behavior attains a certain degree of legitimacy.

If my analysis is correct, the rebels' brutality was in part quite deliberate and strategic, aimed at showing how much they had been wronged in the past, and how legitimate their case was. Moreover, their violence served the rebellion in yet another, subtler way. By perpetrating mass destruction of life and property, the rebels signaled that the dynasty was no longer able to preserve the essential sociopolitical order, which, in Xunzi's eyes (and not only in his) was the crucial watershed between a legitimate and an illegitimate rule. Exacerbating bloodshed and turmoil (*luan*) indicated therefore that the ruling house had lost Heaven's Mandate and should be replaced. Yet to become an appealing alternative, the leader (of the rebels or of one of their foes) had eventually to demonstrate his ability to restore order and put an end to the extremity of violence. Thus, amid chaos, the new regime had to come into being and begin the process of regenerating imperial rule.

Regeneration of Order

The destructiveness of rebellions appears at first glance to challenge the very foundations of the sociopolitical order. How, then, can it correlate with Meadows's assumption, cited at the beginning of this chapter, according to which rebellion was "a chief element of a national stability"? How could rebels of Li Kui's type contribute anything to stability and order? What—if any—were the constructive aspects of rebellion?

To answer these questions we shall return to a consideration of the dynamics of rebellion. Once launched, a rebellion became indeed an extremely devastating force, but from its earliest stages the leadership was clearly prone to restore political stability rather than destroy it once and for all. Most importantly, this restoration was invariably envisioned in terms of the creation of a new imperial dynasty, rather than an alternative political arrangement. The acceptance of the imperial order was clear on the symbolic level: from the very inception of a rebellion, its leaders proclaimed themselves generals, marshals, dukes, and princes, reaffirming thereby that they sought a place within the imperial sociopolitical pyramid rather than outside. This swift and willing adoption of symbolic aspects of the imperial order is indicative of the rebels' fundamental belonging to the imperial political culture—the belonging that was evident even during the most destructive and violent stages of an insurrection.[56]

Successful rebellions advanced to the next stage, when a stable territorial base was secured, and it became possible to begin creating a new order. During this stage, steps were taken to develop an administrative apparatus; to reimpose taxation, levies, population registers, and the like; and, in the late imperial period, even to hold examinations. While each of these steps was usually accompanied by certain modifications of the extant institutions (e.g., the Taiping leaders, as mentioned above, simplified the examinations and expanded the number of successful candidates), the essentials of the imperial system were preserved. It was at this stage that the rebel leaders would downgrade or abandon altogether their egalitarian slogans and promises, and try to entice elite members—including erstwhile officials of the reigning dynasty—to their camp. The stabilization was also accompanied by a reduction in plunder and violence and the adoption of more constructive measures in the conquered areas. If uninterrupted, this process would be crowned with the establishment of a new imperial dynasty.

The evolution of the rebellion from "going to the extreme" back to the normalcy of the imperial order was an uneven process. Not every rebel movement was able—or willing—to transcend the stage of violence and disorder and begin establishing a stable base. Huang Chao, for instance, took significant steps toward creating a new imperial order only after the occupation of the Tang capital, but he failed then to either discipline his supporters or attract a sufficient number of followers from among the Tang officials, which crucially weakened his regime. The late Ming rebel Zhang Xianzhong (1606–1646), who established a short-lived Great Xi dynasty in Sichuan (1644–1646), proved to be even more inept in transforming himself from a "roving bandit" into a state builder; thus, in one of the most notorious massacres under his rule, he called upon the Sichuan literati to participate in the imperial examinations under his aegis, only to butcher them all.[57] But there were other examples, such as Zhu Yuanzhang (and some of his rivals from among the anti-Mongol rebels), who were generally successful in establishing a solid territorial base with a well-run quasi-imperial administration. A more complex pattern is presented by the Taiping rebels, who found it expedient to compromise some of their egalitarian ideals in order to smoothly administer their "Heavenly State of Great Evenness/Peace" but also tried to maintain their ideal system at least within their Heavenly Capital at Nanjing.[58] These differences notwithstanding, it may be confidently asserted that the common trajectory of most, if not all, rebellions was a shift from war and destruction toward the construction of a renovated imperial order.

What prompted the rebels to move from destructiveness to imperial normalcy? Why did none of them—either sectarians or outlaws—try to establish an alternative political order to supplant that against which they supposedly rebelled? The ultimate answer to this question is found in the realm of political culture: namely, the hegemonic position of the imperial political and ideological system. The rebels simply had no alternative to the extant imperial order. They could try to modify it, to reduce exploitation and corruption, to limit abuses of power—but never did they attempt to replace this order with anything "revolutionarily" new. The system in which the absolute and universal monarch sits on the throne, is surrounded by meritorious officials, cares for the people, and relies, at least to a certain extent, on local elites to collect taxes and preserve local stability: this was the default choice of the rebels, just as it was the default choice of alien conquerors of China. Each newcomer to the political game was willing to improve this system and eliminate major malpractices; but none presented any real alternative.

Another major factor that contributed to the swift incorporation of the rebels into the imperial order was the cooperation of elite members with rebel leaders. The early rebel Chen She, "a servant of peasants, an exile among exiles,"[59] succeeded in enlisting in his service several eminent members of the educated elite, including Confucius's descendant Kong Jia (d. 208 BCE) and the court erudite of the Qin dynasty Shusun Tong (fl. 210–190 BCE). This pattern continued throughout imperial history. Some elite members, especially from the lower elite, joined the rebellion from the very beginning; many others followed as the rebellion progressed. Some were coerced to join, while others did so willingly; some rose prominently in the rebels' ranks, while others failed to establish a sustainable mode of cooperation with uncouth bandits; but the trend is uniform: it is remarkable how many literati can be found within the rebel ranks—even around the notoriously murderous Zhang Xianzhong![60] Once again, we can speak of a common pattern of rebellion: the incorporation of the literati into the rebel leadership was the rule no less than the rebels' shift from military struggle to political construction.

This distinctive willingness of elite members to cross class lines, join the ranks of the rebels, and assist even the most disreputable of rebel leaders in establishing the new dynasty is not incidental. It may be understood in the context of the people-oriented discourse discussed above. The ideas that the "people's will" is the ultimate source of the regime's legitimacy, that rebellion against a vicious tyrant or a notoriously inept ruler is justifiable, and that egalitarian slogans do not undermine the rebels' legitimacy—all these served as a bridge between the literati and the rebellious commoners and softened "class antagonism." Also crucial in justifying a shift of allegiances on the part of the literati was the understanding that if a rebellion occurred, it was ipso facto proof of the dynasty's failure, which, in turn, severed the elite's obligations to the ruling family. Although the idea of fidelity to the ruling dynasty was powerful enough to prevent massive defection of high-ranking officials, it was much less effective in preventing cooperation between unemployed or retired intellectuals and the rebels.

The participation of the elite in rebellions provided the rebels with legitimacy and with much-needed manpower for restoring political order. Yet, speaking in class terms, it also "entrapped" the rebels. By joining the rebels' camp, the elite advisers facilitated swift co-optation of the rebels into the imperial political structure. Since, as argued above, the rebels did not intend to destroy the imperial order but just wanted to improve their position within it, this potential for co-optation was shrewdly utilized by the elite advisers, who served as a bridge between the uncouth rebel leaders and the rules of the imperial polity. Through their participation, the literati might substantially help to ensure that a rebellion indeed served, in Meadows's words, "to clear and invigorate a political atmosphere" rather than to destroy the imperial political system.

Epilogue: Rebellions and the Empire's Longevity

From the 1950s to the early 1980s scholars in the People's Republic of China were engaged in lively debates over the long-term role of "peasants' rebellions" in Chinese history. Although greatly influenced by the need to validate Mao Zedong's assertion that the "the peasant uprisings and peasant wars alone formed the real motive force of development in China's feudal society,"[61] the debates yielded many insightful observations with regard to the uprisings' nature, their short- and long-term social and economic impact, and their place within the general trajectory of imperial history. Thus, while few of us today would pose the question in terms of the uprisings' impact on the alleged "transformation from slave-ownership to feudalism" and "from feudalism to capitalism" in China's past, we may still echo many eminent Chinese historians and ask: Were the epic struggles of China's great rebel leaders entirely fruitless? Did lower strata benefit in any way from their sacrifice during the uprisings? Might the constructive (or perhaps reconstructive) elements of the uprisings have compensated for the huge havoc they wreaked in the political and social fabric?[62]

One cannot expect a simple answer to questions that try to make sense of hundreds of small-scale and dozens of large-scale insurrections and civil wars that spanned more than two millennia. Major uprisings had widely different outcomes. Some, like that of the "Way of Great Evenness/Peace" (Taiping Dao, the so-called Yellow Turbans, 184 CE), or that of the nineteenth-century Taipings, were crushed, leaving behind a greatly weakened imperial state and local elites who were more powerful than ever. Others, like those by Zhu Yuanzhang or his predecessor, Liu Bang (d. 195 BCE), succeeded in establishing a viable imperial regime, which, at least initially, was strongly inclined to protect the peasant economy and minimize the burden on peasant households. Exemplifying another pattern were the late Ming rebellions: these were crushed but paved the way for the reconfiguration of power under the new dynasty (the Qing), which became more powerful vis-à-vis the local elites than the Ming dynasty and was able to reinvigorate the economy. Clearly, such divergent outcomes preclude our summarizing the short-term impact of rebellions as serving either to strengthen or to weaken the imperial regime.

Turning from these immediate issues to broader patterns, I believe the rebellions made three positive contributions to the imperial order and, at least to some extent, to the peasants' lot. First, the ruling elite's very awareness of the possibility that "the people could capsize the boat" was a major impetus for much greater concern for the lower strata's needs than would otherwise be expected in a strictly hierarchical and paternalistic regime. While in the aftermath of the imperial unification the peasants' military importance diminished and fears of their absconding to neighboring countries decreased, their role as potential rebels encouraged the perpetuation of the "people-oriented" discourse and the adoption of a variety of people-oriented policies. The persistent concern of power-holders with agricultural production, their efforts to disseminate improved techniques, and to promote land reclamation and hydraulic projects—all these can be interpreted as preventive measures against renewed rebellions. This concern is vividly apparent under any important dynasty, most notably under those established in the aftermath of huge uprisings (e.g., the Han, Tang, Ming, and Qing); and it may doubtless be considered the peasants' major gain from recurrent resurrections.

Second, despite their highly divergent outcomes, major rebellions can be viewed as the single most important factor underlying dynastic changes in Chinese history. The outbreak of a rebellion signaled that the dynasty's malfunction had reached the dangerous level beyond which it should be replaced. In times of prolonged stagnation and persistent corruption, when even the loftiest and most courageous officials failed to convince their colleagues and superiors to mend their ways, when elite malpractices reached their apogee while the peasants' burden became intolerable—rebellion became singularly effective in shattering the system and enabling the eventual restoration of its proper mode of functioning. Rebellions can be interpreted as a peculiar (and very costly) readjustment system, a kind of bloody popular "election," which determined what family would rule for another dynastic cycle, corrected certain wrongs, allowed the influx of new blood into the government apparatus, and thus contributed toward the improvement of the empire's functioning. As such, rebellions became indeed, in Meadows's words, "the storm that clears and invigorates a political atmosphere."

In generating people-focused policies and facilitating dynastic change, rebellions contributed to the improvement of the commoners' lot and to the empire's functioning in general. Yet they had another, subtler impact on the empire's fate: through their persistent willingness to be co-opted into the imperial order, the rebels evidenced this order's exceptional viability. Like nomadic conquerors, rebellious commoners were a formidable enemy of the imperial state; yet even if successful, they proved finally incorporable within the imperial political system. This pattern not only reflected the imperial order's hegemonic position but also further reinforced this position. Any new rebel-turning-emperor served as proof that there was no real alternative to the political system established in the aftermath of the Warring States period. Insofar as the empire's ideological invulnerability remained intact, domestic and external challenges could be accommodated within the extant order and even garnered to improve it. It was not until the late nineteenth century, when alien ideologies backed by alien armies began undermining this invulnerability, that the empire's doom was sealed.

CHAPTER 6

Imperial Political Culture in the Modern Age

> It is too soon to tell.
> —*Zhou Enlai,*
> *on the impact of the 1789 French Revolution*

IN THE EIGHTEENTH CENTURY, the reigning Qing dynasty and the Chinese empire in general reached the peak of their development. For two millennia the empire had withstood countless challenges and recovered from a variety of crises; its statesmen had accumulated historical wisdom enabling them to continuously improve the functioning of the imperial system. Moreover, the Qing dynasty was blessed with a sequence of extraordinarily gifted monarchs, who were skillful in both domestic and external affairs, and under whose aegis China entered one of its lengthiest ages of stability and prosperity, of unprecedented territorial expansion and security on its borders. A casual observer could well have concluded that the empire was truly immortal.

Nonetheless, the seeds of crisis were well sown by then. An unprecedented demographic expansion had dangerously decreased the land/man ratio, driving millions of peasants to the edge of subsistence level, aggravating ecological degradation, and impeding the government's ability to monitor the expanding population. Parallel to these developments a new threat materialized at the dynasty's maritime boundaries, where the increasingly assertive British Empire was no longer prone to tolerate what it perceived as the Qing authorities' discriminatory practices toward British merchants. The dynastic leaders, who were well prepared to combat threats from Inner Asian boundaries, woefully underestimated the potential of Her Majesty's fleet; and when the conflict occurred—in the so-called Opium Wars, 1839–1860—it resulted in the crushing defeat of the Qing armies. In the meantime, a series of domestic uprisings, which culminated in the Taiping apocalypse of 1851–1864, wreaked havoc in the domestic sociopolitical fabric, bringing an end to the lengthy age of peace under the Manchu aegis.

The story of the empire's fall is well known and requires only the most cursory review. Through the second half of the nineteenth century, the Qing leaders desperately tried to restore the fortunes of their battered state through adopting certain achievements of Western civilization, most specifically military technology, while preserving the "essence" (*ti*) of imperial rule intact. The futility of these attempts was mercilessly exposed when China suffered a humiliating defeat in 1894–1895 at the hands of Japan, the country that a generation earlier had introduced much more profound and successful reforms than anything contemplated by the Qing leaders. Immediately thereafter, China fell victim to the great powers' "scramble for concessions," in the process of which its sovereignty and territorial integrity were significantly impaired. Only then (1898) was the first attempt made to introduce truly substantial reforms; but as these reforms were swiftly smashed by the conservative opposition, the imperial court entered the twentieth century in a state of stubborn disregard of new realities. This self-imposed blindness once again extracted a heavy price, as the dynasty entered into a suicidal conflict with the entire "civilized world" of those days, the so-called Boxer War (1900). The subsequent defeat at the hands of Western (and Japanese) expeditionary forces was humiliating enough; moreover, the atrophy of the dynasty's domestic prestige was further demonstrated by the behavior of many regional governors who, ignoring the court's call to arms, proclaimed neutrality in its conflict with the foreign powers. The empire lost not just its military but also its political vigor; change was inevitable.

Imperial China had in the past faced similar combinations of domestic and external threats—but this time it also had to withstand an unprecedented cultural challenge. In marked distinction from the empire's traditional foes, Western powers had no respect for its political system and were not prone to adapt themselves to Chinese ways. While the Westerners in general did not aim at toppling the imperial regime, the demonstrable superiority of their political models in an age of bitter interstate struggle meant that China's erstwhile consensus in favor of imperial rule was steadily eroded. Most fundamentally, the millennia-long insistence on stability as the most essential political virtue came to an end. The narrative of "progress" and "modernization" firmly captivated the minds of the educated elite, becoming a new political paradigm, in light of which the virtues of sociopolitical arrangements had to be measured. By the early twentieth century a broad new consensus emerged: in order to survive, China must modernize itself. Whereas the precise meanings of "progress" and "modernization" were constantly debated, it was increasingly obvious that changes were required not just in the economy and the military but also in the political system and even in basic cultural values. This was the background for the introduction of radical antimonarchical ideas, which in due time ended the once unshakable ideological hegemony of the imperial system. Lacking its ideological legitimacy, the empire collapsed almost instantly in the wake of the somewhat accidental 1911 Republican Revolution. The longest continuous political system in the world abruptly came to its end.

The empire's collapse brought about woeful ideological turmoil. The intellectual elite was unified in its hope to restore "a rich country with a powerful army" (*fu guo qiang bing*)—and its members were increasingly aware that to attain this goal they must dispense with significant aspects of the imperial system or even dismantle it outright. Yet the rapidity of the empire's disintegration had caught them unprepared: few, if any, could clearly envision an alternative to the imperial model. For decades following the collapse of the Qing dynasty China remained a huge battleground of competing ideologies and political systems. Almost any "ism" practiced anywhere throughout the twentieth century was tried in China or parts of it: from experiments in parliamentary democracy to military regimes, from theocracy (e.g., in Tibet) to colonial rule of different kinds; from Leninism and Stalinism to experiments in fascism, anarchism, renovated Confucianism, and Legalism; from an Islamic republic and khanates in Xinjiang to a variety of local idiosyncratic regimes under military and civilian leaders. As evidence of the peculiar ideological openness of twentieth-century China, suffice it to cite the Shanxi warlord Yan Xishan (1883–1960), who proudly proclaimed that he ran his province according to the perfect ideology, one that combined the best features of "militarism, nationalism, anarchism, democracy, capitalism, communism, individualism, imperialism, universalism, paternalism and utopianism."[1] Notably, Confucianism, Daoism, Legalism, Buddhism, and all other traditional "isms" are absent from this ideological supermarket. While twentieth-century Chinese leaders occasionally looked to the native political tradition for answers to persistent crises, more often than not they sought these answers elsewhere—in a variety of novel ideologies introduced into China from the West.

What remained of China's traditional political culture amid these endless twists and turns, in which foreign ideologies appeared incomparably more attractive than the native ones? This question fascinated—and continues to fascinate—scholars in China and in the West. From Joseph Levenson's seminal trilogy *Confucian China and Its Modern Fate* to countless studies by current Chinese, Western, and Japanese scholars, the answers fluctuate tremendously, reflecting ever-changing political and historical perspectives. Naturally, a definitive answer to this question is impossible: as suggested by this chapter's epigraph, a statement ascribed to Zhou Enlai (1898–1976), it is advisable to be humble when dealing with events of the recent past. Perhaps the only clear conclusion that we can draw from the analysis of the last century of historical developments in China is this: any reductionist view—either identifying China's twentieth-century turmoil as nothing but another dynastic change, or, alternatively, arguing that China witnessed a total rupture with its past—is not tenable. David Shambaugh usefully identifies the current

Chinese state as an "eclectic" one, in which "each new departure was never total, although all were sharp and each sought to 'overthrow' and replace the former. In reality, though, each new Chinese state maintained certain features of the old."[2] But which features of the old were adopted by the new state formations, and which—if any—were cast away altogether? To answer this question, I shall focus on the modern trajectory of those major aspects of traditional Chinese political culture that I discussed in previous chapters. I hope that this line of analysis will serve to summarize my study, while adding a few new dimensions to the discussion of continuities and ruptures in the modern Chinese state.[3]

THE QUEST FOR UNITY

The concept of political unity was the most fundamental idea behind the empire's formation, and it remained the least affected by the advent of modernity. While China underwent a painful process of adaptation from an empire with pretensions to world leadership into a nation-state, the idea of unified rule was only marginally affected. Rather, unity, once conceived of as "universal," came to be understood as a "national" one. This readjustment was not entirely nonproblematic, though, especially insofar as postimperial leaders had to preserve huge territories beyond the limits of China proper, inherited from the Qing regime. The process of adaptation to new realities had some painful repercussions on the empire's ethnic frontiers, where former dependencies of the Qing tried—with varying degree of success—to attain independence from the Han-led Chinese Republic. For a short while, as the image of the empire's inclusiveness was profoundly shattered, the possibility of ethnic secession was entertained even by staunch Han nationalists, such as the eminent thinker Zhang Binglin (1868–1936), and even the Republic's "father," Sun Yat-sen (Sun Zhongshan, 1866–1925).[4] Yet soon enough Han nationalists reinterpreted the idea of "national unity" as pertaining inclusively to all the dwellers of the former Qing realm, as it is incorporated nowadays into the official parlance of the People's Republic of China. The close proximity between the traditional idea of unified rule in "All-under-Heaven" and the modern notion of the territorial integrity and sovereignty of a nation-state supported the efforts of China's modern leaders to preserve the former Qing territories intact.[5]

This said, the process of preserving the territorial integrity of the Qing realm was not smooth, and its unity was questioned—even if briefly—not just on the ethnic frontiers but even within the imperial core. Centrifugal forces were set in motion at the very end of Qing rule when the court allowed the formation of provincial assemblies staffed by members of local elites as an entirely new vehicle of political participation. The establishment of the assemblies enabled an unprecedented institutionalization of local interests, turning these new bodies into a powerful instrument in the hands of provincial elites, who sought to protect their economic and administrative interests at the court's expense. The assemblies adopted an increasingly confrontational attitude toward the central government and played an important role in the breakdown of Qing rule. It was the assemblies' declarations of "independence" of the Qing that hastened the empire's collapse in late 1911. These declarations indicated that the new province-oriented discourse, which had emerged in the assemblies, was potentially detrimental to the country's territorial integrity.

The latent threat posed by provincial assemblies to China's unity was duly recognized by the first Republican president, Yuan Shikai (1859–1916), who ordered their dissolution in early 1914, a mere five years after their convention. Yet the idea of provincial autonomy that emerged in the wake of the late Qing reforms did not disappear in the immediate aftermath of the assemblies' dissolution. Rather, it gave rise to a short-lived federalist movement, which articulated provincial identities and local interests as opposed to those of the center. Although not overtly separatist, this movement and the sentiments it generated posed a rare alternative to the millennia-long dominance of "unitism" in China's political tradition.[6]

The "federalist" challenge was short-lived, though. By the 1920s, as the country sank into a civil war led by local military potentates, the so-called warlords, the idea of provincial autonomy rapidly lost its appeal, and the federalist movement evaporated. Some scholars, most notably Prasenjit Duara, lament the demise of federalism, which Duara describes as having been caused by the "interplay of power politics and authoritative language, [which] enabled the hegemonic, centralizing nationalist narrative to destroy and ideologically bury the federalist alternative."[7] Yet this explanation, which reduces political processes to the interplay of "hegemonic narratives," strikes me as somewhat reductionist. From the point of view of the majority of political actors, what was at stake was not just a narrative but the very real survival of China as a unified entity. Rival warlords, who were too ready to pose themselves as champions of regional interests, became the major destabilizing force; they repeatedly defied the central government, became engaged in devastating internecine warfare, and mercilessly plundered the populace. It is against this menace—rather than out of abstract commitment to the "nationalist narrative"—that political unification became an urgent imperative.[8]

The warlord era, with its unmistakable resemblance to earlier periods of political fragmentation in terms of domestic devastation, served as a powerful reminder of the advantages of political unification. The quest for unification duly became the major political factor in the Republican era. It played the decisive role—arguably, more than either anti-imperialist propaganda or promises of social justice—in the success of the Northern Expedition undertaken by the Nation's Party (Guomindang, GMD, a.k.a. Kuomintang, KMT) in 1926–1928. By the same token, the inability to complete an effective unification may be considered the single most unforgivable failure of the GMD leader, Jiang Jieshi (Chiang Kai-shek, 1887–1975), who eventually had to acquiesce—even if grudgingly—in the ongoing autonomy of his warlord allies.[9] Conversely, the successful unification of both China proper and its ethnic peripheries became one of the greatest attainments of the Communist Party of China (CPC) and its leader, Mao Zedong, and an important—perhaps the primary—source of the Party's legitimacy. Unity meant peace and stability—and for Chinese statesmen there was no plausible alternative to it either with or without the emperor.

Nowadays, the quest for unity remains an important factor that influences the complex relations between Mainland China and the fugitive government of the Republic of China on Taiwan. Calls for Taiwan independence emerged strongly in the 1990s in the wake of democratization on the island; they peaked under the rule of native GMD leader Lee Tenghui (Li Denghui, r. 1996–2000) and of his successors from the radically pro-independence Democratic-Progressive Party (DPP). The independence rhetoric adopted by Lee and by the DPP strained the atmosphere across the Taiwan Strait and for a short while even aroused war expectations. As of 2011, the situation has markedly improved, but the Mainland's resolute opposition to Taiwanese independence remains unshaken.

Scholars often analyze Mainland-Taiwan relations from a geopolitical perspective or in terms of Chinese national pride, and these approaches are surely valid. Yet I believe that the Mainland's unwavering opposition to Taiwan independence is also deeply connected to the threat that the independence discourse poses to the principle of political unity, and thereby to the perceived stability of the Mainland itself. The DPP and its allies' claim that a distinct Taiwanese regional identity merits political independence, and this runs counter to the fundamentals of China's political tradition, in which regional differences were widely recognized but were never conceived of as justification for political secession. Should this norm be transgressed, China may face the prospect of disintegration into dozens of independent states, as many provinces in China proper (e.g., Fujian or Guangdong) or even subprovincial units may claim a degree of cultural difference from Beijing similar to that adduced by the supporters of Taiwan independence. Thus if the Pandora's box of distinct identities is opened and the hegemonic position of the unity discourse shattered, one may realistically expect China's descent into deep turmoil akin to that of the early twentieth century. Arguably, it is precisely this fear of potential disintegration that shapes the approach of the Mainland Chinese leadership to the Taiwan issue. Now, as in the past, for the Chinese, Mengzi's twenty-three-centuries-old dictum "Stability is in unity" requires no elaboration.

MONARCHISM

While the concept of unity remains the single most significant legacy bequeathed by the imperial age to China's modernity, the second pillar of the imperial political culture—the principle of monarchism—collapsed immediately with the advent of the new age. The republican form of government, which in the early twentieth century was advocated by only a tiny number of elite radicals, emerged suddenly as a new political norm. Introduced without an intervening age of constitutional monarchy, and amid great confusion, to a largely unprepared population, the Republic, not surprisingly, malfunctioned. Its leaders—presidents, prime ministers, grand marshals, and the like—lacked the emperors' exclusive authority and were unable to effectively perform stabilizing tasks. Since the Republican heads of state owed their nominal authority to a vaguely understood popular will, their position was repeatedly contested, and many political actors refused to comply with the leaders. This lack of sufficient legitimacy became particularly damaging when the Republic's leaders faced the warlords' challenge.

The proliferation of warlordism in the Republic was the direct result of a botched transition from an imperial to a republican form of rule. In the Qing, as in most of the preceding dynasties, the military command structure was decentralized to prevent the emergence of powerful generals who would be able to challenge the emperor's power; yet insofar as substantial numbers of commanders remained fundamentally loyal to the emperor, this decentralization was not inimical to political order. When the Republic inherited this decentralized system, its leaders were unable to rein in powerful warlords. Soon enough, these warlords divided the country among themselves; and while displaying nominal fidelity to the concept of unified rule and to republican legitimacy, they were practically engaged in defending their autonomy. The reason for this situation was self-evident: unlike the emperor, the "republic," the "nation," and the "constitution" were abstract symbols that could not issue orders and demand absolute loyalty. Thus, even when most warlords succumbed to the rule of the GMD, they continued to challenge the Party leader, Jiang Jieshi, causing persistent malfunctioning of the GMD military and civilian structures. The inability of the GMD leaders to subdue holders of the gun became the major source of their disastrous performance vis-à-vis the Japanese aggressors and Communist rebels.[10]

The correlation between the supreme ruler's weakness and the proliferation of domestic disorder was clear to all major leaders of the Republican age, and it may explain why each of these leaders sought quasi-imperial status for himself. Chinese history for much of the twentieth century can actually be interpreted as a process of gradual detoxification from the country's lengthy addiction to imperial rule. One Republican president, Yuan Shikai, fully assumed emperorship in 1915; but his imperial pretensions were rejected by military commanders, and he had to abdicate a few weeks after ascending the throne. Other leaders did not claim the throne directly but developed a variety of personality cults with quasi-imperial pretensions, as is clearly evidenced by the activities of Sun Yat-sen, Jiang Jieshi, and, most blatantly, Mao Zedong. The last was doubtless the most successful candidate for emperorship in the aftermath of the 1911 revolution, and his power over the Party, the army, and society exceeded what the Leninist system could have allowed. The imperial style of Mao, and, to a lesser degree, of Jiang Jieshi, may appall Western observers who are intrinsically averse to dictatorships; but it is worth noting that both leaders were active during a period of transition from monarchism to alternative forms of rule, and their quasi-monarchic behavior may have been requisite to China's gradual adaptation to novel forms of government.

China's "imperial detoxification" accelerated under the next generation of leaders, who were born in the very late years of the empire: Deng Xiaoping (1904–1997) on the Mainland and Jiang Jingguo (Chiang Ching-kuo, 1910–1988) in Taiwan. Both had dramatically reduced personality cults and presided over smooth transitions to essentially nonmonarchical government. Taiwan adopted Western-style parliamentary democracy; yet the advantages and drawbacks of this decision cannot be adequately summarized at this stage and will not be dealt with here. The Mainland, alternatively, evolved into a kind of Leninist oligarchy with power shared by a group of top Party leaders, members of the Politburo Standing Committee. These leaders act as a "collective emperor": while none of them possesses the imperial aura and exclusiveness, as a group they enjoy nearly absolute power and symbolize the state's unity, stability, and prosperity. The transformation from autocratic to collegial rule began with Deng Xiaoping, but it was under his noncharismatic successor, Jiang Zemin (b. 1926), that China truly entered a new age. Jiang instituted the system of mandatory retirement and imposed term limits for top executives; in 2002 he set an example by voluntary stepping down and allowing the next generation of leaders to assume power. As of 2011 it is widely anticipated that the current incumbent, Hu Jintao (b. 1942), and his colleagues would likewise cede power to the next generation of Party leaders in 2012.[11]

Currently (2011) China's experiment with oligarchic leadership appears impressively successful, and it may even be interpreted as a neat solution to the perennial weaknesses of monarchic rule. The principle of collective leadership, term limits, and the introduction of a mandatory retirement age may prevent the rise of inept leaders; these safeguards may also preclude top executives' remaining in office after becoming physically or mentally debilitated, as occurred with the first generation of CPC leaders. Current chief executives undergo lengthy processes of recruitment, training, and socialization into the top leadership, which renders them incomparably fitter for their tasks than were the majority of the emperors. Assuming that this system of leadership selection, training, and rotation is maintained appropriately, then the CPC can be credited with mending one of the weakest aspects of China's imperial system—the emperor's potential inadequacy—without jeopardizing the principle of a single source of legitimate authority. This said, a word of caution is required. The current system can be effectively maintained only insofar as the collective leadership adheres to the Leninist principles of resolving internal contradictions confidentially and presenting a unified front to the outside world. Any deviation from this facade of unity may have the disastrous consequence of exacerbating political conflicts in the Party and in society at large, as happened on the eve of the tragic events of the 1989 Tiananmen incident.[12]

INTELLECTUALS

If the emperor was the major victim of China's drive into modernity, the intellectuals could have been among the major gainers. The abolition of the monarchy ended their humiliating position as the ruler's servitors, while their political and cultural prestige remained—initially—largely intact. This placed them in an ideal situation to exercise unhindered leadership; and in the immediate aftermath of the empire's collapse it seemed that this would be the case. Intellectuals of the early Republican period did not just orchestrate the cultural renovation that profoundly changed Chinese society, but also played an extraordinarily important role in the political dynamics of that age. For a considerable period, one can discern clear continuity in the position and self-image of Chinese intellectuals as their society's moral and, potentially, political leaders; yet far-reaching changes that occurred in the nature, composition, and social role of the intellectual stratum brought about gradual erosion in its political power.

It was the abolition of the imperial examinations in 1905, not the Republican Revolution of 1911, that had the most profound impact on the intellectuals' life. This abolition, and the accompanying educational reforms, brought an end to the millennia-old association between education and political careers. New avenues of social advancement were open, and many ambitious individuals were able thenceforth to pursue prestigious careers outside the government sphere. Gradually, the composition of the intellectual stratum changed, an increasing proportion of it becoming skilled professionals with minimal, if any, political involvement. Members of the new intelligentsia (*zhishifenzi*, literally "the knowledgeable elements") differed markedly from the imperial literati in the nature of their education, in their career patterns, and most notably in the degree of their attachment to the political realm.

This said, a sizable group within the newly emerging intelligentsia has inherited and perpetuated the tradition of the imperial literati as wide-ranging sociopolitical critics and as bearers of a solemn political mission. This numerically small but politically and culturally extraordinarily important group will stand at the focus of my discussion in this section. These men and women had to navigate their way in the aftermath of the collapse of the sociopolitical system within which Chinese intellectuals had operated for more than two millennia, and amid the profound ideological crisis that accompanied the end of the imperial order. They had to formulate anew their "True Way": a value system that would fit the new circumstances and allow them to resume the traditional role of the intellectuals as moral and political guides of society.

This task was performed primarily by a young generation of politically active intellectuals whose worldview was formed in the last years of the Qing or in the early years of the Republic, and who were not constrained by venerated imperial traditions. For them, patriotism (often coupled with many other "isms") replaced the erstwhile commitment to the throne; while the burning desire to save the country from domestic and external perils led some of them to turn their backs on the past, in what Lin Yü-sheng laments as "totalistic iconoclasm." Not only was the imperial political system discarded as obsolete and inadequate; the very "national essence," namely, the Confucian cultural legacy, was stigmatized as an obstacle on the road to modernity. Chen Duxiu (1879–1942), the renowned leader of the iconoclastic "New Culture Movement" and the future first General Secretary of the CPC, plainly declared in 1916 that the "national essence" should be sacrificed lest "our nation . . . die out because of its unfitness for living in the modern world."[13] These words epitomize the choice made by many—although by no means all— young intellectuals of the first decades of the twentieth century. For the sake of the supreme political goal of national salvation, any cultural change was permissible. Facing the choice between their two roles, as political leaders of the society and as custodians of its cultural values, these intellectuals decisively opted for the former, thereby facilitating tremendous cultural and intellectual change in the world's oldest continuous civilization within an amazingly short historical period.

The New Culture Movement began in 1915 as an internal ferment within the intellectual community; but four years later, it merged with patriotic upheaval to give birth to the May Fourth Movement of 1919, one of the most significant events in China's modern history. It began as a tiny demonstration against the unjust treatment of China in the soon-to-be-signed Versailles Treaty, but it grew into a powerful wave of protests against warlordism, against corrupt politicians, and against political and cultural stagnation. Both major Chinese political parties of the twentieth century, the CPC and the (renovated) GMD, were born in the immediate aftermath of these events, which are widely considered the true watershed in China's path to modernity. While many recent studies aim at "decentralizing" the May Fourth Movement from the narrative of China's entrance into the modern age, the movement's overall importance is undeniable; Mao Zedong himself viewed it as a turning point in the history of China's "bourgeois-democratic revolution."[14] That a tiny intellectual community could reshape the political dynamic in China in the heyday of the warlord era testifies to the ongoing power of the men of letters and to their exceptional political potency. And yet, while intellectuals continued to play an important role throughout much of subsequent Republican history, soon enough new trends emerged that were not conducive to the future political and cultural leadership of the intellectuals in Chinese society.

The intellectuals' eventual loss of their leadership position was curiously linked to the processes that they themselves had set in motion, namely, the collapse of the monarchy and the advancement of new, participatory modes of mass behavior. In the republican polity the intellectuals lost their erstwhile function as speakers on behalf of the people before the throne; and they no longer sought to fulfill the role of the natural representatives of "the masses." Rather, their overt goal was "to enlighten" or "to awaken" the people and to advance their political and cultural emancipation. In the process, even the traditional written language, the hallmark of the literati's culture, was sacrificed and replaced (in 1920) with the colloquial language, a move that was meant to put an end to the intellectuals' traditional elitism. This assault on elitism in the cultural sphere eventually hastened the end of the intellectuals' dominance in the political sphere as well. As noted by Vera Schwarcz, while during the May Fourth Movement intellectuals still retained the sense of their "unique cultural mission" and behaved as undisputed social leaders, soon thereafter their position changed. They "could no longer hold on to their previous self-image as pioneer-prophets of enlightenment . . . [and] transformed themselves into *zhishi fenzi*—members of a politicized intelligentsia, or, more literally, knowledgeable members of a larger, class-conscious body politic."[15]

In the 1920s, as politically involved intellectuals were losing both political prestige and the elitist stance characteristic of the imperial literati, a new sociopolitical force emerged that began filling in the void. The newly formed Leninist parties (primarily the CPC, but to a certain extent also the GMD) began replacing the scholar-officials of the past as a new ruling stratum. Like the imperial literati, these parties acted as a political and ideological elite, supposedly united by common values, and having preferential access to sources of political power and social prestige. Many intellectuals were active in the formation of both parties, and some preserved important positions within their party's establishment, which allowed them to sustain their traditional role as the rulers' advisers; yet theirs were individual success stories. As a social stratum the intellectuals were no longer considered exceptionally fit to hold office; gone was their political leadership. The CPC's victory in the lengthy civil war and the establishment of the People's Republic in 1949 marked the end of an active political role for intellectuals outside the Party establishment. The new power configuration was completed.

Mao Zedong's period in power (1949–1976) was greatly disadvantageous to the intelligentsia as a whole. No longer the collective possessor of correct values (a position they had lost to the proletariat), the intellectuals—especially those who remained politically involved—witnessed an unprecedented assault on their stratum, which peaked in the tragic farce wherein scores of professors and students were rusticated in order to "learn from poor peasants" and remold their consciousness. The decade of the Cultural Revolution (1966–1976), during which the intellectuals were defined as the "stinking old ninth [category of class enemies]," marked the nadir of their status. Yet even under these adverse circumstances the erosion of the intellectuals' power was neither unidirectional nor irreversible. Their traditional prestige, their ideological expertise, and their widely respected contribution to the nation's rejuvenation and to the revolutionary movements—all these prevented the complete marginalization of the intelligentsia even under Mao Zedong. Prior to the Cultural Revolution, many intellectuals remained prominent within the Party establishment, continuing to seek the restoration of their traditional role as moral and intellectual leaders of society, or what Timothy Cheek somewhat derisively calls the position of "priest-rentiers, serving the cosmic state (Confucian or Leninist)."[16] The continuation of traditional patterns is clearly evident in the relations of some of these establishment intellectuals with the Party leadership led by the quasi-emperor, Mao Zedong, as traditional dramas of loyal self-sacrifice were repeatedly reenacted.[17] Moreover, even campaigns that targeted intellectuals (and, no less significantly, periodic attempts to court them, as in the "Hundred Flowers" movement of 1956–1957) testify to the ongoing importance of that stratum. Being designated as the "stinking old ninth" was humiliating, to be sure; but behind the humiliation were Mao's profound fears of the intellectuals' ability to influence the state in a negative ("revisionist," "capitalist," or "bureaucratic") direction.

In retrospect, Mao's fears were justified: shortly after his death, the intellectuals briefly reemerged as a powerful stratum, whose support was crucial to the successful restoration of Deng Xiaoping and the subsequent dismantling of radical aspects of Maoist practices.[18] Furthermore, in the 1980s China witnessed a brief revival of the intellectuals' political importance as a social group, and this revival was not limited to establishment figures. In the aftermath of Mao's era the country searched intensively for a new course of development, and the prestige of those with demonstrable ideological expertise soared. By the late 1980s, as the Party leadership vacillated between conflicting programs, intellectuals became particularly vociferous, and their impact on the country's political dynamics rapidly increased. It peaked in 1989, when, in an emulation of the May Fourth Movement, student demonstrations on Beijing's Tiananmen Square intoxicated much of the country's urban population, bringing millions to voice their grievances and to protest against corruption and against the ineptitude of the Party leadership. At the end, the beleaguered Party elders fought back, brutally suppressing the student movement; but the power of a tiny student community to trigger broad protests caused many observers to refocus on perceived continuities in the intellectuals' political role in traditional and modern China. For a short while it seemed that the pendulum had swung back to 1919, and that the Beijing protests would change the course of China's history.[19]

Twenty years after these events, with the advantage of hindsight, it is possible to contextualize the 1980s within the gradual process of erosion of the intellectuals' power, and to conclude that the student movement's temporary success did not mark the intellectuals' return as autonomous actors to the forefront of political processes. The student radicals' ability to influence national politics derived from a peculiar confluence: an atmosphere of intensive ideological search for a new course coincided with deep cleavages within the CPC leadership; but once these factors had ebbed, the intellectuals' impact on social and political life receded as well. While the termination of the class-oriented discourse enabled the intellectuals to recoup some of their cultural prestige, and their position within the Party and the government has markedly improved since the end of Mao's era, this stratum has by no means been reconstituted as China's political elite. The changes in China's political and social structure that I have outlined, which weakened the intellectuals' leadership, appear currently to be irreversible.

It may be tempting here to speculate that in due time the CPC—despite the obvious ideological, organizational, numerical, and social differences—might replace the imperial scholar-officials as China's cultural, ideological, and sociopolitical elite. The transformation of the Party from a revolutionary organization of have-nots into a managerial organization—one that successfully absorbs members of newly emerging professional and economic elites—lends credibility to this comparison. Like the literati of the past, the Party lays claim to exclusive understanding of the proper ways to ensure China's international prestige, domestic stability, and prosperity; and it is because of their monopoly on this collective wisdom that its members are supposed to have preferential access to government positions. Party members are, moreover, expected to cultivate their morality, to behave public-mindedly and "serve the people" in a quasi-Confucian fashion, and as such they are expected to be moral leaders of society.[20] Yet the Party is still much weaker than the imperial educated elite in terms of its ideological cohesiveness, and in terms of its ability to secure ideological hegemony over society. Should these weaknesses be overcome (which currently appears unlikely, at least in the short term—but see more below), the comparison of the CPC to the literati of the past may become even more appealing.

As for "pure intellectuals," their political reemergence does not seem likely. Massive expansion in higher education has eroded their elite status, despite its partial resurgence in the 1980s; while the ongoing diversification of employment opportunities and a proliferation of prestigious careers outside the government, and outside the public sphere, further decrease their erstwhile political engagement. The only notable exceptions to this dissociation of the intellectuals from politics are influential "establishment intellectuals" and their peers who find ways to promote their ideas and ideals through the Party organization or through a variety of affiliated think tanks, which have become increasingly important for decision makers in recent decades. In contrast, those intellectuals who opt to disengage from the governing structures are losing their political impact. Cheek predicted in 1994 that "the price of autonomy for Chinese intellectuals will be not only to let go of their priestly vocation, . . . but to become as irrelevant as Western intellectuals in their nations' politics."[21] This may be too gloomy, but Cheek's estimate does grasp current trends—at least with regard to a significant segment of the intelligentsia.

ELITES AND THE "MASSES"

Descending the traditional social ladder, we arrive at two groups whose positions changed dramatically in the wake of the twentieth-century upheavals: local elites and the commoners. The first were, along with the emperor, the chief victims of China's entrance into modernity; the latter—whom we can no longer aptly term "commoners" but must refer to, in the modern parlance, as "the masses"—were supposed to be its major beneficiaries, and certainly gained a lot, though less than what might have been expected. It is with regard to two these groups that we find the most significant departures from traditional patterns of power configuration.

In the early twentieth century local elites briefly emerged as the most powerful political force in China. They benefited first from the weakening of the central government, which was losing its ability to monitor the elite's activities and to rein in their abuses; and, second, from the late Qing reforms. As mentioned above, the establishment of provincial assemblies staffed almost exclusively by elite members was an important step toward the institutionalization of elite power. Moreover, with the abrupt abolition of the examination system in 1905, the dynasty lost its major leverage vis-à-vis the elites. These developments, which brought about comprehensive change in the balance of power between the court and the elites, emboldened the elite members, encouraging many of them to adopt an oppositional stance toward the imperial government, and even to endorse the republican movement. Yet in retrospect this sudden profession of republicanism by the dynasty's traditional supporters was an ill-conceived gamble. The collapse of the old order had profoundly undermined the elites' position and has hastened their demise.

From the beginning of the Republican era, the elite's power began to wane. In the very first year of the Republic, massive expansion in the electorate deprived the elites of their exclusivity as the only responsible political class; then the replacement of parliamentarianism with the politics of the gun further undermined the elites' preferential access to sources of political power. Perennial warfare, banditry, extractions by rival warlord armies, and the general loss of stability were detrimental to the interests of many elite members; yet these troubles were not exceptional to the Republican age, and normally would have resulted in changes in the elites' personnel but not in their grasp over local society. Yet deeper changes were unfolding—and these fundamentally weakened local elites as a social stratum.

What most eroded elite power were not temporary political developments but the proliferation of the new discourse, the one directed at the creation of a modern Chinese nation. When Sun Yat-sen lamented in 1924 that "the Chinese people have only family and clan solidarity; they do not have national spirit . . . they are just a heap of loose sand,"[22] he reflected the widely shared belief of contemporaneous leaders that, to survive, China must be transformed into a modern nation-state, and its people imbued with national spirit. Yet if the nation-state was to be formed, it would be necessary to abolish the elite's role as mediators between the masses and the government; and the Republic duly endorsed this course. Attempts were made to build new institutions that would increase the state's direct reach into peasant society and obliterate the need for elite intermediaries; and while these were not entirely successful prior to the Communist revolution, they were indicative of the new state's desire to eliminate local elites. The very ideology of cooperation with, and co-optation of, these elites was discontinued. In his seminal study of this topic, Prasenjit Duara summarizes:

> The Republican state was unable to hold on to [the elite] identification [with the new nation-state] and build on it. The budding alliance between modernizing state and rural elites . . . failed to flower. The new ideology of the modernizing state did not succeed in providing a viable alternative to the cultural nexus that had generated legitimacy for both local leaders and for the state.[23]

Putting aside Duara's concept of the "cultural nexus," his summary grasps well the fate of local elites in the new Republican state. The abandonment of the traditional ideology, according to which the state should cultivate the elite's support while the latter should serve as a voluntary upholder of local order, meant that the rationale of cooperation was lost, and the fate of the elites was doomed. Although the elites were natural allies of the GMD government in the anti-Communist struggle, GMD support of their cause remained halfhearted at best. Abandoned by the state, having lost their preferential access to sources of political power and their role as brokers and mediators between local society and the central authorities, the elites could not withstand the Communist assault.

The CPC ascendancy epitomizes an inverse process to that of the elites' demise: namely, the rise of "the masses" as the major political actor. The tendency to elevate the masses to the forefront of politics was embedded in the republican ethos, which identified "the people" as the source of sovereignty and not just as recipients of the ruler's and the elite's munificence. The fundamental distinction between "superior men" and "petty men," which had guided the Chinese polity for millennia, was obliterated. "The people" were no longer an amorphous and benighted mass, whose only desirable political contribution would be to behave morally in their communities and to abide by the laws; rather, they were now appealed to as members of China's nation, as potential agents who must be "awakened" and who would ultimately take the future in their own hands.[24] This "masses-oriented" discourse permeated the political spectrum, but it was the self-proclaimed champions of the people, the Communists, who succeeded in turning it into the vehicle of their struggle, and who also contributed more than anybody else to the masses' political emancipation.

The revolutionary nature of the CPC brought it from its very inception into the realm of popular uprisings, which had traditionally been the lower strata's only effective means of political participation. Like many rebel groups in the past, the Communists acted as a kind of local "counterelite," effectively mobilizing the have-nots against the existing order; but there were fundamental differences between the CPC and past rebels. Unlike traditional rebels, the Party aimed not just at seizing power from the current "dynasty," but also at profound restructuring of the entire socioeconomic order. Inspired by their vision of "modernity" and of conscious and politically involved citizens, the party made mass mobilization and politicization of the people its primary goal, and not just a tool of temporary struggle. Mao Zedong succinctly summarized the party's role vis-à-vis the masses in his formulation of the so-called mass line: the party should, first, absorb the "unsystematic and scattered ideas" of the masses; second, rework them; and third, bring the reworked ideas back to the masses "until the masses embrace them as their own."[25] This notion aptly represents both the elitist and the participatory strands in the Chinese Communist ideology. The masses were still unenlightened and required the party's guidance, but once properly educated and imbued with the party line they would—and should!—become active political actors.

The Communists' new type of elitism—a Leninist rather than Confucian one—had a profound impact on both the elites and the masses. The Communists were not rebels but revolutionaries: they refused to be coopted into the extant sociopolitical order but rather wanted to topple it. In particular, they were committed to uprooting the elite's economic, social, and political dominance. This was achieved through a series of careful steps that created new organizational frameworks for mass action, and gave birth to a new state, which was carefully constructed in the bottom-up fashion. Amid this construction, local society was profoundly restructured.[26] The elites were treated as natural enemies—both as exploiters and as the Party's competitors for societal power—and were identified as the Revolution's immediate target. Their political elimination was finalized immediately after the CPC's nationwide victory in 1949. It was achieved not just through terror from above, but in a much deeper fashion, through mass mobilization to the land reform. The landlords' lands were expropriated and redistributed, while rich landowners—the backbone of local elites—were identified as "enemies of the people," deprived of basic rights, struggled against, humiliated, and—quite often—executed by incited peasants. Cruel as it was, the process of land reform was extraordinarily successful. It not only eliminated the elites from the local arena but, more significantly, prevented their reemergence. Under the new norms of land distribution, the resurrection of the landowning elite became impossible. Gone was the social class that had dominated China for millennia.[27]

The land reform had multiple political and social consequences. From its initial attempts to redistribute the landowners' possessions, back in the 1930s, and in a more comprehensive way after 1949, the Party learned how to arouse the peasants and mobilize them against the landlords, and for the party's cause. The overwhelming success of this method may have strengthened the Party's belief in mass mobilization as the ultimate remedy for a variety of political, social, and economic ills. From its first moments in power, the Party launched a series of mass campaigns among the rural and urban populace. These campaigns tremendously increased both the Party's hold over the population and the degree of party-state penetration into the lowest social levels, yet the Party was not satisfied with mere control. Rather, mass mobilization and politicization of the citizens continued on an unprecedented scale, resulting in the broadest—often involuntary—involvement of the population in state affairs. These mass campaigns were continued long after they had outlived their political utility, and even when they became obviously counterproductive economically, as was the case with the disastrous Great Leap Forward (1958–1961).[28]

Mao's desire repeatedly to galvanize the masses and to preserve a semblance of popular political participation finally led him into conflict with moderate Party leaders, who began realizing that the once-effective policy had become pernicious. The conflict ultimately brought about the most devastating mass campaign in China, if not in human history: the Great Proletarian Cultural Revolution.[29] During the early stages of this tumultuous campaign, the intoxicated "revolutionary masses" were expected to scrutinize the deeds of top Party and state officials, and—at certain moments—were encouraged to "seize power" from the discredited Party establishment. The campaign not only violated the Leninist principles of the party leadership but endangered the very foundations of political order; yet Mao remained adamant. That Mao opted to mobilize the masses, rather than purge his rivals through routine intraparty procedures,[30] is indicative of his unwavering commitment to the notion of mass politicization. As such, the Cultural Revolution can be considered the true peak of the antielitist and pro-masses trend in twentieth-century Chinese politics.

Eventually, the Cultural Revolution, with its images of violence, disorder, and the collapse of normal ways of life, became a powerful antidote against continued political mobilization of the masses in the aftermath of Mao's era. The new generation of leaders, many of whom had been primary targets of the Cultural Revolution campaigns, considered excessive politicization of the population counterproductive, and shifted their concern from fostering new citizens to developing the economy. Gradually, the political realm became less masses-oriented: input from below (e.g., through localized protests or, increasingly, through a variety of Internet debates) is tolerated,[31] but mass actions—even in support of party policies—are actively discouraged. The leadership is no longer prone to mobilize the masses; rather, it prefers to educate them through such campaigns as "character education" (*suzhi jiaoyu*) and "patriotic education" (*aiguozhuyi jiaoyu*), and to monitor their activities. Simultaneously, the Party acts subtly but steadily to dissociate the majority of the population from political life and to professionalize the political realm. The new generations of cadres are valued for their educational level and managerial abilities, rather than for their ability to manipulate the masses. These elitist trends divorce the Party from the "mass line" of the past and increase its resemblance to the erstwhile "Confucian" elite.

This shift toward political elitism coincides—not incidentally—with the partial resurrection of socioeconomic elites. Although currently this process is still in its infancy, and the newly emerging elites are incomparably more diversified, less stable, and less powerful than their late imperial counterparts, the likelihood of their future importance in China's increasingly stratified society cannot be easily dismissed. May we expect, then, a resurrection of politically active social elites in some distant or not-so-distant future? Will the party-state opt to ignore the newly emerging elites, suppress them, or try to co-opt them and relegate some of its burdensome responsibilities to them, mirroring the trend of the imperial age?[32] Can we expect the rise of new forms of elite voluntarism? Is it imaginable that the future will see the reemergence of an intermediary stratum between the state apparatus and the populace? While currently it is too early to attempt to answer these questions, the mere fact that we can reasonably pose them is indicative of the surprising relevance of past patterns for evaluating possible development trajectories for the Chinese state in the future.

EPILOGUE: STABILITY VERSUS PROGRESS

Many scholars of the history of China's Communist Party have noted the pendulum-like trajectory of the Party's course: a certain policy is first adopted and radically pursued, then discarded and discontinued, and then recurs again, sometimes in a more radical form than before. The last section of the discussion above suggests that at times this pattern of development may be identified, mutatis mutandis, in longer historical arcs as well. Having discarded the imperial system as a source of stagnation and an impediment to "modernization" and "progress," the renovated

Chinese political elite is gradually shifting toward a more accommodative view of the past. Having lost its revolutionary zeal, the CPC leadership in particular has come to appreciate the value of stability and tranquillity. Hence the lessons embodied by the imperial political system, which excelled at ensuring long-term stability, cannot be ignored.

Interest in the legacy of the past is increasing in China almost daily, paralleling the rise in national pride and the resultant more affirmative view of the imperial enterprise. This interest has copious manifestations. On the popular level it is promoted through a variety of popular publications, movies, TV serials, and even Internet games that deal with emperors, meritorious ministers, generals, and other heroes from the past. On the level of official discourse it is reflected in the adoption of new terminology, such as Hu Jintao's invocation of the term "harmonious society" (*hexie shehui*) as a substitute for the class-based ideology of the past. On a more substantial level we see the work of certain members of the academic community who are eager to promote a "Confucian revival."[33] Even if largely superficial, these phenomena cannot be ignored.

With the diminishing appeal of Marxism-Leninism, China faces a dangerous ideological void that should sooner or later be filled in. While a few Chinese intellectuals—and many foreign observers—would like China to embrace Western liberal ideals, and while the ideological gap between China and Western democracies is indeed narrowing, it is highly doubtful that Western democratic discourse will prevail in the long term. Aside from being potentially detrimental to CPC power, and lacking demonstrable advantages in ensuring prosperity and stability for non-Western countries, the democratic discourse of the West is problematic in China owing to its patently alien roots. Should China fully embrace it, the country would forever be compelled to follow the ideological lead of alien powers, who would oversee and judge its "advancement" on the path toward democracy and human rights, much as the USSR dominated China ideologically when the latter embraced the Soviet model of development. This situation is incompatible with China's growing power, prestige, and assertiveness. In this context, the search in China's immensely rich past for appropriate ideological solutions to the country's current problems, followed by the synthesis of these traditional elements with modern Western (either Marxist or liberal or both) ideas, appears by far the more advantageous course.

Which aspects of Chinese traditional political culture are applicable nowadays? Perhaps the single most important one is the legacy of the political center maintaining its hegemonic position vis-à-vis a variety of social groups and local interests, and reining in centrifugal socioeconomic and political forces. In this context, the ability of the Party leadership to act as "a collective emperor" and maintain a single legitimate locus of power on Chinese soil is the most essential precondition for China's political stability and governability. The idea that "oneness [of the ruler] brings orderly rule; doubleness brings chaos"[34] in its modified (oligarchic rather than monarchic) form remains broadly acceptable to the vast majority of China's political actors—or so, at least, the present observer remains convinced.

The second—closely related—pillar of traditional political culture that retains ongoing relevance is the concept of political unity. As argued above, this concept was least influenced by China's entrance into modernity; and it arguably reflects the broadest consensus on the Chinese mainland. Both the turmoil of the Republican period, and, more recently, the disintegration of the USSR and Yugoslavia, contributed toward the ever-stronger belief that "stability is in unity." Significantly, the actualization of this ideal—much as in the past, especially under the Qing—remains highly flexible: as the cases of Hong Kong and Macao exemplify, the central government can grant certain areas real autonomy, much beyond what is acceptable in most nation-states. It may be expected that China will apply similar flexibility in settling the Taiwan issue, and, perhaps (though this is less likely), in resolving tensions on the country's ethnic frontiers. Insofar as the overarching principle of political unity is not compromised, China may well be able to allow a considerable degree of local variation with regard to its practical implementation.

The third, and perhaps most controversial, pillar of traditional order that may be of relevance today is political elitism. Surely, after a century of "masses-oriented" discourse one can expect neither a reemergence of the stratum of "scholar-officials" in its traditional form, nor a reappearance of the erstwhile rigid bifurcation between "superior" and "petty" men. Yet the advantages of meritocratic rather than excessively egalitarian modes of rule are evident to many in China, and it is plausible to expect further professionalization of the political elite amid ongoing depoliticization of the "masses." It is also possible that attempts will be made to utilize the power of the newly emerging socioeconomic elites, turning them from the state's and the Party's potential competitors into their voluntary aides. However, in this regard the trends are still unclear, and the Party's radically egalitarian past may prevent successful co-optation of the members of new proprietary classes.[35] Concomitantly, the Party's strongly pronounced commitment to the economic interests of "the people"—which clearly echoes not only modern concerns but also the "people-oriented" discourse of the past—may ensure that it continues to enjoy a sufficient degree of popular support, at least insofar as it is able to satisfy the rising economic expectations of the masses.

Time will show whether the CPC will be able to creatively synthesize China's traditional values and norms with current social and ideological realities, forming a new viable ideological framework for Chinese society. Yet the very possibility that the lessons of the Chinese empire—the most durable political entity in human history—have relevance for the rapidly advancing and innovating Chinese society of the twenty-first century testifies to the empire's remarkable posthumous strength. Now, as always, studying China's past is essential for an understanding of China's future.

Notes

INTRODUCTION

1. For a brief summary of changing Western attitudes concerning the Chinese model, see Blue, "China."

2. Major English-language studies that directly address the relations between China's past and its present include Ho and Tsou, *China's Heritage*, especially Ho's "Salient Aspects" therein; Solomon, *Mao's Revolution*; Metzger, *Escape from Predicament*; Pye, *The Spirit of Chinese Politics*; in addition many other studies of premodern China were clearly influenced by the modern perspective (e.g., de Bary, *Waiting for the Dawn*).

3. Elizabeth Perry ("Introduction") demonstrates how political scientists' interest in China's historical peculiarity increased during periods of radical upheaval (e.g., the Communist victory, the Cultural Revolution [1966–1976], or the Tiananmen drama [1989]), and decreased during periods when China's political processes were relatively predictable and "normal."

4. Montesquieu (1689–1755) was among the first to associate "Oriental despotism" (including that of China) with climatic conditions (Blue, "China," 88); and this "environmental determinism" peaked in Wittfogel's seminal *Oriental Despotism*. The fallacy of this approach is evident, however. Suffice it to mention that China is the most climatically heterogeneous land empire on earth (see McNeill, "China's Environmental History"), and its historical trajectory simply cannot be reduced to environmental factors. Besides, Wittfogel's "hydraulic" theory ignores the fact that massive hydraulic works began in China at a relatively late stage of its history, and that during much of its formative age—especially during the so-called Springs-and-Autumns period (770–453 BCE) its political structure was quite similar to the European "multicentric" system, which, according to his theory, could not emerge in the arid areas of the loess plateau (see more in chapter 4). Alternatively, the view that China's "authoritarianism" reflects weaknesses in its national character became popular among Chinese liberal thinkers in the early twentieth century, most notably during the so-called New Culture Movement (1915–); it curiously resonates with behavioral approaches toward Chinese political culture, such as those of Solomon, *Mao's Revolution*; Pye, *The Spirit of Chinese Politics*.

5. For detailed analysis of the empire's ideological foundations, see Pines, *Envisioning Eternal Empire*.

6. Eisenstadt, "Frederic Wakeman's Oeuvre," xv–xvi. For Gramsci's notion of hegemony, see, e.g., Femia, *Gramsci's Political Thought*; Adamson, *Hegemony and Revolution*.

7. See, especially, Pines, *Envisioning Eternal Empire*.

8. It is still regrettably common to reduce the analysis of Chinese political culture to a few allegedly primordial features of Chinese civilizations, such as the notion of "divine kingship" or the importance of patrilineal kinship (see, e.g., Baum, "Ritual and Rationality"; Jin Taijun and Wang Qingwu, *Zhongguo chuantong zhengzhi wenhua*).

9. See Liu Zehua's introduction to Ge Quan's *Quanli zaizhi lixing*, 1–3.

10. Tu, "The Creative Tension between *Jen* and *Li*." In a slightly different context, Philip Huang insightfully identifies paradoxes and tensions within the Chinese legal system as the reasons for its flexibility and its longevity (*Civil Justice*, 15–18); and this observation is valid for the imperial political system in general.

11. Balazs, "L'Histoire." The importance of these alternative materials is particularly vivid in studies of the late imperial period; but even for the preimperial and early imperial periods we are now less dependent on official historiography, especially because of the successful incorporation of material and epigraphic evidence.

12. These are the words of a peer reviewer of this book at the manuscript stage.

13. For earlier studies, see, e.g., Eisenstadt, *The Political System of Empires*; Doyle, *Empires* (the latter being a strictly Eurocentric study). Among recent publications, see Alcock, *Empires*; Mutschler and Mittag, *Conceiving the Empire*; Scheidel, *Rome and China*; Burbank and Cooper, *The Empires in World History*; and, most notably, Morris and Scheidel, *The Dynamics of Ancient Empires*.

14. Jack Goldstone and John Haldon provide a refreshing analysis of empires' life span, which combines sociological and historical approaches. They argue that empires were "the normal or model form of large political entity throughout Eurasia until quite recently," and identify the empire as "a territory . . . ruled from a distinct organizational center . . . with clear ideological and political sway over varied elite, who in turn exercise power over a population in which a majority have neither access to nor influence over position of imperial power" (Goldstone and Haldon, "Ancient States," 18–19).

15. The role of ideological factors in empires' varying trajectories is still highly contestable, as is illustrated by two very recent publications. Goldstone and Haldon place ideological factors on a par with institutional developments as essential for state formation in general and for the maintenance of an empire in particular ("Ancient States," 18ff.). In contrast, Walter Scheidel, who specifically compares the Chinese and Roman empires, is dismissive of the importance of ideology in the Chinese case, which, in my eyes, greatly impoverishes his discussion ("From the 'Great Convergence,'" 21–22).

16. See, for example, Cao Deben, *Zhongguo chuantong zhengzhi wenhua de xiandai jiazhi*.

17. For ecological challenges to China, see, e.g., Elvin, *The Retreat of the Elephants*.

CHAPTER 1
THE IDEAL OF "GREAT UNITY"

1. For China's geographic heterogeneity, see McNeill, "China's Environmental History." For the diversity of the core "Han" population, see, e.g., Honig, *Creating Chinese Ethnicity*; Leong, *Migration and Ethnicity*.

2. For the history of the Shang dynasty, see Keightley, "The Shang."

3. See details in Li Feng, *Landscape and Power*.

4. For instance, in an inscription on the Guai Bo-*gui* vessel, the author, a leader of a non-Zhou polity, refers to his father as "king" but reserves the designation "Son of Heaven" for the Zhou monarch (see ibid., 183–185). Even centuries later, in the Warring States period (453–221 BCE), as major regional lords elevated their status to that of "kings," none dared proclaim himself "Son of Heaven."

5. See more in Pines, *Envisioning Eternal Empire*, 17–20; idem, "The Question of Interpretation," 4–23.

6. This and subsequent discussion is largely based on Pines, "'The One that Pervades All.'"

7. For the dynamics of international relations during the Springs-and-Autumns period, see Pines, *Foundations*, 105–135; for the cultural cohesiveness of the Zhou aristocratic elites, see Falkenhausen, *Chinese Society*.

8. *Chunqiu Zuo zhuan*, Xiang 29:959.

9. For details of the "disarmament conferences," see Kano, "Chūgoku."

10. *Zhanguo ce*, "Qin ce 1" 3.2:74.

11. For military developments of the Warring States period, see Lewis, "Warring States," 625–629; idem, *Sanctioned Violence*, 53–96.

12. See, e.g., Pines et al., "General Introduction," for Qin; and articles in Cook and Major, *Defining Chu*, for Chu. It should be recalled, however, that during the Warring States period, the centrifugal tendencies were counterbalanced by forces of renewed cultural integration, promulgated by members of the educated elite; see more below in the text.

13. The following discussion largely elaborates upon Pines, "'The One That Pervades All.'"

14. See Lewis, *The Construction of Space*, 192–212.

15. *Lunyu*, "Ji shi" 16.2: 174.

16. *Mozi*, "Shang tong shang" III. 11:109–110.

17. See *Boshu Laozi*, 25: 351, and Pines, *Envisioning Eternal Empire*, 36–44.

18. *Mengzi*, "Liang Hui Wang A" 1.6: 12–13.

19. *Shang jun shu*, "Qu qiang" I.4: 27.

20. See *Mengzi*, "Li Lou A" 7.14:175; *Shang jun shu*, "Hua ce," IV.18: 107.

21. This notion is most vividly seen in the recently unearthed manuscript *Rong Cheng shi*, which was apparently produced in the state of Chu ca. 300 BCE. See translation and analysis of this text in Pines, "Political Mythology"; cf. idem, "Imagining the Empire?"

22. See Lewis, *The Construction of Space*.

23. *Xunzi*, "Wang zhi" V.9: 171.

24. For attitudes toward Qin, see Pines, "Biases." Our sources contain only two references to attempts to restore the vanquished states, Zhao and Chu, and the rebellion in the conquered lands of the state of Han (not to be confused with the later Han dynasty). Paleographic sources suggest that small-scale resistance, particularly in the Chu territories, might have continued throughout the Qin era.

25. Modified from Watson, *Records* [Qin], 80–81.

26. For citations from the Qin steles, see Kern, *The Stele Inscriptions*, 14, 21, 32, 39, 49 (I modify Kern's translation). For the Qin marketplace propaganda, see Wang and Cheng, *Qin wenzi*, 63–69; Sanft, "Communication and Cooperation."

27. *Shiji* 6:239; cf. Watson, *Records* [Qin], 44.

28. See Giele, "Signatures," 363–364. Qianling County, from which the unearthed documents come, was inhabited by over 250,000 persons (Zhang Chunlong, "Liye").

29. For the Qin transportation system, see Sanft, "Communication and Cooperation"; for the potentially negative impact of Qin's tightly organized administrative system on the dynasty's viability, see Shelach, "Collapse or Transformation?"

30. For Xiang Yu, see Watson, *Records* [Han], I: 17–48; for the course of the early Han recentralization, see Loewe, "The Former Han Dynasty," 110–152.

31. For the evolution of the system of provincial rule, see Guy, *Qing Governors*, especially pp. 21–46.

32. See details in Wechsler, "T'ai-tsung," 210–212.

33. See details in Twitchett, "Hsüan-tsung," and Graff, *Medieval Chinese Warfare*, 205–226.

34. See Peterson, "Court and Province," for this and the next passage.

35. For financial reforms, see Twitchett, *Financial Administration*; for the Uighur role in the dynasty's survival, see Mackerras, *The Uighur Empire*.

36. Peterson, "Court and Province."

37. See Somers, "The End of the T'ang."

38. See, e.g., Wang Gungwu, *Divided China*, 7–82; Wang shows that even individual prefectures could maintain a high degree of autonomy in the age of Tang's collapse, which suggests much higher degree of disintegration than, e.g., in the Warring States period.

39. For Zhu Wen's career, see ibid., 46–116; for his legitimation efforts, see Fang Cheng-hua, "The Price of Orthodoxy." For general discussions of dynastic legitimacy, see Wechsler, *Offerings*; Chan, *Legitimation*; cf. Rao Zongyi, *Zhongguo shixue shang zhi zhengtong*. It is important to distinguish between what may be dubbed "cultural legitimation," as discussed in these studies, and "practical legitimation," which in the ages of division was attained primarily by those with demonstrable ability to reunify the realm. See more in the text below.

40. For the history of southern regimes in the tenth century, see Clark, "The Southern Kingdoms"; see also Worthy, "Diplomacy for Survival."

41. Standen, *Unbounded Loyalty*, 42. Standen's study focuses primarily on frontier crossing between Northern Chinese regimes and the Khitan Liao state; but her observations are easily applicable to other frontiers as well, and also to other periods of disunion.

42. One of these symbolic demonstrations of one's aspiration to unify the realm was enfeoffing one's relatives and generals with territories that were situated deep within the enemy's jurisdiction. For instance, leaders of southern regimes during ages of disunion routinely appointed princes of Qi, Qin, or Jin, that is, territories in the north. Few modern scholars pay attention to this "symbolic aggression," yet it would be the equivalent of, say, the Russian Federation appointing the governor of Alaska or of Finland. Naturally, these actions—which were fairly common—precluded the possibility of long-term peaceful coexistence among rival regimes.

43. Cited, e.g., in *Mengzi*, "Wan Zhang A" 9.4: 215.

44. See, e.g., an example depicted by David Graff, "Dou Jiande's Dilemma." A similar "unification momentum" was achieved by Li Cunxu of the Later Tang dynasty (r. 923–936) in 923, but, as mentioned above in the text, he failed to capitalize on his initial success, and his realm disintegrated.

45. See Standen, "The Five Dynasties," 112–132; Lau and Huang, "Founding and Consolidation," 206–247. For the Southern Tang regime, see Kurz, "The Yangzi"; Ren Shuang, *Nan Tang*.

46. Ouyang Xiu, *Historical Records*, 62: 504.

47. Mather, *Biography of Lü Kuang*, 25. Charles Holcombe, "The Last Lord of the South," makes a similar observation with regard to elites of southern ("native Chinese") states of the same period: even after the Southern Dynasties had existed independently for two and a half centuries (318–589), "there was surprisingly little evidence of . . . long-term southern separatist sentiment" in the aftermath of the Sui conquest of 589; the southerners acquiesced in the northern triumph with "surprising alacrity" (p. 101).

48. For the early history of the term *jiu zhou* and its geographic scope, see Dorofeeva-Lichtman, "Ritual Practices"; throughout the imperial age this term was occasionally employed to distinguish between China proper and the nomadic realm in the north.

49. For an extreme view of China's supposed "racism," see Dikötter, *The Discourse of Race*, 1–30; for a more balanced approach, see Townsend, "Chinese Nationalism."

50. See Pines, "Beasts or Humans" and "Imagining the Empire?"; Goldin, "Steppe Nomads."

51. For nomads, see Di Cosmo, *Ancient China*. If preimperial thinkers were aware of the existence of other major civilization beyond the East Asian subcontinent, this awareness is not attested to in our sources.

52. Cited with modifications from Kern, *The Stele Inscriptions*, 32–33. Those "whose doors face north" are dwellers in the areas to the south of the Tropic of Cancer, where people reportedly "open their door north to face the sun" (33n76).

53. For the peculiar mind-set of the First Emperor, see Pines, "The Messianic Emperor."

54. For the Great Wall, see Di Cosmo, *Ancient China*, 138–158. I rely heavily on Di Cosmo's analysis of the Xiongnu interaction with the Qin and Han empires.

55. For the nomads and their long-term interaction with China, see, e.g., ibid.;

Barfield, *The Perilous Frontier*; Jagchid and Symons, *Peace, War, and Trade*. For a broader perspective, see Khazanov, *Nomads and the Outside World*.

56. *Han shu*, 48: 2240.

57. See details in Di Cosmo, *Ancient China*, 190–206.

58. For the *Gongyang zhuan*, see Gentz, *Das Gongyang zhuan*; for its impact on Emperor Wu's policy, see Chen Suzhen, *Handai zhengzhi*, especially pp. 222–246. The *Gongyang zhuan* explicitly identifies progressive expansion into the alien periphery as the proper task of the True Monarch. See *Chunqiu Gongyang*, Cheng 15, 18: 2297; cf. Xi 4, 10: 2249; and Pines, "Imagining the Empire?" 79–81.

59. On Han foreign relations, see Yü Ying-shih, "Han Foreign Relations," especially pp. 381–383 on the "tribute system." The nature of this system and its usefulness as an analytical tool in the understanding of China's foreign relations is subject to continuous dispute, which cannot be adequately dealt with here. For the classical presentation of the system, see Fairbank, "A Preliminary Framework"; cf. Rossabi, "Introduction."

60. For the Southern Tang courtiers' self-congratulatory rhetoric following the arrival of the Khitan "tribute" (actually trade) mission, see Ren Shuang, *Nan Tang*, 108; for the importance of the tribute rhetoric for masking the dynasty's weakness vis-à-vis foreign polities, see Wang Gungwu, "The Rhetoric of a Lesser Empire."

61. Wang Gungwu, "The Rhetoric of a Lesser Empire."

62. See Goncharov, *Kitajskaia Srednevekovaia Diplomatiia*.

63. *Qing Shizong shilu*, 83, cited from Liu Zehua, *Zhongguo de Wangquanzhuyi*, 19. For the context of the controversy that spurred the emperor's statement, see Spence, *Treason by the Book*, 116–134.

64. For fluctuations in Yongzheng's foreign policy, see Dai, *The Sichuan Frontier*, 92–100.

65. For the Qianlong Emperor's polemic with his critics, see Millward, *Beyond the Pass*, 20–43, especially 38–40. Millward illustrates there how in the process of the Qing territorial expansion the borders between "internal" and "external" realms were continuously redrawn. For more about the Qing expansion policy, see Perdue, *China Marches West*; Dai, *The Sichuan Frontier*.

66. See Honey, "Stripping Off Felt and Fur."

67. See Golden, "Imperial Ideology"; Di Cosmo, "State Formation," especially p. 20; Biran and Amitai, "Introduction." For the evolution of the nomads' political ideology in the aftermath of Chinggis Khan (ca. 1162–1227), see Elverskog, *Our Great Qing*, 14–62.

68. For the military history of that age, see Graff, *Medieval Chinese Warfare*, 54–120; for Fu Jian's reign, see Fang Xuanling, *The Chronicle of Fu Chien*; for more details, see Wang Zhongluo, *Wei Jin*.

69. For the complexity of Liao relations with the North China political and military leaders, and for its occupation and subsequent abandonment of Kaifeng, see Standen, "What Nomads Want."

70. See Tao Jing-shen, *Two Sons of Heaven*. For a detailed account of Liao history, see Twitchett and Tietze, "The Liao."

71. For the impact of the Xi Xia on Song-Liao relations, and for Song at-

tempts to avoid recognition of the Tangut leader as yet another emperor, see Tao Jing-shen, *Two Sons of Heaven*.

72. For the recognition of Liao's exceptionality, see Tao Jing-shen, "Barbarians or Northerners"; for the bifurcation between rhetoric and reality, see Wang Gungwu, "The Rhetoric of a Lesser Empire."

73. For these essays, see, respectively, *Zizhi tongjian* 69: 2187; Ouyang Xiu, *Zhengtong lun*. See discussion in Pines, "Name or Substance?"; cf. Rao Zongyi, *Zhongguo shixue shang zhi zhengtong*.

74. For "irredentism" as a prime mover of late Northern Song politics, see Smith, "Irredentism as Political Capital," and idem, "Shen-Tsung's Reign." For Huizong's disastrous foreign policy, see Goncharov, *Kitajskaia Srednevekovaia Diplomatiia*.

75. For the end of the Song resistance, see Davis, *Wind against the Mountain*.

76. See Biran, *Chinggis Khan*, 137–162.

77. The importance of the concept of unification in Mongol propaganda and in their legacy is discussed by Timothy Brook in "Unification as a Political Ideal." Brook even opines that the very notion of Great Unity originated with the Mongols.

78. See, e.g., Duara, "Provincial Narratives," 184; Schafer, "The Yeh Chung chi," 148.

79. De Crespigny, *Generals of the South*, 512.

80. *Song shu*, 95: 2359; the last sentence refers to the *Laozi*'s political idyll (*Boshu Laozi* 80: 150–155).

CHAPTER 2
THE MONARCH

1. Thus Liu Zehua, the leading scholar of Chinese political culture, summarized his lifetime of research in a book titled *China's Monarchism* (*Zhongguo de Wangquanzhuyi*); see also note 3 below.

2. For aspects of the emperor's ritual and symbolic supremacy, see, e.g., Wechsler, *Offerings*; Rawski, *The Late Emperors*; McDermott, *State and Court Ritual*. For the emperor's "presence" at lower social levels, see, e.g., Faure, "The Emperor in the Village."

3. There is as yet no comprehensive discussion in English of China's emperorship; yet there are many insightful studies of individual monarchs, especially from the late imperial period. The most notable of these, in my eyes, is Huang, *1587*; see also Ebrey and Bickford, *Emperor Huizong*; Dardess, *Confucianism and Autocracy*; Farmer, *Zhu Yuanzhang*; Schneewind, *Long Live the Emperor*. In China, by contrast, the nature of emperorship is comprehensively treated in manifold monographs and articles, of which I am most indebted to Liu Zehua's *Zhongguo de Wangquanzhuyi*; see also Zhang Fentian, *Zhongguo diwang guannian*; Zhou Liangxiao, *Huangdi*; Wang Yi, *Zhongguo huangquan zhidu*.

4. For Montesquieu, see his *The Spirits of the Laws*, bk. 2, chap. 1 (cited from Richter, *The Political Theory of Montesquieu*). For the assault on monarchism in early Chinese republican thought, see Liang Qichao, "Zhongguo zhuanzhi."

5. For the Shang political system, see Keightley, "The Shang."

6. See Zhang Rongming, *Yin Zhou*; cf. Bilsky, *The State Religion*.

7. *Chunqiu Zuo zhuan*, Xiang 26: 1112. For more on the weakness of rulers in the Springs-and-Autumns period, see Pines, *Foundations*, 136–163.

8. See Lewis, "Warring States," 597. For the importance of the Jin successor states in fostering political reforms, see ibid., 598–600.

9. See, e.g., Lewis, "Warring States."

10. For a detailed discussion, see Pines, *Envisioning Eternal Empire*, 25–53.

11. *Lüshi chunqiu*, "Zhi yi" 17.8: 1132. See also *Guanzi*, "Qi chen qi zhu" XVII.52: 998–999; *Xunzi*, "Wang ba" VII.11: 223–224; *Han Feizi*, "Er bing" II.7:39–43.

12. For views of rulership during the imperial millennia, see Liu Zehua, *Zhongguo zhengzhi sixiang shi*, vols. 2–3 (specifically for Deng Mu and Huang Zongxi, see 3: 412–416 and 600–618). For Huang Zongxi, see also de Bary, *Waiting for the Dawn*; cf. Jiang Yonglin, "Denouncing."

13. See Pines, "To Rebel Is Justified?"

14. For attempts to establish an alternative to the dynastic principle of rule and their fiasco, see Pines, *Envisioning Eternal Empire*, 54–81.

15. Puett, *To Become a God*.

16. See *Mengzi*, "Gongsun Chou xia" 4.13: 109.

17. *Xunzi*, "Zheng lun" XII.18: 331.

18. See, e.g., *Xunzi*, "Fu guo" VI.10: 182–183; "Zheng ming" XVI.22: 431; and the detailed discussion in Pines, *Envisioning Eternal Empire*, 86–90.

19. *Xunzi*, "Wang ba" VII.11: 223–224.

20. See discussion in Pines, *Envisioning Eternal Empire*, 90–96.

21. De Bary, *Waiting for the Dawn*, 100–103. Interestingly, similar views were expressed even by an early modern critic of monarchical abuses, Liang Qichao ("Zhongguo zhuanzhi," 1662–1667).

22. For Han Feizi's complex views of rulership, see Pines, *Envisioning Eternal Empire*, 97–102, and idem, "Submerged by Absolute Power."

23. See details in Pines, "The Messianic Emperor."

24. Citations are from the First Emperor's stele inscriptions (Kern, *The Stele Inscriptions*, 33, 22, 36, 28, 33, and 42); see more in Pines, "The Messianic Emperor."

25. An anecdote describes the emperor examining daily the documents he dealt with, and not going to rest until a certain weight was reached (*Shiji* 6: 258).

26. This change in the monarch's self-presentation emerged in the early Han dynasty, in the immediate aftermath of the fall of Qin (Pines, "The Messianic Emperor").

27. The predominantly negative image of Qin through much of imperial history (Pines, "The First Emperor") encouraged many critics of dynastic rule, such as Deng Mu and Huang Zongxi (see note 12 above), to identify it as the progenitor of all abuses perpetrated by the imperial system. Yet even admirers of this system, such as Wang Fuzhi (*Du Tongjian* 1: 1–3), credited the Qin with its establishment.

28. Montesquieu, *The Spirits of the Laws*, bk. 2, chap. 1, cited from Richter, *The Political Theory of Montesquieu*, 178.

29. Huang, *1587*, 46.

30. *Zizhi tongjian* 1: 2–3. For Sima Guang's political views, see Bol, "Government, Society and State."

31. These cases of the emperors' "unorthodox" self-divinization could derive from their personal predilections (e.g., Chao Shin-yi, "Huizong"), or from political expediency (Crossley, *A Translucent Mirror*, 223–280), or from the combination of the two (Janousch, "The Emperor as Bodhisattva").

32. McDermott, "Emperor, Élites and Commoners."

33. For massive loyalist suicides, see, e.g., Davis, *Wind against the Mountain*; Wakeman, *The Great Enterprise*. Such instances of extreme zeal were rare in Chinese established religions, and were associated either with sectarians (see chapter 5) or with segments of the Buddhist establishment (Benn, *Burning for the Buddha*).

34. Patricia Ebrey notes that "the relative rarity of reverencing likenesses of rulers makes China stand out among the early civilizations of Eurasia" ("Portrait Sculptures," 46n13). While imperial portraits were produced, their circulation generally remained limited to members of the upper elite; in the Ming dynasty "it was made illegal to make or possess an image of a ruler or former rulers, apparently out of fear that it would be used for anti-dynastic ends" (46n13); cf. Ching, "Visual Images."

35. For the "ten abominations," see Jiang Yonglin, *The Great Ming Code*, 18–19; for an example of the sacred power of an edict sealed by the emperor, see, e.g., Holmgren, "Politics of the Inner Court," 300.

36. *A Dream of Red Mansions* 18: 255.

37. For the example of the Eastern Jin dynasty (318–420), see Holcombe, "The Exemplar State"; cf. the trajectory of the Tang dynasty in the aftermath of An Lushan's rebellion, discussed in chapter 1. For "loyal criticism" and its perils, see Zhang Xiangming, "A Preliminary Study of the Punishment of Political Speech."

38. See Goodrich, *The Literary Inquisition*; Guy, *The Emperor's Four Treasuries*, 157–200; Kutcher, "The Death of the Xiaoxian Empress"; Elman, *Cultural History*, 211–212; Wu Fusheng, *Written at Imperial Command*, 14.

39. The earliest attempts to reshape the popular pantheon are traceable to the First Emperor of Qin, and they were repeated by many other rulers, albeit with limited success. See Bujard, "State and Local Cults," for the early imperial period, and Taylor, "Official and Popular Religion," for the later one.

40. See, e.g., Weinstein, *Buddhism under the Tang*; Brook, "At the Margin"; Martynov, "Gosudarstvo i religii." For Liang Emperor Wu's example, see Janousch, "The Emperor as Bodhisattva."

41. See Weinstein, *Buddhism under the Tang*, 114–136, for a detailed account of this event.

42. For the Byzantine case, see Gregory, *A History of Byzantium*, 198–241.

43. For Huan Xuan's initiative and the resultant exchange, see Zürcher, *The Buddhist Conquest of China*, 231–259; cf. Komissarova, "Monakh."

44. *Mao shi zhengyi*, "Bei shan" 13: 463 (Mao 205); cf. Waley, *The Book of Songs*, 189.

45. For private ownership of land as recognized de facto, even if not de jure, see Philip Huang, *Civil Justice*.

46. See the detailed discussion of Northern Wei reforms in Wang Zhongluo, *Wei Jin*, 522–557; for certain aspects of these reforms, see Chase, "The Edict of 495 Reconsidered."

47. For Huang Zongxi and Gu Yanwu, see Liu Zehua, *Zhongguo zhengzhi sixiang shi*, 3: 600–630, and note 12 above; for Liang Qichao, see his "Zhongguo zhuanzhi"; for a classical exposition of the "descent into despotism" thesis, see Mote, "The Growth of Chinese Despotism." For negative comments, see, e.g., Endicott-West, "Imperial Governance"; Bol, *Neo-Confucianism*, 115–152. For Chinese scholars who adopt this thesis, see, e.g., Wang Yi, *Zhongguo huangquan zhidu*; Zhou Liangxiao, *Huangdi*.

48. Ray Huang's *1587* is a classical exposition of the weakness of the throne vis-à-vis powerful bureaucracy.

49. Rawski, *The Last Emperors*, 212–213.

50. Farmer, *Zhu Yuanzhang*, 105; for Huang Zongxi, see de Bary, *Waiting for the Dawn*, 100–103.

51. The Sui Emperor Wen (r. 581–604), initiated a series of administrative reforms amid which the position of a "prime minister" had been abolished, and his functions divided among a group of chief ministers (Xiong, *Emperor Yang*, 109–110). This system continued into the early Tang, when there was no single chief minister but rather a group of ad hoc appointees to chief ministerial positions; only gradually did the position of these ministers strengthen and domineering chief ministers evolve in the court (see Twitchett, "Hsüan-tsung," 349–350; Dalby, "Court Politics," 590–591). For the early Song concentration of executive powers in the emperor's hands and the absence of the prime minister office, see Lau and Huang, "Founding and Consolidation," 239–240.

52. Cited from Spence, *Emperor of China*, 146–147. For the complaint of Kangxi's son, the Yongzheng Emperor, that in order to make a proper appointment he "often goes without sleep all night," see Zelin, "The Yung-cheng Reign," 195.

53. Robinson, "The Ming Court and the Legacy of the Yuan Mongols," 400; for the classical study of the disempowerment of the emperors in the late Ming dynasty, see Huang, *1587*.

54. *The August Ming Ancestral Instruction*, cited from Farmer, *Zhu Yuanzhang*, 117.

55. For training of the heir apparent, see, e.g., Twitchett, "The T'ang Imperial Family"; cf. Huang, *1587*.

56. For Taizong's career, see Eisenberg, *Kingship*, 167–194.

57. See *Xunzi*, "Zheng lun" XII.18: 333. For the contraction of the emperors' ritual space from the beginning to the end of the Han dynasty, see Lewis, *The Construction of Space*, 169–186, and Puett, "Combining the Ghosts"; for later trends, see Chang, *A Court on Horseback*, 34–113, 423–438.

58. For the gradual deterioration of the ministers' status vis-à-vis the throne, see Du Jiaji, "Zhongguo gudai junchen"; for its harshest manifestation—public flogging of court officials—which proliferated beginning in the Jin (1115–1234) and Yuan (1271–1368) dynasties, see Endicott-West, "Imperial Governance."

59. See Fletcher, "Turco-Mongolian Monarchic Tradition"; Biran, *Chinggis Khan*. In my discussion here I do not distinguish between pure nomadic regimes (e.g., the Mongols) and the seminomadic ones (e.g., the Manchus), because both shared the same fundamental traits of a tribal and military-oriented political culture. For different assessments of the importance of these differences, see Barfield, *The Perilous Frontier*; cf. Franke and Twitchett, "Introduction," especially pp. 21–30.

60. It is not my intention here to deal with the much-debated issue of cultural aspects of the "Sinicization" of China's conquerors; generally, I share misgivings about this term as expressed, e.g., in Elliott, *The Manchu Way*, 20–35. What really matters for me is the process of the conqueror's political adaptation to the norms of a sedentary (in this case, Chinese) world—particularly modification of the form of rulership.

61. For the *qurlitai* in Mongol political culture and its gradual fading away under Khubilai, see Endicott-West, "Imperial Governance."

62. For Khubilai Khan, see Rossabi, *Khubilai*; for subsequent Mongol history, see Dardess, *Conquerors and Confucians*. David Robinson (*Empire's Twilight*, 18–21) questions the widespread denigration of Toghon Temür as a weakling but fails to produce compelling evidence to overturn the negative verdict. For the Qianlong Emperor's indignation with regard to Toghon Temür's loss of nomadic prowess, see Chang, *A Court on Horseback*, 108–111.

63. See Dardess, *Confucianism and Autocracy*, 186.

64. For the power of pre-1800 Qing emperors, see, e.g., Rawski, *The Last Emperors* (especially pp. 206–207); Chang, *A Court on Horseback*; Spence, "The Kang-hsi Reign." For the Yongzheng reign, see Zelin, "The Yung-cheng Reign," and idem, *The Magistrate's Tael*; Bartlett, *Monarchs and Ministers*; Spence, *Treason by the Book*. For the Qing territorial expansion see chapter 1, note 65.

65. For the first of these instances, see Fisher, *The Chosen One*; for the second, Huang, *1587*.

66. For the struggle of one of the Ming emperors, Wuzong (r. 1505–1521), to preserve his individuality and "construct a portfolio of identities in harmony more with his vision of imperial rule rather than with the models advanced by the civil bureaucracy," see Robinson, "The Ming Court and the Legacy of the Yuan Mongols," 405; cf. Ray Huang, *1587*, 95–102.

67. See, respectively, Goncharov, *Kitajskaia Srednevekovaia Diplomatiia*; Wakeman, *The Great Enterprise*; idem, *The Fall of Imperial China*.

68. To explain "even": in the eyes of the Chinese literati a female presence in the public realm, especially in the capacity of a ruler, was absolutely intolerable.

69. See Holmgren, "Seeds of Madness."

CHAPTER 3
THE LITERATI

1. Fan Zhongyan, "Yueyang Lou ji," in *Fan Zhongyan quanji*, 168–169. For Fan Zhongyan's career and thought, see James T. C. Liu, "An Early Sung Reformer"; Bol, *"This Culture,"* 166–175.

2. See, for instance, Yu Yingshi, *Shi yu Zhongguo wenhua*, 1–3; cf. Wakeman, "The Price of Autonomy," 137–138. Many studies analyze what it meant to be a *shi* at different stages of China's history: see, e.g., Pines, *Envisioning Eternal Empire*, 115–135; Ebrey, "Toward a Better Understanding"; Bol, *"This Culture."*

3. My discussion in this chapter is greatly indebted to several major Chinese studies, most notably Liu Zehua, *Xian Qin shi ren yu shehui*; Yu Yingshi, *Shi yu Zhongguo wenhua*; Ge Quan, *Quanli zaizhi lixing*. See also Yan Buke, *Shidafu zhengzhi yansheng shi*.

4. My discussion in this and the next section is based overwhelmingly on Pines, *Envisioning Eternal Empire*, 115–186. For alternative views, see, e.g., Hsu, *Ancient China*; Lewis, *Writing and Authority*, 53–97.

5. See Pines, *Envisioning Eternal Empire*, 119–121.

6. See more in ibid., 115–135.

7. See, e.g., *Lunyu* "Wei zheng" 2.14: 17; "Zilu" 13.23: 141; 13.25–26: 143.

8. *Lunyu*, "Xian wen" 14.42: 159.

9. See Pines, *Envisioning Eternal Empire*, 123–131.

10. See Pines, *Foundations*.

11. Pines, *Envisioning Eternal Empire*, 123–131.

12. *Lüshi chunqiu*, "Shi jie" 12.2: 622–623.

13. The citations are, respectively, from the *Lüshi chunqiu*, "Bo zhi" 24.5: 1618, and *Zhanguo ce*, "Qin ce 1" 3.2: 75.

14. *Lunyu*, "Yang Huo" 17.5: 182.

15. See, respectively, *Mengzi*, "Teng Wen Gong xia" 6.3: 142–143; "Li Lou shang" 7.20: 180; "Gaozi xia" 12.7: 287; "Li Lou shang" 7.14: 175; "Liang Hui Wang shang" 1.6: 12–13. See more in Pines, *Envisioning Eternal Empire*, 147–150.

16. See Pines, "Friends or Foes."

17. *Xunzi*, "Chen Dao" IX.13: 249.

18. *Xunzi*, "Chen Dao" IX. 13: 250.

19. See Pines, "Friends or Foes." The market simile for the relations of the *shi* with the rulers is not exclusively modern; it was employed by an astute contemporaneous observer, Han Feizi (*Han Feizi*, "Nan yi" XV.36: 352).

20. *Mengzi*, "Liang Hui Wang B" 2.6: 40.

21. See Pines, "From Teachers to Subjects."

22. *Xunzi*, "Fei shi'er zi" III.6: 98.

23. *Han Feizi*, "Wu du" XIX.49: 452.

24. *Shiji* 6: 255, modifying Watson, *Records* [Qin], 56.

25. Watson, *Records* [Qin], 56; see also discussion in Petersen, "Which Books."

26. For Liu An's activities, see Vankeerberghen, *The Huainanzi*.

27. *Han shu* 56: 2523.

28. See Lewis, *Writing and Authority*, 337–362.

29. For the concept of the "victory of Confucianism," see, e.g., Yao, *The Introduction to Confucianism*, 81–83; for the syncretism of Han thought, see, e.g., Nylan, "A Problematic Model"; for the elevation of Confucius after Emperor Wu's reign, see Liu Zehua, *Zhongguo zhengzhi sixiang shi*, 2: 134–142.

30. The major "Confucian" text from which Emperor Wu drew inspiration, the *Gongyang zhuan*, is of disputed relation to the mainstream legacy of Confucius and his disciples. See more in chapter 1, note 58.

31. *Shiji* 47: 1947.

32. For criticism of Emperor Wu and indirect comparison of his policies to those of the First Emperor, see van Ess, "Emperor Wu"; cf. Declerq, *Writing against the State*, 20–38. This criticism notwithstanding, Emperor Wu's treatment by subsequent historians was incomparably milder than that of the First Emperor.

33. See Goodrich, *The Literary Inquisition*; Guy, *The Emperor's Four Treasuries*; cf. Brook, "State Censorship."

34. For the most powerful presentation of this point, see Ge Quan, *Quanli zaizhi lixing*.

35. See, e.g., Farmer, *Zhu Yuanzhang*.

36. For an example of such active imperial support for a single ideological current, see Smith, "Shen-Tsung's Reign."

37. See Elman, *Cultural History*, 78–105.

38. For Han Yu's views and career, see Hartman, *Han Yü*; the citations are from his most famous essay, "On the Origins of the True Way" (*Yuan Dao*) (*Han Changli*, 13–19).

39. For printing, see Brook, "State Censorship." For academies, see Walton, *Academies and Society*; Meskill, *Academies in Ming China*.

40. See Elman, *Cultural History*, 173–238ff.

41. See Bol, *"This Culture,"* 48–58.

42. See Levine, *Divided by a Common Language*.

43. Cited from Chafee, *The Thorny Gates*, 79. All the tabooed phrases are closely associated with views of Wang Anshi's opponents.

44. See Bol, "Examination and Orthodoxies"; idem, *Neo-Confucianism*; see also James T. C. Liu, *China Turns Inward*. For the attempt to persecute "Neo-Confucians," see Schirokauer, "Neo-Confucians under Attack."

45. Brook, "State Censorship."

46. These are the words of the eminent historian Sima Qian (ca. 145–90 BCE) (*Han shu*, 62: 2732); see also an excellent discussion in Declercq, *Writing against the State*, 21–38 and passim. For earlier examples, see Sima Qian's "Biographies of Confucian Scholars" (*Shiji* 121: 3115–3129).

47. *Zizhi tongjian* 19: 638; cited from Wu Fusheng, *Written at Imperial Command*, 14.

48. *Lunyu*, "Wei zheng" 2.12: 17.

49. These long-term patterns are summarized by Du Jiaji, "Zhongguo gudai

junchen." See also Liu Zehua, *Zhongguo de Wangquanzhuyi*, 263–279; Ge Quan, *Quanli zaizhi lixing*, passim.

50. Liu Zehua, *Zhongguo de Wangquanzhuyi*, 175–181 and passim.

51. See details in Berkowitz, *Patterns of Disengagement*; Declercq, *Writing against the State*. For the background of the idea of disengagement, see Vervoorn, *Men of the Cliffs*.

52. Citations from the accounts concerning recluses in the *New Tang History* (*Xin Tang shu*), cited from Wong, "On the Reclusion," 148–149.

53. To illustrate this point, suffice it to adduce the case of a lofty recluse, Fan Ying, who finally heeded the summons of Han Emperor Shun (r. 125–144), but even in the court behaved haughtily and provocatively. Emperor Shun, nonetheless, "respected [Fan's] reputation" and continued to treat him courteously despite Fan's affronts (*Hou Han shu* 82: 2723). By contrast, the Xiongnu emperor of the Xia dynasty, Helian Bobo (381–425, r. 407–425), was appalled by the too-swift positive response of a famous recluse, Wei Xuan, to Helian's summons and had Wei executed (see Berkowitz, *Patterns of Disengagement*, 134).

54. The major exception to this rule was shunning the office out of loyalty to the fallen dynasty—a matter of far-reaching consequences in the ages of dynastic change (e.g., Mote, "Confucian Eremitism").

55. Saying by Ming Shizong, cited from Chu, "The Jiajing Emperor's Interaction," 222; cf. Huang, *1587*, 223–225.

56. Huang, *1587*, 135; the entire Hai Rui story is told on pp. 130–155.

57. For Shizong's career, see Fisher, *The Chosen One*; Geiss, "The Chia-ching Reign."

58. For "commemorative immortality," see Pines, "Chinese History-Writing," 335–340. For an example of the ups and downs of an official's reputation during his life and after his martyrdom, see Hammond, *Pepper Mountain*.

59. For details, see Dardess, *Blood and History*; cf. Wakeman, "The Price of Autonomy."

60. Huang, *1587*, 136.

61. The dramatic power the Hai Rui affair resurfaced in the late 1950s when this model remonstrator became associated with loyal critics of Mao Zedong. See Wagner, "In Guise."

62. For Zhu Xi's view of the rulers, see, e.g., Huang, "Imperial Rulership"; for his quest for an enlightened monarch, see Yu Yingshi, *Zhu Xi*, 13–15 and passim. For Huang Zongxi, see de Bary, *Waiting for the Dawn*, 92 (translation modified).

63. This point is powerfully made by Eisenstadt in his "Frederic Wakeman's Oeuvre."

64. For a marked example to the contrary, see Levine, *Divided by a Common Language*.

CHAPTER 4
LOCAL ELITE

1. Many insightful studies have been published in recent decades on the nature of Chinese local elites and their interaction with the imperial state. See, espe-

cially, essay collections edited by Dien (*State and Society*) for the early imperial period; by Hymes and Schirokauer (*Ordering the World*) for the Song dynasty; and by Rankin and Esherick (*Chinese Local Elites*) for the late imperial period. For monographs, see references below.

2. See Esherick and Rankin, "Introduction," and Rankin and Esherick, "Concluding Remarks," for further elaboration and criticism of previous scholarship.

3. Wittfogel, *Oriental Despotism*.

4. Hobsbawm, *Nations and Nationalism*, 80.

5. For details of Qin's policies, see Pines et al., "General Introduction."

6. For socioeconomic functions of the preimperial state, see, e.g., Liu Zehua, *Zhongguo de Wangquanzhuyi*, 19–42. For the economic dependence of the *shi* on the power-holders, see Pines, *Envisioning Eternal Empire*, 136–140. For the role of village elders in preimperial and early imperial society, and Qin's attempt to co-opt them into its administrative apparatus, see insightful observations by Perelomov, *Imperiia Tsin'*; cf. Bu Xianqun, "Cong jiandu kan."

7. See Loewe, "The Former Han Dynasty," 110–153, for further details.

8. See discussion in Mao Han-kuang, "The Evolution"; Cui Xiangdong, *Han dai haozu*.

9. These policies are summarized by Sima Qian in chapter 30 of the *Shiji* (Watson, *Records* [Han] II: 61–85).

10. See details in Loewe, *Crisis and Conflict*.

11. These discussions are presented (not necessarily in their original form) in *Yantie lun*; see Gale, *Discourses*.

12. For a somewhat apologetic account of Wang Mang's reign, see Bielenstein, "Wang Mang."

13. See Ebrey, "The Economic and Social History of Later Han"; for the abolition of mass conscription in the Han dynasty, see Lewis, "The Han Abolition."

14. See Ebrey, "The Economic and Social History of Later Han." For the Han taxation system as benefiting large estates, see Mao Han-kuang, "The Evolution," 74–75.

15. See Graffin, "Reinventing China," 145–155, for the function of the new system.

16. For aspects of the systemic difficulties faced by the southern dynasties in that era, see Holcombe, *In the Shadow*, 34–72; Graff, *Medieval Chinese Warfare*, 76–96; Crowell, "Northern Émigrés."

17. For the equal field system, see Wang Zhongluo, *Wei Jin*, 522–538; for militia, see Graff, *Medieval Chinese Warfare*, 109–111.

18. For the Tang recruitment system, see Herbert, *Examine the Honest*.

19. See Johnson, *The Medieval Chinese Oligarchy*; Bol, *"This Culture,"* 36–48; Tackett, "Great Clansmen."

20. The precise nature of the processes that hastened the demise of the old aristocratic oligarchy and changed the composition of the elite during the Tang-Song interregnum is still debatable. For a recent attempt to readdress it, see Tackett, "The Transformation."

21. See Bol, *"This Culture,"* 48–58.

22. For the manifold aspects of the examination system and its cultural im-

pact, see Elman, *Cultural History*; see also Chafee, *The Thorny Gates*, for the Song dynasty.

23. See Chafee, *The Thorny Gates*; Bol, *"This Culture,"* 48–58 and 148ff.

24. For ideological trends of the Song period, see Hymes and Schirokauer, *Ordering the World*.

25. Bol, *Neo-Confucianism*, 218–269.

26. My discussion of Wang Anshi is based on Bol, "Government, Society and State"; Smith, "State Power and Economic Activism"; idem, "Shen-Tsung's Reign."

27. Smith, "State Power and Economic Activism," 85.

28. For the *baojia* system, see Smith, "Shen-Tsung's Reign," 407–414.

29. See Bol, "Government, Society and State."

30. See ibid.

31. For political collisions around the New Policies, see Levine, *Divided by a Common Language*.

32. See James T. C. Liu, *China Turns Inward*, 63–67.

33. For various aspects of these processes, see Schirokauer and Hymes, "Introduction"; Hymes, *Statesmen and Gentlemen*; James T. C. Liu, *China Turns Inward*.

34. See the summary in Bol, *Neo-Confucianism*, 246–253.

35. For Buddhist antecedents of Zhu Xi's activism, see, e.g., Glahn, "Community and Welfare"; for the lineage activities under the Song, see Ebrey, "The Early Stages."

36. See Dardess, "Confucianism," and Rowe, *Crimson Rain*, 85–90. It is worth noting that in both cases redistribution of the tax burden did not aim at increasing the state's revenues but rather at avoiding a potentially explosive situation resulting from unequal distribution of the burden within the community.

37. See discussion in Esherick and Rankin, "Introduction," 5–9; cf. Hejidra, "The Socio-economic Development," 552–564.

38. See Chü, *Local Government*, 14–35ff.

39. See ibid., 36–55; Reed, *Talons and Teeth*; Rowe, *Saving the World*, 339–344.

40. See Rankin and Esherick, "Concluding Remarks," 322–324.

41. For the complexity of these issues, see Rowe, *Saving the World*, 363–405. For the lineage organization in late imperial China, see Ebrey, "The Early Stages," and studies in Ebrey and Watson, *Kinship Organization*.

42. The examples are scattered through Rowe, *Crimson Rain*, and idem, *Saving the World*; Hejidra, "The Socio-economic Development"; Perdue, *Exhausting the Earth*; Huang, *Civil Justice*. The tension between the "orthodox" status of the lineage organization and disruptive lineage practices is insightfully discussed in Lamley, "Lineage and Surname Feuds."

43. For Hai Rui's case, see Huang, *1587*, 130–155.

44. Cited from Crawford, "Eunuch Power," 118.

45. For discussions of Zhu Yuanzhang's personality and his policies, see, e.g., Mote, *Imperial China*, 517–582; Dardess, *Confucianism and Autocracy*, 183–

254; Langlois, "The Hung-wu Reign"; Farmer, *Zhu Yuanzhang*; Jiang Yonglin, "In the Name of 'Taizu.'"

46. For this comparison, see Andrew and Rapp, *Autocracy*; for the shifting perspectives on Zhu Yuanzhang, see Schneewind, *Long Live the Emperor*; cf. Jiang Yonglin, "In the Name of 'Taizu.'"

47. Rowe notes that "much of the lineage elite that dominated the entire Middle and Lower Yangzi regions over the late-imperial and Republican eras was a systematic creation of the Hongwu [i.e., Zhu Yuanzhang's] reign" (*Crimson Rain*, 66). Surely, many elite lineages perished during the prolonged uprisings that marred the last decades of Yuan rule; but it seems that Zhu Yuanzhang's purges were an equally important factor behind the overhaul in the composition of the elite in the early Ming.

48. Bol, *Neo-Confucianism*, 256–261. My discussion of Zhu Yuanzhang's policies is based on Schneewind, "Visions and Revisions."

49. See Hejidra, "The Socio-economic Development," 552–575.

50. See, e.g., Bol, *Neo-Confucianism*, 261–269; see also discussion in the next section below in the text.

51. For the tense relations between the Manchu conquerors and Chinese local elites, especially in the prosperous Lower Yangzi area, see Wakeman, *The Great Enterprise*; for the Yongzheng Emperor's experiments, see Zelin, "The Yungcheng Reign," and idem, *The Magistrate's Tael*.

52. For an insightful, even if partly outdated, study of Chinese local society in the nineteenth century, see Hsiao, *Rural China*.

53. This issue is dealt extensively in Rowe, *Saving the World*, 326–405.

54. See Pines, *Foundations*, 187–199.

55. See *Lunyu*, "Xue er" 1.2: 2.

56. See *Han Feizi*, "Wu du" 49: 445.

57. See Liu Kwang-Ching, "Socioethics as Orthodoxy," and other studies in idem, ed., *Orthodoxy in Late Imperial China*.

58. See Liu Kwang-Ching, "Introduction" and "Socioethics as Orthodoxy."

59. Keith Knapp identifies a correlation between the consolidation of elite lineages in the Later Han dynasty (25–220) and in its aftermath, and the parallel strengthening of family-oriented morality (*Selfless Offspring*, 13–26). A similar process recurred with the renewed proliferation of the lineage organization in the Song dynasty and thereafter (Ebrey, "The Early Stages"). In both cases, and particularly in the latter, the government was enthusiastic in promoting kinship values (see, e.g., Elvin, "Female Virtue").

60. For the latter, see Rowe, *Saving the World*, 397.

61. See details in Ebrey, "The Early Stages," 30, 42.

62. See Elvin, "Female Virtue."

63. For problems connected with this policy and its modification under the Qing, see Kutcher, *Mourning in Late Imperial China*; see also Huang, *1587*, 21–26, for the crisis around the mourning leave of the all-important imperial secretary, Zhang Juzheng.

64. Farmer, *Zhu Yuanzhang*, 202.

65. For the Qing edict's text and the history of its dissemination, see Mair, "Language and Ideology" (translation on pp. 325–326).

66. McDermott, "Emperor, Élites and Commoners."

67. For an example of the elites' mobilization for the dynasty's cause, see Kuhn, *Rebellion and Its Enemies.*

68. Rankin and Esherick, "Concluding Remarks," 338.

69. See, e.g., Perdue, *Exhausting the Earth*; Will and Bin Wong, *Nourish the People*; Will, *Bureaucracy and Famine.*

70. Huang, "The Ming Fiscal Administration," 111.

71. See Eisenstadt, "Multiple Modernities," for the latter point.

72. See Huang, "The Ming Fiscal Administration," for the lasting impact of Zhu Yuanzhang's model. For the Kangxi Emperor's preference for fiscal "leniency" even at the expense of government revenues, see Zelin, *The Magistrate's Tael*, 21–24.

CHAPTER 5
THE PEOPLE

1. See Meadows, *The Chinese and their Rebellions*, pp. 23, 24, 401–403; italics in original.

2. See Kuhn, *Rebellion and Its Enemies*; for the "orthodoxy-heterodoxy" juxtaposition, see the two volumes edited by Liu Kwang-Ching: *Orthodoxy in Late Imperial China* and (Liu and Shek) *Heterodoxy in Late Imperial China*; see, in particular, Liu's and Shek's "Introduction" to the latter volume.

3. The class character of popular rebellions (which are often dubbed in Marxist parlance "peasant wars," echoing Friedrich Engels's *The Peasant War in Germany*), was systematically studied by Soviet and Chinese scholars. For a summary of Chinese views, see Cen and Liu, *Zhongguo nongmin zhanzheng*; for Soviet studies, see, e.g., Smolin, "Problemy." For a recent inspiring discussion of the rebellions' class nature, see Rowe, *Crimson Rain*, especially pp. 53–59.

4. The discussion in this section is largely based on Pines, *Envisioning Eternal Empire*, 187–218; see also Zhang Fentian, *Min ben sixiang*; Sanft, "Communication and Cooperation."

5. Both citations are from the now lost "Tai shi" (Great Pledge) document, allegedly composed on the eve of the overthrow of the Shang (it should be distinguished from the eponymous forged chapter in the current collection of the *Book of Documents*). See *Mengzi*, "Wan Zhang A" 9.5: 219; and *Chunqiu Zuo zhuan*, Xiang 31: 1184.

6. See Pines, *Envisioning Eternal Empire*, 190–191.

7. See Lewis, *The Construction of Space*, 136–150; cf. Pines, "Bodies," 174–181.

8. See details in Pines, *Envisioning Eternal Empire*, 198–203; for the impact of mass armies, see Lewis, *Sanctioned Violence*, 128–133; for the "iron revolution," see Wagner, *Iron and Steel.*

9. Pines, *Envisioning Eternal Empire*, 201–210.

10. *Lunyu* "Ji shi," 16.2: 174; *Mengzi*, "Teng Wen Gong A," 5.4: 124.

11. For the establishment of the office of song-collectors in the Han period, and its ritual background, see Kern, "The Poetry of Han Historiography," 33–35. For the evolution of the complaint system, see Fang, "Hot Potatoes"; Fang fails to notice that the system he discusses invariably favored the educated segment of society. For the importance of "public opinion" for late imperial policy makers, see Rowe, *Saving the World*, 373–377; cf. Rowe's discussion of the elite as natural leaders of the "stupid people," on pp. 295–300.

12. Tu Wei-ming, "The Structure and Function of the Confucian Intellectual," 20.

13. See detailed discussion in Pines, "To Rebel Is Justified?"

14. *Mengzi*, "Liang Hui Wang B" 2.8: 42.

15. *Han Feizi*, "Zhong xiao" XX.52: 465–466.

16. See *Xunzi*, "Zheng lun" XII.18: 322–325, and discussion in Pines, "To Rebel Is Justified?" 16–20.

17. I adopt "egalitarian" here from Chinese scholars who usually define rebel ideology in this way (*pingjunzhuyi*). See, e.g., Dong Chuping, *Nongmin zhanzheng yu pingjunzhuyi*.

18. The Chinese debates are neatly summarized in Cen and Liu, *Zhongguo nongmin zhanzheng*, 221–239; for Soviet studies, see, e.g., Smolin, "Problemy." To remind the readers, mainstream Marxist historiography in China and the Soviet Union defines imperial China as a "feudal" state.

19. See Liu Kwang-Ching and Shek, "Introduction."

20. See Liu Kwang-Ching and Shek, "Early Daoism." See, however, Donald Munro's attempt to analyze concepts of equality in mainstream Confucian thought (*A Chinese Ethics*, 3–20).

21. *Xunzi*, "Xing'e" XVII.23: 443.

22. *Xunzi*, "Wang zhi" V.9: 148–49.

23. *Mozi*, "Shang xian shang" II.8: 67.

24. *Shiji* 48: 1952.

25. For the Taiping examinations, see, e.g., Zhou Lasheng, "Da Xi, Taiping tianguo keju."

26. This said, it should be mentioned that among certain rebel leaders the brigands' brotherhood was valued more than strict social distinctions; hence they disliked attempts to institutionalize the rebels' camp. See details in Dong Chuping, *Nongmin zhanzheng yu pingjunzhuyi*, 39.

27. See *Lunyu*, "Ji shi" 16.1: 172; *Mengzi*, "Teng Wen Gong A" 5.3: 118.

28. *Mozi*, "Shang tong shang" III.11:109.

29. *Liji*, "Li yun" XXI.9: 582.

30. See articles in Deliusin and Borokh, *Kitajskie Sotsial'nye Utopii*.

31. My discussion of banditry draws primarily on such studies as Perry, "Social Banditry"; Antony, "Peasants, Heroes, and Brigands"; and Robinson, "Banditry."

32. The literature on Chinese sects is plentiful and fast growing. See the very important study by Ter-Haar, *White Lotus*, for a challenge to established views

of sectarian movements; cf. articles in Liu and Shek, *Heterodoxy*. For the sects' ideology, see Overmyer, "Attitudes toward the Ruler and State." For an in-depth study of sectarian rebellions, see, especially, Naquin, *Millenarian Rebellion*, and idem, *Shantung Rebellion*.

33. For an excellent introduction to millenarian beliefs in China, see Zürcher, "Prince Moonlight"; see also Naquin, *Millenarian Rebellion*.

34. See Naquin, *Millenarian Rebellion* and *Shantung Rebellion*; Liu Kwang-Ching, "Religion and Politics"; Shek and Noguchi, "Eternal Mother Religion."

35. See Perry, "Heterodox Rebellion?"

36. See, e.g., Liu Kwang-Ching, "Religion and Politics," 307. Even the Muslim rebels in Xinjiang employed this slogan in 1864, probably anticipating that they would thereby add legitimacy to their rebellion. See Kim, *Holy War*, 53.

37. *Shiji* 48: 1950, cited with slight modifications from Watson, *Records* [Qin], 218.

38. See details in Xiong, *Emperor Yang*.

39. For a statistical analysis of the correlation between economic hardships and social unrest, see Tong, *Disorder under Heaven*, 76–95.

40. For the impact of population growth on China's economy, see Chao, *Man and Land*; for ecological changes in China over the centuries, see Elvin, *The Retreat of the Elephants*; for an insightful case study of Hunan Province in the late imperial period, see Perdue, *Exhausting the Earth*.

41. See Wong, "Food Riots"; Perry, "Protective Rebellion"; cf. Tong, *Disorder under Heaven*.

42. See Perry, "Permanent Rebellion?"

43. For a good analysis of the balance of power between the government and the rebels, see Naquin, *Millenarian Rebellion* and *Shantung Rebellion*.

44. These factors are discussed in Naquin, *Millenarian Rebellion* and *Shantung Rebellion*.

45. Cited from Lai Chi-tim, "Daoism and Political Rebellion," 90.

46. See, e.g., Teng Xincai, "Lun Huang Chao," 137–138.

47. Levy, *Biography of Huang Ch'ao*, 34 and 42.

48. See Rowe, *Crimson Rain*, and Naquin, *Millenarian Rebellion*, for further details. For systematic cannibalism as employed by the government forces against the "bandits," see Tong, *Disorder under Heaven*, 3.

49. In this regard, the Chinese rebels' violence can be compared to that of the peasants in the Spanish Civil War, depicted in the immortal *For Whom the Bell Tolls* by Ernest Hemingway.

50. For this topic see Ter Haar, "Rethinking 'Violence' "; cf. Lewis, *Sanctioned Violence*.

51. Mao Zedong, *Selected Works* 1: 28–29.

52. For the *Report*'s background, see Van de Ven, *War and Nationalism in China*, 109–118.

53. See more in James J. Y. Liu, *The Chinese Knight Errant*; Pines, "A Hero Terrorist."

54. See details in Plaks, *The Four Masterworks*, 279–358.

55. *Shui hu zhuan* 41: 606; translation cited from Shapiro, *Outlaws of the Marsh*, 662.

56. See more in Aubin, "The Rebirth of Chinese Rule."

57. See Zhou Lasheng, "Da Xi, Taiping tianguo keju," 32–34; Parsons, "The Culmination," 393.

58. See Kuhn, *Rebellion and Its Enemies*; cf. Bernhardt, "Elite and Peasant."

59. *Shiji* 6: 281; cf. Watson, *Records* [Qin], 80.

60. This presence of elite members within the rebel ranks calls into question Kuhn's identification of the elites as natural "enemies" of the rebellions (*Rebellion and Its Enemies*). For a more nuanced approach to the Taiping case, see Zheng Xiaowei, "Loyalty, Anxiety, and Opportunism."

61. Mao, "The Chinese Revolution and the Chinese Communist Party" (1939), in Mao, *Selected Works* 2: 308.

62. Chinese debates are conveniently summarized in Cen and Liu, *Zhongguo nongmin zhanzheng*; see also Liu Kwang-Ching, "World View and Peasant Rebellion."

CHAPTER 6
IMPERIAL POLITICAL CULTURE IN THE MODERN AGE

1. Cited from Spence, *The Search for Modern China*, 284.

2. Shambaugh, "Introduction," 2.

3. The secondary literature on the topics covered in this chapter is enormous; I limit myself in what follows to references to those studies that directly influenced my perspective. Needless to say, many nuances of the twentieth-century developments cannot be adequately addressed here.

4. For Zhang Binglin's views, see Esherick, "How the Qing Became China," 237; for Sun Yat-sen, see Bergere, *Sun Yat-sen*, 265–266.

5. The only major exception to this rule was China's recognition of the independence of the Mongolian People's Republic in the wake of strong pressure from the USSR.

6. For a positive treatment of federalism, see Duara, "Provincial Narratives"; Chen, *Chen Jiongming*.

7. Duara, "Provincial Narratives," 177–178.

8. Fitzgerald, *Awakening China*, is also sympathetic toward federalism, but acknowledges that "Warlord armies supplied federalists with their most potent argument for retaining provincial autonomy and offered Nationalist revolutionaries the most cogent of reasons for downgrading the province in the hierarchy of political places" (p. 166).

9. For the Northern Expedition, see Wilbur, *The Nationalist Revolution*; for Jiang Jieshi's inability to attain full unification of China under his control, see, e.g., Van de Ven, *War and Nationalism in China*.

10. See details in McCord, *The Power of the Gun*, and Van de Ven, *War and Nationalism*.

11. For Jiang's transmission of power, see Nathan and Gilley, *China's New Rulers*.

206 • Notes to Chapter 6

12. For an analysis of the events that led to the Tiananmen tragedy, see Baum, "The Road to Tiananmen." For speculations about the potential for divisiveness in the next ("fifth") generation of CPC leaders, see Li Cheng, "The Chinese Communist Party."

13. Cited from Lin Yü-sheng, *The Crisis of Chinese Consciousness*, 66.

14. Mao, "On New Democracy" (1940), in *Selected Works*, 2: 347–348. For revisionist approaches to the May Fourth Movement, see Ip, Hon, and Lee, "The Plurality of Chinese Modernity."

15. Schwarcz, *The Chinese Enlightenment*, 9–10; cf. Wakeman, "The Price of Autonomy," 163–170. For "awakening" the masses, see Fitzgerald, *Awakening China*.

16. See Cheek, "From Priests to Professionals," 185. For the establishment intellectuals in general, see articles collected in Hamrin and Cheek, *China's Establishment Intellectuals*.

17. See, e.g., Cheek, *Propaganda and Culture*.

18. For the importance of intellectuals in facilitating Deng's "restoration," see MacFarquhar, "The Succession to Mao," 311–327.

19. For an example of the 1980s observation, see, e.g., Moody, "The Political Culture"; for the post-1989 analysis, see, e.g. Cheek, "From Priests to Professionals," and other articles in Wassertrom and Perry, *Popular Protest*.

20. It should be recalled here that one of the most important essays in CPC history, "How to Be a Good Communist" (1939) by Liu Shaoqi (*Selected Works of Liu Shaoqi*, 107–168), depicts an ideal Communist in overtly Confucian terms. Needless to say, in both cases there were plenty of hypocrites who hid their selfishness behind lofty pronouncements.

21. Cheek, "From Priests to Professionals," 200.

22. Sun Yat-sen, *San min chu i*, 12.

23. Duara, *Culture, Power, and the State*, 248.

24. Fitzgerald, *Awakening China*.

25. Cited from Schram, *The Thought of Mao Tse-tung*, 46.

26. For the Communist social restructuring prior to their victory, see, e.g. Perry, *Rebels and Revolutionaries*, 239–247.

27. This generalization should be qualified with the knowledge that many elite families were able to survive the land reform upheaval and even join the new regime (for one example, see, e.g., He, "The Death of a Landlord," especially pp. 131–133). These and other exceptions notwithstanding, it remains true that the landowning rural elite disappeared as a distinct social stratum in the aftermath of the Land Reform.

28. For the nature of the Great Leap Forward, see Lieberthal, "The Great Leap Forward"; cf. MacFarquhar, *The Origins of the Cultural Revolution 2*; for early campaigns, see, e.g., Teiwes, "The Establishment and Consolidation."

29. The reasons for the launch of the Cultural Revolution are still obscure despite the best efforts of the most profound analysts (e.g., Lieberthal, "The Great Leap Forward"; MacFarquhar, *The Origins of the Cultural Revolution*, vols. 1–3; Harding, "The Chinese State in Crisis"). Among other sources of intra-Party conflict, Mao's attempts to launch mass campaigns in the early 1960s, and

the recalcitrant attitude of the Party establishment toward these initiatives, figure prominently.

30. For Mao's purge of some of his rivals through the normal intraparty procedure just a few weeks before the launch of the mass campaigns of the Cultural Revolution, see MacFarquhar and Shoenhals, *Mao's Last Revolution*, 14–51. For the events of the Cultural Revolution, see MacFarquhar and Shoenhals, *Mao's Last Revolution*, and Harding, "The Chinese State in Crisis."

31. For local protests in contemporary China and the parallels with the past, see Perry, "Permanent Rebellion?"; for the political impact of the Internet, see Zheng, *Technological Empowerment*.

32. For an interesting example of the Party's attempt to co-opt private entrepreneurs, see Dickson, *Red Capitalists*; for more recent developments, see Li Cheng, "The Chinese Communist Party."

33. See Bell, *China's New Confucianism*, especially pp. 175–191.

34. See chapter 2, note 11.

35. See Dickson, *Red Capitalists*, and Li Cheng, "The Chinese Communist Party," for some preliminary estimates.

Bibliography

Adamson, Walter L. *Hegemony and Revolution: A Study of Antonio Gramsci's Political and Cultural Theory*. Berkeley: University of California Press, 1980.

Alcock, Susan E., et al., eds. *Empires: Perspectives from Archaeology and History*. Cambridge: Cambridge University Press, 2001.

Andrew, Anita M., and John A. Rapp, authors and eds. *Autocracy and China's Rebel Founding Emperors: Comparing Chairman Mao and Ming Taizu*. Lanham, MD: Rowman and Littlefield, 2000.

Antony, Robert J. "Peasants, Heroes, and Brigands: The Problems of Social Banditry in Early Nineteenth-Century South China." *Modern China* 15.2 (April 1989): 123–148.

Aubin, Françoise. "The Rebirth of Chinese Rule in Times of Trouble: North China in the Early Thirteenth Century." In *Foundations and Limits of State Power in China*, edited by Stewart Schram, 113–146. Hong Kong: Chinese University Press, 1987.

Balazs, Etienne. "L'Histoire comme guide de la pratique bureaucratique." In *Historians of China and Japan*, edited by William G. Beasley and Edwin G. Pulleyblank, 78–94. London: Oxford University Press, 1961.

Barfield, Thomas. *The Perilous Frontier: Nomadic Empires and China*. Oxford: Basil Blackwell, 1989.

Bartlett, Beatrice S. *Monarchs and Ministers: The Grand Council in Mid-Ch'ing China, 1723–1820*. Berkeley: University of California Press, 1991.

de Bary, William Theodore. *Waiting for the Dawn. A Plan for the Prince: Huang Tsung-hsi's Ming-i-tai-fang lu*. New York: Columbia University Press, 1993.

Baum, Richard. "Ritual and Rationality: Religious Roots of the Bureaucratic State in Ancient China." *Social Evolution & History* 3.1 (March 2004) (http://www.socionauki.ru/journal/articles/130061/).

———. "The Road to Tiananmen: Chinese Politics in the 1980s." In *The Politics of China: The Eras of Mao and Deng*, 2nd ed., edited by Roderick MacFarquhar, 340–471. Cambridge: Cambridge University Press, 1997.

Bell, Daniel A. *China's New Confucianism: Politics and Everyday Life in a Changing Society*. Princeton, NJ: Princeton University Press, 2008.

Benn, James A. *Burning for the Buddha: Self-immolation in Chinese Buddhism*. Kuroda Institute Studies in East Asian Buddhism 19. Honolulu: University of Hawai'i Press, 2007.

Bergere, Marie-Claire. *Sun Yat-sen*. Translated by Janet Lloyd. Stanford, CA: Stanford University Press, 1998.

Berkowitz, Alan J. *Patterns of Disengagement: The Practice and Portrayal of Reclusion in Early Medieval China*. Stanford, CA: Stanford University Press. 2000.

Bernhardt, Kathryn. "Elite and Peasant during the Taiping Occupation of the Jiangnan, 1860–1864." *Modern China* 13.4 (1987): 379–410.

Bielenstein, Hans. "Wang Mang, the Restoration of the Han Dynasty, and Later Han." In *The Cambridge History of China*, vol. 1, *The Ch'in and Han Empires, 221 B.C.–A.D. 220*, edited by Denis Twitchett and Michael Loewe, 223–290. Cambridge: Cambridge University Press, 1986.

Bilsky, Lester J. *The State Religion of Ancient China*. Taipei: Orient Cultural Service, 1975.

Biran, Michal. *Chinggis Khan*. Oxford: Oneworld, 2007.

Biran, Michal, and Reuven Amitai. "Introduction." In *Eurasia Nomads as Agents of Cultural Change*, edited by Reuven Amitai and Michal Biran. Honolulu: University of Hawai'i Press, forthcoming.

Blue, Gregory. "China and Western Social Thought in the Modern Period." In *China and Historical Capitalism: Genealogies of Sinological Knowledge*, edited by Timothy Brook and Gregory Blue, 57–109. Cambridge: Cambridge University Press, 1999.

Bol, Peter K. "Examination and Orthodoxies: 1070 and 1313 Compared." In *Culture and State in Chinese History*, edited by Theodore Huters, R. Bin Wong, and Pauline Yu, 29–57. Stanford, CA: Stanford University Press, 1997.

———. "Government, Society and State: On the Political Visions of Ssu-ma Kuang and Wang An-shih." In *Ordering the World: Approaches to State and Society in Sung Dynasty China*, edited by Robert R. Hymes and Conrad Schirokauer, 128–192. Berkeley: University of California Press, 1993.

———. *Neo-Confucianism in History*. Cambridge, MA: Harvard University Asia Center, 2008.

———. *"This Culture of Ours": Intellectual Transitions in T'ang and Sung China*. Stanford, CA: Stanford University Press, 1992.

Boshu Laozi jiaozhu 帛書老子校注. Compiled and annotated by Gao Ming 高明. Beijing: Zhonghua shuju, 1996.

Brook, Timothy. "At the Margin of Public Authority: The Ming State and Buddhism." In idem, *Chinese State in Ming Society*, 139–158. London: RoutledgeCurzon, 2006.

———. "State Censorship and the Book Trade." In idem, *Chinese State in Ming Society*, 118–136. London: RoutledgeCurzon, 2006.

———. "Unification as a Political Ideal: An Effect of the Mongol Conquest of China." Paper presented at the Roundtable on the Nature of the Mongol Empire and Its Legacy with Respect to Political and Spiritual Relations among Asian Leaders and Polities, Austrian Academy of Sciences, Vienna, 6 November 2010.

Bu Xianqun 卜憲群. "Cong jiandu kan Qin dai xiangli de liyuan shezhi yu xingzheng gongneng" 從簡牘看秦代鄉里的吏員設置與行政功能. In *Liye gucheng: Qin jian yu Qin wenhua yanjiu* 里耶古城·秦簡與秦文化研究, edited by Zhongguo shehuikexueyuan Kaogu Yanjiusuo 中國社會科學院考古研究所 et al., 103–113. Beijing: Kexue chubanshe, 2009.

Bujard, Marianne. "State and Local Cults in Han Religion." In *Early Chinese Religion. Part One: Shang through Han (1250 BC –AD 220)*, edited by John Lagerwey and Marc Kalinowski, 783–784. Leiden: Brill, 2009.

Burbank, Jane, and Frederick Cooper. *The Empires in World History: Power and the Politics of Difference*. Princeton, NJ: Princeton University Press, 2010.

Cao Deben 曹德本, ed. *Zhongguo chuantong zhengzhi wenhua de xiandai jiazhi* 中國傳統政治文化的現代價值. Beijing: Qinghua daxue chubanshe, 2006.

Cen Dali 岑大利 and Liu Yuebin 李悅斌. *Zhongguo nongmin zhanzheng shi lunbian* 中國農民戰爭史論辯. Edited by Li Wenhai 李文海 and Gong Shuduo 龔書鐸. Nanchang: Baihuazhou wenyi chubanshe, 2004.

Chafee, John W. *The Thorny Gates of Learning in Sung China: A Social History of Examinations*. Albany: State University of New York Press, 1995.

Chan, Hok-lam. *Legitimation in Imperial China: Discussions under the Jurchen-Chin Dynasty (1115–1234)*. Seattle: University of Washington Press, 1984.

Chang, Michael G. *A Court on Horseback: Imperial Touring & the Construction of Qing Rule, 1680–1785*. Cambridge, MA: Harvard University Asia Center, 2007.

Chao, Kang. *Man and Land in Chinese History: An Economic Analysis*. Stanford, CA: Stanford University Press, 1986.

Chao, Shin-yi. "Huizong and the Divine Empyrean Palace 神霄宮 Temple Network." In *Emperor Huizong and Late Northern Song China*, edited by Patricia B. Ebrey and Maggie Bickford, 324–358. Cambridge, MA: Harvard University Asia Center, 2006.

Chase, Kenneth W. "The Edict of 495 Reconsidered." *Journal of the Economic and Social History of the Orient* 39.4 (November 1996): 383–97.

Cheek, Timothy. "From Priests to Professionals: Intellectuals and the State under the CCP." In *Popular Protest and Political Culture in Modern China*, 2nd ed., edited by Jeffrey N. Wassertrom and Elizabeth J. Perry, 184–205. Boulder, CO: Westview, 1994.

———. *Propaganda and Culture in Mao's China: Deng Tuo and the Intelligentsia*. Oxford: Clarendon Press, 1997.

Chen, Leslie H. Dingyan. *Chen Jiongming and the Federalist Movement: Regional Leadership and Nation Building in Early Republican China*. Ann Arbor: Center for Chinese Studies, the University of Michigan, 1999.

Chen Suzhen 陳蘇鎮. *Handai zhengzhi yu 'Chunqiu' xue* 漢代政治與《春秋》學. Beijing: Guangbo dianshi chubanshe, 2001.

Ching, Dora C. Y. "Visual Images of Zhu Yuanzhang." In *Long Live the Emperor! Uses of the Ming Founder across Six Centuries of East Asian History*, edited by Sarah Schneewind, 171–210. Minneapolis, MN: Society for Ming Studies, 2008.

Chu, Hung-lam. "The Jiajing Emperor's Interaction with His Lecturers." In *Culture, Courtiers and Competition: The Ming Court (1368–1644)*, edited by David M. Robinson, 186–230. Cambridge, MA: Harvard University Asia Center; distributed by Harvard University Press, 2008.

Chü, T'ung-tsu. *Local Government in China under the Ch'ing*. Cambridge, MA: Harvard University Press, 1962.

Chunqiu Gongyang zhuan zhushu 春秋公羊傳注疏. Annotated by He Xiu 何休 and Xu Yan 徐彥. Reprinted in *Shisanjing zhushu* 十三經注疏, compiled by Ruan Yuan 阮元, 2: 2189–2355. Beijing: Zhonghua shuju, 1991.

Chunqiu Zuo zhuan zhu 春秋左傳注. Annotated by Yang Bojun 楊伯峻. Beijing: Zhonghua shuju, 1981.

Clark, Hugh, R. "The Southern Kingdoms between the T'ang and the Sung, 907–

979." In *The Cambridge History of China*, vol. 5, *Part One: The Sung Dynasty and Its Precursors, 907–1279*, edited by Denis Twitchett and Paul Jakov Smith, 133–205. Cambridge: Cambridge University Press, 2009.

Cook, Constance A., and John S. Major, eds. *Defining Chu: Image and Reality in Ancient China*. Honolulu: University of Hawai'i Press, 1999.

Crawford, Robert B. "Eunuch Power in the Ming Dynasty." *T'oung Pao* 49.3 (1961): 115–148.

de Crespigny, Rafe. *Generals of the South: The Foundation and Early History of the Three Kingdoms State of Wu*. Canberra: Australian National University, 1990.

Crossley, Pamela K. *A Translucent Mirror: History and Identity in Qing Imperial Ideology*. Berkeley: University of California Press, 1999.

Crowell, William G. "Northern Émigrés and the Problems of Census Registration under the Eastern Jin and Southern Dynasties." In *State and Society in Early Medieval China*, edited by Albert E. Dien, 171–209. Stanford, CA: Stanford University Press, 1990.

Cui Xiangdong 崔向東. *Han dai haozu yanjiu* 漢代豪族研究. Wuhan: Chongwen shuju, 2003.

Dai Yingcong. *The Sichuan Frontier and Tibet: Imperial Strategy in the Early Qing*. Seattle: University of Washington Press, 2009.

Dalby, Michael T. "Court Politics in Late T'ang Times." In *The Cambridge History of China*, vol. 3, *Sui and T'ang China, 589–906 AD*, pt. 1, edited by Denis C. Twitchett, 561–681. Cambridge: Cambridge University Press, 1979.

Dardess, John W. *Blood and History in China: The Donglin Faction and Its Repression, 1620–1627*. Honolulu: University of Hawai'i Press, 2002.

———. *Confucianism and Autocracy: Professional Elites in the Founding of the Ming Dynasty*. Berkeley: University of California Press, 1983.

———. "Confucianism, Local Reform, and Centralization in Late Yüan Chekiang, 1342–1359." In *Yüan Thought: Chinese Thought and Religion under the Mongols*, edited by Hok-lam Chan and William Theodore de Bary, 327–374. New York: Columbia University Press, 1982.

———. *Conquerors and Confucians: Aspects of Political Change in Late Yüan China*. New York: Columbia University Press, 1973.

Davis, Richard L. *Wind against the Mountain: The Crisis of Politics and Culture in Thirteenth-century China*. Cambridge, MA: Council on East Asian Studies, Harvard University; distributed by Harvard University Press, 1996.

Declercq, Dominik. *Writing against the State: Political Rhetorics in Third and Fourth Century China*. Leiden: Brill, 1998.

Deliusin L. P., and L. N. Borokh, eds. *Kitajskie Sotsial'nye Utopii*. Moscow: Nauka, 1987.

Dickson, Bruce J. *Red Capitalists in China: The Party, Private Entrepreneurs, and Prospects for Political Change*. Cambridge: Cambridge University Press, 2003.

Di Cosmo, Nicola. *Ancient China and Its Enemies: The Rise of Nomadic Power in East Asian History*. Cambridge: Cambridge University Press, 2002.

———. "State Formation and Periodization in Inner Asian History." *Journal of World History* 10 (1999): 1–40.

Dien, Albert, ed. *State and Society in Early Medieval China*. Stanford, CA: Stanford University Press, 1990.

Dikötter, Frank. *The Discourse of Race in Modern China*. Stanford, CA: Stanford University, Press, 1992.

Dong Chuping 董楚平. *Nongmin zhanzheng yu pingjunzhuyi* 農民戰爭與平均主義. Beijing: Fangzhi chubanshe, 2003.

Dorofeeva-Lichtman, Vera. "Ritual Practices for Constructing Terrestrial Space (Warring States—early Han)." In *Early Chinese Religion. Part One: Shang through Han (1250 BC–220 AD)*, edited by John Lagerwey and Marc Kalinowski, 1: 595–644. Leiden: Brill, 2009.

Doyle, Michael W. *Empires*. Ithaca, NY: Cornell University Press, 1986.

A Dream of Red Mansions, by Tsao Hsueh-Chin (Cao Xueqin) and Kao Ngo (Gao E). Translated by Yang Hsien-Yi and Gladys Yang. Peking (Beijing): Foreign Languages Press, 1978–1980.

Du Jiaji 杜家驥. "Zhongguo gudai junchen zhi li yanbian kaolun" 中國古代君臣之禮演變考論. In *Zhongguo shehui lishi pinglun* 中國社會歷史評論, edited by Zhang Guogang 張國剛, 1: 255–269. Tianjin: Guji chubanshe, 1999.

Duara, Prasenjit. *Culture, Power, and the State: Rural North China, 1900–1942*. Stanford, CA: Stanford University Press, 1988.

———. "Provincial Narratives of the Nation: Federalism and Centralism in Modern China." In idem, *Rescuing History from the Nation: Questioning Narratives of Modern China*, 177–204. Chicago: University of Chicago Press, 1995.

Ebrey, Patricia B. "The Early Stages in Development of Descent Group Organization." In *Kinship Organization in Late Imperial China 1000–1940*, edited by Patricia B. Ebrey and James L. Watson, 16–61. Berkeley: University of California Press 1985.

———. "The Economic and Social History of Later Han." In *The Cambridge History of China*, vol. 1, *The Ch'in and Han Empires, 221 B.C.–A.D. 220*, edited by Denis Twitchett and Michael Loewe, 608–648. Cambridge: Cambridge University Press, 1986.

———. "Portrait Sculptures in Imperial Ancestral Rites in Song China." *T'oung Pao* 83.1–3 (1997): 42–92.

———. "Toward a Better Understanding of the Later Han Upper Class." In *State and Society in Early Medieval China*, edited by Albert Dien, 49–72. Stanford, CA: Stanford University Press, 1990.

Ebrey, Patricia B., and Maggie Bickford, eds. *Emperor Huizong and Late Northern Song China*. Cambridge, MA: Harvard University Asia Center, 2006.

Ebrey, Patricia B., and James L. Watson, eds. *Kinship Organization in Late Imperial China 1000–1940*. Berkeley: University of California Press 1985.

Eisenberg, Andrew. *Kingship in Early Medieval China*. Leiden: Brill, 2008.

Eisenstadt, Shmuel N. "Frederic Wakeman's Oeuvre in the Framework of World and Comparative History." In Frederic E. Wakeman, Jr., *Telling Chinese History: A Selection of Essays*, selected and edited by Lea H. Wakeman, xi–xix. Berkeley: University of California Press, 2009.

———. "Multiple Modernities." *Daedalus* 129.1 (2000): 1–29.

————. *The Political System of Empires*. London: Free Press of Glencoe, 1963.

Elliott, Mark C. *The Manchu Way: The Eight Banners and Ethnic Identity in Late Imperial China*. Stanford, CA: Stanford University Press, 2001.

Elman, Benjamin A. *A Cultural History of Civil Examinations in Late Imperial China*. Berkeley: University of California Press, 2000.

Elverskog, Johan. *Our Great Qing: The Mongols, Buddhism and the State in Late Imperial China*. Honolulu: University of Hawai'i Press, 2006.

Elvin, Mark. "Female Virtue and State in China." Reprinted in Mark Elvin, *Another History: Essays on China from a European Perspective*, 302–351. Sydney: Wild Peony, 1996.

————. *The Retreat of the Elephants: An Environmental History of China*. New Haven, CT: Yale University Press, 2004.

Endicott-West, Elizabeth. "Imperial Governance in Yüan Times." *Harvard Journal of Asiatic Studies* 46.2 (1986): 523–549.

Esherick, Joseph E. "How the Qing Became China." In *Empire to Nation: Historical Perspectives on the Making of the Modern World*, edited by Joseph Esherick, Hasan Kayali and Eric Van Young, 229–259. Lanham, MD: Rowman & Littlefield, 2006.

Esherick, Joseph E., and Mary B. Rankin. "Introduction." In *Chinese Local Elites and Patterns of Dominance*, edited by Mary B. Rankin and Joseph E. Esherick, 1–24. Berkeley: University of California Press, 1990.

Ess, Hans van. "Emperor Wu of the Han and the First August Emperor of Qin in Sima Qian's *Shiji*." In *The Birth of Empire: The State of Qin Revisited*, edited by Yuri Pines, Lothar von Falkenhausen, Gideon Shelach, and Robin D. S. Yates. Berkeley: University of California Press, forthcoming.

Fairbank, John K. "A Preliminary Framework." In *The Chinese World Order: Traditional China's Foreign Relations*, edited by John K. Fairbank, 1–20. Cambridge, MA: Harvard University Press, 1968.

Falkenhausen, Lothar von. *Chinese Society in the Age of Confucius (1050–250 BC): The Archeological Evidence*. Los Angeles: Cotsen Institute of Archaeology at UCLA, 2006.

Fan Zhongyan quanji 范仲淹全集, by Fan Zhongyan 范仲淹. Compiled by Fan Nengjun 范能濬. Collated by Xue Zhengxing 薛正興. Nanjing: Fenghuang chubanshe, 2004.

Fang Cheng-hua [Fang Zhenhua 方震華]. "The Price of Orthodoxy: Issues of Legitimacy in the Later Liang and Later Tang." *Taida lishi xuebao* 臺大歷史學報 35 (2005): 55–84.

Fang, Qiang. "Hot Potatoes: Chinese Complaint Systems from Early Times to the Late Qing (1898)." *Journal of Asian Studies* 68.4 (2009): 1105–1135.

Fang Xuanling. *The Chronicle of Fu Chien: A Case of Exemplar History*. Translated and annotated, with prolegomena, by Michael C. Rogers. Berkeley: University of California Press, 1968.

Farmer, Edward L. *Zhu Yuanzhang and Early Ming Legislation: The Reordering of Chinese Society Following the Era of Mongol Rule*. Leiden: Brill, 1995.

Faure, David. "The Emperor in the Village: Representing the State in South China." In *State and Court Ritual in China*, edited by Joseph P. McDermott, 299–351. Cambridge: Cambridge University Press, 1999.

Femia, Joseph V. *Gramsci's Political Thought: Hegemony, Consciousness, and the Revolutionary Process*. Oxford: Clarendon Press, 1981.

Fisher, Carney T. *The Chosen One: Succession and Adoption in the Court of Ming Shizong*. Boston: Allen & Unwin, 1990.

Fitzgerald, John. *Awakening China: Politics, Culture, and Class in the Nationalist Revolution*. Stanford, CA: Stanford University Press, 1966.

Fletcher, Joseph. "Turco-Mongolian Monarchic Tradition in the Ottoman Empire." *Harvard Ukrainian Studies* 3–4 (1979–1980): 236–251.

Franke, Herbert, and Denis Twitchett. "Introduction." In *The Cambridge History of China*, vol. 6, *Alien Regimes and Border States, 907–1368*, edited by Herbert Franke and Denis Twitchett, 1–42. Cambridge: Cambridge University Press, 1994.

Gale, Esson M., trans. *Discourses on Salt and Iron: A Debate on State Control of Commerce and Industry in Ancient China*. Leiden: Brill, 1931.

Ge Quan 葛荃. *Quanli zaizhi lixing: shiren, chuantong zhengzhi wenhua yu Zhongguo shehui* 權力宰制理性—士人、傳統政治文化與中國社會. Tianjin: Nankai daxue chubanshe, 2003.

Geiss, James. "The Chia-ching Reign, 1522–1566." In *The Cambridge History of China*, vol. 7, *The Ming Dynasty, 1368–1644, Part I*, edited by Frederick W. Mote and Denis Twitchett, 440–510. Cambridge: Cambridge University Press, 1988.

Gentz, Joachim. *Das Gongyang zhuan: Auslegung und Kanoniesierung der Frühlings und Herbstannalen (Chunqiu)*. Wiesbaden: Harrassowitz Verlag, 2001.

Giele, Enno. "Signatures of 'Scribes' in Early Imperial China." *Asiatische Studien / Études Asiatique* 59.1 (2005): 353–387.

Glahn, Richard von. "Community and Welfare: Chu Hsi's Community Granary in Theory and Practice." In *Ordering the World: Approaches to State and Society in Sung Dynasty China*, edited by Robert R. Hymes and Conrad Schirokauer, 221–254. Berkeley: University of California Press, 1993.

Golden, Peter B. "Imperial Ideology and the Sources of Political Unity amongst the Pre-Chinggisid Nomads of Western Eurasia." *Archivum Eurasiae Medii Aevi* 2 (1982): 37–77.

Goldin, Paul R. "Steppe Nomads as a Philosophical Problem in Classical China." In *Mapping Mongolia: Situating Mongolia in the World from Geologic Time to the Present*, edited by Paula L. W. Sabloff, 220–246. Philadelphia: University of Pennsylvania Museum of Archaeology and Anthropology, 2010.

Goldstone, Jack A., and John F. Haldon. "Ancient States, Empires and Exploitation: Problems and Perspectives." In *The Dynamics of Ancient Empires: State Power from Assyria to Byzantium*, edited by Ian Morris and Walter Scheidel, 3–29. Oxford: Oxford University Press, 2009.

Goncharov, S.N. *Kitajskaia Srednevekovaia Diplomatiia: Otnosheniia Mezhdu Imperiiami Tszin' i Sun, 1127–1142*. Moscow: Nauka, 1986.

Goodrich, Luther C. *The Literary Inquisition of Ch'ien-Lung*. 2nd ed. New York: Paragon Book Reprint Corp., 1966.

Graff, David A. "Dou Jiande's Dilemma: Logistics, Strategy, and State." In *Warfare in Chinese History*, edited by Hans van de Ven, 77–105. Leiden: Brill, 2000.

————. *Medieval Chinese Warfare, 300–900*. London: Routledge, 2002.

Graffin, Dennis. "Reinventing China: Pseudobureaucracy in the Early Southern Dynasties." In *State and Society in Early Medieval China*, edited by Albert Dien, 139–170. Stanford, CA: Stanford University Press, 1990.

Gregory, Timothy E. *A History of Byzantium*. Malden, MA: Blackwell, 2005.

Gu Yanwu 顧炎武. "Ren zhu hu renchen zi" 人主呼人臣字. In idem, *Ri zhi lu jishi* 日知錄集釋, edited by Huang Rucheng 黃如成. Changsha: Yuelu, 1994.

Guanzi jiaozhu 管子校注. Compiled by Li Xiangfeng 黎翔鳳. Beijing: Zhonghua shuju, 2004.

Guy, R. Kent. *The Emperor's Four Treasuries: Scholars and the State in the Late Ch'ien-lung Era*. Harvard East Asian Monographs 129. Cambridge, MA: Harvard University Press, 1987.

————. *Qing Governors and Their Provinces: The Evolution of Territorial Administration in China, 1644–1796*. Seattle: University of Washington Press, 2010.

Hammond, Kenneth J. *Pepper Mountain: The Life, Death and Posthumous Career of Yang Jisheng*. London: Kegan Paul, 2007.

Hamrin, Carol Lee, and Timothy Cheek, eds. *China's Establishment Intellectuals*. Armonk, NY: Sharpe, 1986.

Han Changli wenji jiaozhu 韓昌黎文集校注, by Han Yu 韓愈. Annotated by Ma Qichang 馬其昶. Edited by Ma Maoyuan 馬茂元. Shanghai: Guji chubanshe, 1986.

Han Feizi jijie 韩非子集解. Compiled by Wang Xianshen 王先慎. Beijing: Zhonghua shuju, 1998.

Han shu 漢書, by Ban Gu 班固 et al. Annotated by Yan Shigu 顏師古. Beijing: Zhonghua shuju, 1997.

Harding, Harry. "The Chinese State in Crisis, 1966–1969." In *The Politics of China, 1949–1989*, edited by Roderick MacFarquhar, 148–247. Cambridge: Cambridge University Press, 1993.

Hartman, Charles. *Han Yü and the T'ang Search for Unity*. Princeton, NJ: Princeton University Press, 1986.

He Jianfei. "The Death of a Landlord: Moral Predicament in Rural China, 1968–1969." In *The Chinese Cultural Revolution as History*, edited by Joseph W. Esherick, Paul G. Pickowicz, and Andrew G. Walder, 124–152. Stanford, CA: Stanford University Press, 2006.

Hejidra, Martin. "The Socio-economic Development of Rural China during the Ming." In *The Cambridge History of China*, vol. 8, *The Ming Dynasty, 1368–1644, Part 2*, edited by Frederick W. Mote and Denis Twitchett, 417–578. Cambridge: Cambridge University Press, 1998.

Herbert, Penelope A. *Examine the Honest, Appraise the Able: Contemporary Assessments of Civil Service Selection in Early T'ang China*. Canberra: Faculty of Asian Studies, Australian National University Press, 1988.

Ho Ping-ti. "Salient Aspects of China's Heritage." In *China's Heritage and the Communist Political System*, edited by Ho Ping-ti and Tsou Tang, 1–37. Chicago: University of Chicago Press, 1968.

Ho Ping-ti and Tsou Tang, eds. *China's Heritage and the Communist Political System*. Chicago: University of Chicago Press, 1968.

Hobsbawm, Eric J. *Nations and Nationalism since 1780: Programme, Myth Reality*. 2nd ed. Cambridge: Cambridge University Press, 1992.

Holcombe, Charles. "The Exemplar State: Ideology, Self-Cultivation, and Power in Fourth-Century China." *Harvard Journal of Asiatic Studies* 49.1 (1989): 93–139.

———. *In the Shadow of the Han: Literati Thought and Society at the Beginning of the Southern Dynasties*. Honolulu: University of Hawai'i Press, 1994.

———. "The Last Lord of the South: Chen Houzhu (r. 583–589) and the Reunification of China." *Early Medieval China* 12 (2006): 91–121.

Holmgren, Jennifer. "Politics of the Inner Court under the Hou-chu of Northern Ch'i." In *State and Society in Early Medieval China*, edited by Albert Dien, 269–330. Stanford, CA: Stanford University Press, 1990.

———. "Seeds of Madness: A Portrait of Kao Yang, First Emperor of Northern Ch'i, 530–560 A.D." *Papers on Far Eastern History* 24 (1981): 83–134.

Honey, David B. "Stripping Off Felt and Fur: An Essay on Nomadic Sinification." *Papers on Inner Asia* 21 (1992): 1–39.

Honig, Emily. *Creating Chinese Ethnicity: Subei People in Shanghai, 1850–1980*. New Haven, CT: Yale University Press, 1992.

Hou Han shu 後漢書. Compiled by Fan Ye 范曄 et al. Annotated by Li Xian 李賢. Beijing: Zhonghua shuju, 1997.

Hsiao Kung-chuan. *Rural China: Imperial Control in the Nineteenth Century*. Seattle: University of Washington Press, 1960.

Hsu Cho-yun. *Ancient China in Transition: An Analysis of Social Mobility, 722–222 B.C.* Stanford, CA: Stanford University Press, 1965.

Huang Chün-chieh. "Imperial Rulership in Cultural History: Chu Hsi's Interpretation." In *Imperial Rulership and Cultural Change in Traditional China*, edited by Frederick P. Brandauer and Huang Chün-chieh, 188–205. Seattle: University of Washington Press, 1994.

Huang, Philip C. C. *Civil Justice in China: Representation and Practice in the Qing*. Stanford, CA: Stanford University Press, 1996.

Huang, Ray. *1587: A Year of No Significance*. New Haven, CT: Yale University Press, 1981.

———. "The Ming Fiscal Administration." In *The Cambridge History of China*, vol. 8, *The Ming Dynasty, 1368–1644, Part 2*, edited by Frederick W. Mote and Denis Twitchett, 106–171. Cambridge: Cambridge University Press, 1998.

Hymes, Robert P. *Statesmen and Gentlemen: The Elite of Fu-chou, Chiang-hsi, in Northern and Southern Sung*. Cambridge: Cambridge University Press, 1986.

Hymes, Robert R., and Conrad Schirokauer, eds. *Ordering the World: Approaches to State and Society in Sung Dynasty China*. Berkeley: University of California Press, 1993.

Ip, Hung-Yok, Tze-Ki Hon, and Chiu-Chun Lee. "The Plurality of Chinese Modernity: A Review of Recent Scholarship on the May Fourth Movement." *Modern China* 29 (October 2003): 490–509.

Jagchid, Sechin, and Van Jay Symons. *Peace, War, and Trade along the Great Wall: Nomadic-Chinese Interaction through Two Millennia*. Bloomington: Indiana University Press, 1989.

Janousch, Andreas. "The Emperor as Bodhisattva: The Bodhisattva Ordination and Ritual Assemblies of Emperor Wu of the Liang Dynasty." In *State and Court Ritual in China*, edited by Joseph P. McDermott, 112–147. Cambridge: Cambridge University Press, 1999.

Jiang Yonglin. "Denouncing the 'Exalted Emperor': Huang Zongxi's Uses of Zhu Yuanzhang's Legal Legacy in *Waiting for the Dawn.*" In *Long Live the Emperor: Uses of the Ming Founder across Six Centuries of East Asian History*, edited by Sarah Schneewind, 245–274. Ming Studies Research Series. Minneapolis, MN: Society for Ming Studies, 2008.

———, trans. *The Great Ming Code / Da Ming lü*. Seattle: University of Washington Press, 2005.

———. "In the Name of 'Taizu': The Construction of Zhu Yuanzhang's Legal Philosophy and Chinese Cultural Identity in the *Veritable Records of Taizu.*" *T'oung Pao* 96 (2011): 408–470.

Jin Taijun 金太军 and Wang Qingwu 王庆五. *Zhongguo chuantong zhengzhi wenhua xin lun* 中国传统政治文化新论. Beijing: Shehui kexue wenxian chubanshe, 2006.

Johnson, David G. *The Medieval Chinese Oligarchy*. Boulder, CO: Westview, 1977.

Kano Osamu 河野収. "Chūgoku kodai no aru hibusō heiwa undō" 中國古代の或る非武裝平和運動. *Gunji shigaku* 軍事史學13.4 (1978): 64–74.

Keightley, David N. "The Shang: China's First Historical Dynasty." In *The Cambridge History of Ancient China*, edited by Michael Loewe and Edward L. Shaughnessy, 232–291. Cambridge: Cambridge University Press, 1999.

Kern, Martin. "The Poetry of Han Historiography." *Early Medieval China* 10–11.1 (2004): 23–65.

———. *The Stele Inscriptions of Ch'in Shih-huang: Text and Ritual in Early Chinese Imperial Representation*. New Haven, CT: American Oriental Society, 2000.

Khazanov, Anatoly M. *Nomads and the Outside World*. Translated by Julia Crookenden. Cambridge: Cambridge University Press, 1984.

Kim Hodong. *Holy War in China: The Muslim Rebellion and State in Chinese Central Asia, 1864–1877*. Stanford, CA: Stanford University Press, 2004.

Knapp, Keith, N. *Selfless Offspring: Filial Children and Social Order in Medieval China*. Honolulu: University of Hawai'i Press, 2005.

Komissarova T. G. " 'Monakh ne dolzhen byt' pochtitel'nym k imperatoru.' Iz buddijskoj polemiki v Kitae v IV–V vv." In *Buddism i Gosudarstvo na Dal'nem Vostoke*, edited by Lev P. Deliusin, 47–70. Moscow: Nauka, 1987.

Kuhn, Philip A. *Rebellion and Its Enemies in Late Imperial China: Militarization and Social Structure, 1796–1864*. Cambridge, MA: Harvard University Press, 1970.

Kurz, Johannes L. "The Yangzi in the Negotiations between the Southern Tang and Its Northern Neighbors (mid-tenth century)." In *China and Her Neighbours: Borders, Visions of the Other, Foreign Policy 10th to 19th Century*, edited by Sabine Dabringhaus, Roderich Ptak, and Richard Teschke, 29–47. Wiesbaden: Harrassowitz, 1997.

Kutcher, Norman. "The Death of the Xiaoxian Empress: Bureaucratic Betrayals and the Crises of Eighteenth-Century Chinese Rule." *Journal of Asian Studies* 56.3 (August 1997): 708–725.

———. *Mourning in Late Imperial China: Filial Piety and the State.* New York: Cambridge University Press, 1999.

Lai, Chi-tim. "Daoism and Political Rebellion during the Eastern Jin Dynasty." In *Politics and Religion in Ancient and Medieval Europe and China*, edited by Frederick Hok-ming Cheung and Ming-chiu Lai, 77–100. Hong Kong: Chinese University Press, 1999.

Lamley, Harry, J. "Lineage and Surname Feuds in Southern Fukien and Eastern Kwnagtung under the Ch'ing." In *Orthodoxy in Late Imperial China*, edited by Liu Kwang-Ching, 255–280. Berkeley: University of California Press, 1990.

Langlois, John D., Jr. "The Hung-wu Reign, 1368–1398." In *The Cambridge History of China*, vol. 7, *The Ming Dynasty, 1368–1644, Part I*, edited by Frederick W. Mote and Denis Twitchett, 107–181. Cambridge: Cambridge University Press, 1988.

Lau Nap-yin and Huang K'uan-chung. "Founding and Consolidation of the Sung Dynasty under T'ai-tsu (960–976), T'ai-tsung (976–997), and Chen-tsung (997–1022)." In *The Cambridge History of China*, vol. 5, *Part One: The Sung Dynasty and Its Precursors, 907–1279*, edited by Denis Twitchett and Paul Jakov Smith, 206–278. Cambridge: Cambridge University Press, 2009.

Leong Sow-Theng. *Migration and Ethnicity in Chinese History: Hakkas, Pengmin, and Their Neighbors.* Edited by Tim Wright. Stanford, CA: Stanford University Press, 1997.

Levenson, Joseph R. *Confucian China and Its Modern Fate: The Problem of Intellectual Continuity.* 3 vols. London: Routledge and Kegan Paul, 1958–1965.

Levine, Ari Daniel. *Divided by a Common Language: Factional Conflict in Late Northern Song China.* Honolulu: University of Hawai'i Press, 2009.

Levy, Howard S., trans. *Biography of Huang Ch'ao.* Berkeley: University of California Press, 1955.

Lewis, Mark E. *The Construction of Space in Early China.* Albany: State University of New York Press, 2006.

———. "The Han Abolition of Universal Military Service." In *Warfare in Chinese History*, edited by Hans Van de Ven, 33–76. Leiden: Brill, 2000.

———. *Sanctioned Violence in Early China.* Albany: State University of New York Press, 1990.

———. "Warring States: Political History." In *The Cambridge History of Ancient China*, edited by Michael Loewe and Edward L. Shaughnessy, 587–650. Cambridge: Cambridge University Press, 1999.

———. *Writing and Authority in Early China.* Albany: State University of New York Press, 1999.

Li, Cheng. "The Chinese Communist Party: Recruiting and Controlling the New Elites." *Journal of Current Chinese Affairs* 38.3 (2009): 13–33.

Li Feng. *Landscape and Power in Early China: The Crisis and Fall of the Western Zhou 1045–771 BC.* Cambridge: Cambridge University Press, 2006.

Liang Qichao 梁啟超. "Zhongguo zhuanzhi zhengzhi jinhua shi lun" 中國專制政治進化史論. In idem, *Yin bing shi wenji dianjiao* 飲冰室文集點校, collated by

Wu Song 吳松 et al., 3: 1649–1667. Kunming: Yunnan jiaoyu chubanshe, 2003.

Lieberthal, Kenneth. "The Great Leap Forward and the Split in the Yan'an Leadership, 1958–1965." In *The Politics of China, 1949–1989*, edited by Roderick MacFarquhar, 87–125. Cambridge: Cambridge University Press, 1993.

Liji jijie 禮記集解. Compiled by Sun Xidan 孫希旦. Beijing: Zhonghua shuju, 1995.

Lin Yü-sheng. *The Crisis of Chinese Consciousness: Radical Antitraditionalism in the May Fourth Era*. Madison: University of Wisconsin Press, 1979.

Liu, James J. Y. *The Chinese Knight Errant*. London: Routledge and Kegan Paul, 1967.

Liu, James T. C. (Liu Zijian 劉子健). *China Turns Inward: Intellectual-Political Changes in the Early Twelfth Century*. Cambridge, MA: Harvard University Press, 1989.

———. "An Early Sung Reformer: Fan Chung-yen." In *Chinese Thought and Institutions*, edited by John K. Fairbank, 105–131. Chicago: University of Chicago Press, 1957.

Liu Kwang-Ching. "Introduction: Orthodoxy in Chinese Society." In *Orthodoxy in Late Imperial China*, edited by Liu Kwang-Ching, 1–24. Berkeley: University of California Press, 1990.

———, ed. *Orthodoxy in Late Imperial China*. Berkeley: University of California Press, 1990.

———. "Religion and Politics in the White Lotus Rebellion of 1796 in Hubei." In *Heterodoxy in Late Imperial China*, edited by Liu Kwang-Ching and Richard Shek, 281–322. Honolulu: University of Hawai'i Press, 2004.

———. "Socioethics as Orthodoxy." In *Orthodoxy in Late Imperial China*, edited by Liu Kwang-Ching, 53–100. Berkeley: University of California Press, 1990.

———. "World View and Peasant Rebellion: Reflections on Post-Mao Historiography." *Journal of Asian Studies* 40.2 (1981): 295–326.

Liu Kwang-Ching and Richard Shek. "Early Daoism in Retrospect: Cosmology, Ethics and Eschatology." In *Heterodoxy in Late Imperial China*, edited by Liu Kwang-Ching and Richard Shek, 29–72. Honolulu: University of Hawai'i Press, 2004.

———, eds. *Heterodoxy in Late Imperial China*. Honolulu: University of Hawai'i Press, 2004.

———. "Introduction." In *Heterodoxy in Late Imperial China*, edited by Liu Kwang-Ching and Richard Shek, 1–28. Honolulu: University of Hawai'i Press, 2004.

Liu Shaoqi. *Selected Works of Liu Shaoqi*. Beijing: Foreign Languages Press, 1984.

Liu Zehua 劉澤華. *Xian Qin shi ren yu shehui* 先秦士人與社會. Rev. ed. Tianjin: Tianjin renmin chubanshe, 2004.

———. *Zhongguo de Wangquanzhuyi* 中國的王權主義. Shanghai: Renmin chubanshe, 2000.

———, ed. *Zhongguo zhengzhi sixiang shi* 中國政治思想史. 3 vols. Hangzhou: Zhejiang renmin chubanshe, 1996.

Loewe, Michael. *Crisis and Conflict in Han China: 104 BC to AD 9*. London: George Allen & Unwin, 1974.

———. "The Former Han Dynasty." In *The Cambridge History of China*, vol. 1, *The Ch'in and Han Empires, 221 B.C.–A.D. 220*, edited by Denis Twitchett and Michael Loewe, 103–222. Cambridge: Cambridge University Press, 1986.

Lunyu yizhu 論語譯注. Annotated by Yang Bojun 楊伯峻. Beijing: Zhonghua shuju, 1992.

Lüshi chunqiu jiaoshi 呂氏春秋校釋. Compiled and annotated by Chen Qiyou 陳奇猷. Shanghai: Xuelin, 1990.

MacFarquhar, Roderick. *The Origins of the Cultural Revolution*, vol. 1, *Contradictions among the People, 1956–1957*. New York: Columbia University Press, 1974.

———. *The Origins of the Cultural Revolution*, vol. 2, *The Great Leap Forward, 1958–1960*. New York: Columbia University Press, 1983.

———. *The Origins of the Cultural Revolution*, vol. 3, *The Coming of the Cataclysm, 1961–1966*. Oxford: Oxford University Press; New York: Columbia University Press, 1997.

———. "The Succession to Mao and the End of Maoism, 1969–82." In *The Politics of China, 1949–1989*, edited by Roderick MacFarquhar, 248–339. Cambridge: Cambridge University Press, 1993.

MacFarquhar, Roderick, and Michael Shoenhals. *Mao's Last Revolution*. Cambridge MA: Belknap Press of Harvard University Press, 2006.

Mackerras, Colin. *The Uighur Empire according to the T'ang Dynastic Histories: A Study in Sino-Uighur Relations, 744–840*. 2nd ed. Columbia: University of South Carolina Press, 1973.

Mair, Victor H. "Language and Ideology in the Written Popularisations of the *Sacred Edict*." In *Popular Culture in Late Imperial China*, edited by David Johnson, Andrew J. Nathan, and Evelyn S. Rawski, 325–359. Berkeley: University of California Press, 1985.

Mao shi zhengyi 毛詩正義. Annotated by Zheng Xuan 鄭玄 and Kong Yingda 孔穎達. Reprinted in *Shisanjing zhushu* 十三經注疏, compiled by Ruan Yuan 阮元, 1: 259–629. Beijing: Zhonghua shuju, 1991.

Mao Han-kuang. "The Evolution in the Nature of the Medieval Genteel Families." In *State and Society in Early Medieval China*, edited by Albert Dien, 73–109. Stanford, CA: Stanford University Press, 1990.

Mao Zedong. *Selected Works of Mao Tse-Tung* [*Mao Zedong*]. 4 vols. Peking [Beijing]: Foreign Languages Press, 1975.

Martynov, Aleksander S. "Gosudarstvo i religii na Dal'nem Vostoke (vmesto predisloviia)." In *Buddism i Gosudarstvo na Dal'nem Vostoke*, edited by Lev P. Deliusin, 3–46. Moscow: Nauka, 1987.

Mather, Richard B., trans. *Biography of Lü Kuang*. Berkeley: University of California Press, 1959.

McCord, Edward A. *The Power of the Gun: The Emergence of Modern Chinese Warlordism*. Berkeley: University of California Press, 1993.

McDermott, Joseph P. "Emperor, Élites and Commoners: The Community Pact

Ritual of the Late Ming." In *State and Court Ritual in China*, edited by Joseph P. McDermott, 299–351. Cambridge: Cambridge University Press, 1999.

———, ed. *State and Court Ritual in China*. Cambridge: Cambridge University Press, 1999.

McNeill, John R. "China's Environmental History in World Perspective." In *Sediments of Time: Environment and Society in Chinese History*, edited by Mark Elvin and Liu Ts'ui-jung, 31–49. Cambridge: Cambridge University Press, 1998.

Meadows, Thomas T. *The Chinese and their Rebellions: Viewed in Connection with their National Philosophy, Ethics, Legislation, and Administration, to which is added, an Essay on Civilization and its Present State in the East and West*. Stanford, CA: Academics Reprints, 1959.

Mengzi yizhu 孟子譯注. Annotated by Yang Bojun 楊伯峻. Beijing: Zhonghua shuju, 1992.

Meskill, John. *Academies in Ming China: A Historical Essay*. Tucson: University of Arizona Press, 1982.

Metzger, Thomas A. *Escape from Predicament: Neo-Confucianism and China's Evolving Political Culture*. New York: Columbia University Press, 1977.

Millward, James, A. *Beyond the Pass: Economy, Ethnicity, and Empire in Qing Central Asia, 1759–1864*. Stanford, CA: Stanford University Press, 1998.

Moody, Peter R., Jr. "The Political Culture of Chinese Students and Intellectuals: A Historical Examination." *Asian Survey* 28.11 (November 1988): 1140–1160.

Morris, Ian, and Walter Scheidel. *The Dynamics of Ancient Empires: State Power from Assyria to Byzantium*. Oxford: Oxford University Press, 2009.

Mote, Frederick W. "Confucian Eremitism in the Yuan Period." In *Confucianism and Chinese Civilization*, edited by Arthur F. Wright, 252–290. Stanford, CA: Stanford University Press, 1964.

———. "The Growth of Chinese Despotism: A Critique of Wittfogel's Theory of Oriental Despotism as Applied to China." *Oriens Extremus* 8 (1961): 1–41.

———. *Imperial China, 900–1800*. Cambridge, MA: Harvard University Press, 1999.

Mozi jiaozhu 墨子校注. Compiled and annotated by Wu Yujiang 吳毓江. Beijing: Zhonghua shuju, 1994.

Munro, Donald J. *A Chinese Ethics for the New Century: The Ch'ien Mu Lectures in History and Culture, and Other Essays on Science and Confucian Ethics*. Hong Kong: Chinese University Press, 2005.

Mutschler, Fritz-Heiner, and Achim Mittag, eds. *Conceiving the Empire: China and Rome Compared*. Oxford: Oxford University Press, 2008.

Naquin, Susan. *Millenarian Rebellion in China: The Eight Trigrams Uprising of 1813*. New Haven, CT: Yale University Press, 1976.

———. *Shantung Rebellion: The Wang Lun Uprising of 1774*. New Haven, CT: Yale University Press, 1976.

Nathan, Andrew J., and Bruce Gilley. *China's New Rulers: The Secret Files*. 2nd rev. ed. New York: New York Review Books, 2003.

Nylan, Michael. "A Problematic Model: The Han 'Orthodox Synthesis,' Then and Now." In *Imagining Boundaries: Changing Confucian Doctrines, Texts, and*

Hermeneutics, edited by Chow Kai-wing, On-cho Ng, and John B. Henderson, 17–56. Albany: State University of New York Press, 1999.

Ouyang Xiu. *Historical Records of the Five Dynasties.* Translated with an introduction by Richard L. Davis. New York: Columbia University Press, 2004.

———. *Zhengtong lun* 正統論. In idem, *Wenzhong ji* 文忠集 16, *Siku quanshu* 四庫全書 e-edition.

Overmyer, Daniel L. "Attitudes toward the Ruler and State in Chinese Popular Religious Literature: Sixteenth and Seventeenth Century *Pao-chüan.*" *Harvard Journal of Asiatic Studies* 44.2 (1984): 347–379.

Parsons, James B. "The Culmination of a Chinese Peasant Rebellion: Chang Hsien-chung in Szechwan, 1644–46." *Journal of Asian Studies* 16.3 (1957): 387–400.

Perdue, Peter C. *China Marches West: The Qing Conquest of Central Eurasia.* Cambridge, MA: Belknap Press of Harvard University Press, 2005.

———. *Exhausting the Earth: State and Peasant in Hunan, 1500–1850.* Cambridge, MA: Harvard University Press, 1987.

Perelomov, Leonard S. *Imperiia Tsin': Pervoe Tsentralizovannoe Gosudarstvo v Kitae.* Moscow: Nauka, 1961.

Perry, Elizabeth J. "Heterodox Rebellion? The Mystery of Yellow Cliff." In idem, *Challenging the Mandate of Heaven: Social Protest and State Power in China*, 76–107. New York: M. E. Sharpe, 2001.

———. "Introduction: Chinese Political Culture Revisited." In *Popular Protest and Political Culture in Modern China*, 2nd ed., edited by Jeffrey N. Wassertrom and Elizabeth J. Perry, 1–14. Boulder, CO: Westview, 1994.

———. "Permanent Rebellion? Continuities and Discontinuities in Chinese Protest." In *Popular Protest in China*, edited by Kevin J. O'Brien, 205–216. Cambridge MA: Harvard University Press, 2008.

———. "Protective Rebellion: Tax Protest in Late Qing China." In idem, *Challenging the Mandate of Heaven: Social Protest and State Power in China*, 47–75. New York: M. E. Sharpe, 2001.

———. *Rebels and Revolutionaries in North China, 1845–1945.* Stanford, CA: Stanford University Press, 1980.

———. "Social Banditry Revisited: The Case of Bai Lang, a Chinese Brigand." *Modern China* 9.3 (July 1983): 355–382.

Petersen, Jens Østergård. "Which Books Did the First Emperor of Ch'in Burn? On the Meaning of *Pai Chia* in Early Chinese Sources." *Monumenta Serica* 43 (1995): 1–52.

Peterson, Charles A. "Court and Province in Mid- and Late T'ang." In *The Cambridge History of China*, vol. 3, *Sui and T'ang China, 589–906 AD, Part I*, edited by Denis C. Twitchett, 464–560. Cambridge: Cambridge University Press, 1979.

Pines, Yuri. "Beasts or Humans: Pre-Imperial Origins of Sino-Barbarian Dichotomy." In *Mongols, Turks and Others*, edited by Reuven Amitai and Michal Biran, 59–102. Leiden: Brill, 2005.

———. "Biases and Their Sources: Qin History in the *Shiji.*" *Oriens Extremus* 45 (2005–2006): 10–34.

———. "Bodies, Lineages, Citizens, and Regions: A Review of Mark Edward

Lewis' *The Construction of Space in Early China.*" *Early China* 30 (2005): 155–188.

———. "Chinese History-Writing between the Sacred and the Secular." In *Early Chinese Religion. Part One: Shang through Han (1250 BC–220 AD)*, edited by John Lagerwey and Marc Kalinowski, 1: 315–340. Leiden: Brill, 2009.

———. *Envisioning Eternal Empire: Chinese Political Thought of the Warring States Era.* Honolulu: University of Hawai'i Press, 2009.

———. "The First Emperor and His Image." In *The Birth of Empire: The State of Qin revisited*, edited by Yuri Pines, Lothar von Falkenhausen, Gideon Shelach, and Robin D. S. Yates. Berkeley: University of California Press, forthcoming.

———. *Foundations of Confucian Thought: Intellectual Life in the Chunqiu Period, 722–453 B.C.E.* Honolulu: University of Hawai'i Press, 2002.

———. "Friends or Foes: Changing Concepts of Ruler-Minister Relations and the Notion of Loyalty in Pre-Imperial China." *Monumenta Serica* 50 (2002): 35–74.

———. "From Teachers to Subjects: Ministers Speaking to the Rulers from Yan Ying 晏嬰 to Li Si 李斯." In *Addressing the Autocrat: The Drama of Early Chinese Court Discourse*, edited by Garret Olderding. Cambridge MA: Harvard University Press, forthcoming.

———. "A Hero Terrorist: Adoration of Jing Ke Revisited." *Asia Major*, 3rd ser., 21.2 (2008): 1–34.

———. "Imagining the Empire? Concepts of 'Primeval Unity' in Pre-imperial Historiographic Tradition." In *Concepts of Empire in Ancient China and Rome— An Intercultural Comparison*, edited by Achim Mittag and Fritz-Heiner Muetschler, 67–90. Oxford: Oxford University Press, 2008.

———. "The Messianic Emperor: A New Look at Qin's Place in China's History." In *The Birth of Empire: The State of Qin Revisited*, edited by Yuri Pines, Lothar von Falkenhausen, Gideon Shelach, and Robin D. S. Yates. Berkeley: University of California Press, forthcoming.

———. "Name or Substance? Between *zhengtong* 正統 and *yitong* 一統." *History: Theory and Criticism* 2 (2001): 105–138.

———. "'The One That Pervades All' in Ancient Chinese Political Thought: Origins of the 'Great Unity' Paradigm." *T'oung Pao* 86.4–5 (2000): 280–324.

———. "Political Mythology and Dynastic Legitimacy in the *Rong Cheng shi* Manuscript." *Bulletin of the School of Oriental and Asian Studies* 73.3 (2010): 503–529.

———. "The Question of Interpretation: Qin History in Light of New Epigraphic Sources." *Early China* 29 (2004): 1–44.

———. "Submerged by Absolute Power: The Ruler's Predicament in the *Han Feizi.*" In *Dao Companion to the Philosophy of Han Fei*, edited by Paul Goldin. Berlin: Springer, forthcoming.

———. "To Rebel Is Justified? The Image of Zhouxin and Legitimacy of Rebellion in Chinese Political Tradition." *Oriens Extremus* 47 (2008): 1–24.

Pines, Yuri, with Lothar von Falkenhausen, Gideon Shelach, and Robin D. S. Yates. "General Introduction: Qin History Revisited." In *The Birth of Empire: The State of Qin Revisited*, edited by Yuri Pines, Lothar von Falkenhausen,

Gideon Shelach, and Robin D. S. Yates. Berkeley: University of California Press, forthcoming.

Pines, Yuri, Lothar von Falkenhausen, Gideon Shelach, and Robin D. S. Yates, eds. *The Birth of Empire: The State of Qin Revisited*. Berkeley: University of California Press, forthcoming.

Plaks, Andrew. *The Four Masterworks of the Ming Novel*. Princeton, NJ: Princeton University Press, 1987.

Puett, Michael J. "Combining the Ghosts and Spirits, Centering the Realm: Mortuary Ritual and Political Organization in the Ritual Compendia of Early China." In *Early Chinese Religion. Part One: Shang through Han (1250 BC–AD 220)*, edited by John Lagerwey and Marc Kalinowski, 2: 695–720. Leiden: Brill, 2009.

———. *To Become a God: Cosmology, Sacrifice, and Self-Divinization in Early China*. Cambridge: Cambridge University Press, 2002.

Pye, Lucian W. *The Spirit of Chinese Politics*. New ed. Cambridge, MA: Harvard University Press, 1992.

Rankin, Mary B., and Joseph E. Esherick, eds. *Chinese Local Elites and Patterns of Dominance*. Berkeley: University of California Press, 1990.

———. "Concluding Remarks." In *Chinese Local Elites and Patterns of Dominance*, edited by Mary B. Rankin and Joseph E. Esherick, 305–346. Berkeley: University of California Press, 1990.

Rao Zongyi 饒宗頤. *Zhongguo shixue shang zhi zhengtong lun* 中國史學上之正統. Reprint. Shanghai: Yuandong chubanshe, 1996.

Rawski, Evelyn S. *The Last Emperors: A Social History of Qing Imperial Institutions*. Berkeley: University of California Press, 1998.

Reed, Bradly W. *Talons and Teeth: County Clerks and Runners in the Qing Dynasty*. Stanford, CA: Stanford University Press, 2000.

Ren Shuang 任爽. *Nan Tang shi* 南唐史. Changchun: Dongbei shifan daxue chubanshe, 1995.

Richter, Melvin. *The Political Theory of Montesquieu*. Cambridge: Cambridge University Press, 1977.

Robinson, David M. "Banditry and the Subversion of State Authority in China: The Capital Region during the Middle Ming Period (1450–1525)." *Journal of Social History* 33.3 (2000): 527–563.

———. *Empire's Twilight: Northeast Asia under the Mongols*. Cambridge MA: Harvard University Asia Center; distributed by Harvard University Press, 2009.

———. "The Ming Court and the Legacy of the Yuan Mongols." In *Culture, Courtiers and Competition: The Ming Court (1368–1644)*, edited by David M. Robinson, 365–422. Cambridge MA: Harvard University Asia Center; distributed by Harvard University Press, 2008.

Rossabi, Morris. "Introduction." In *China among Equals: The Middle Kingdom and Its Neighbors, 10th–14th Centuries*, edited by Morris Rossabi, 1–13. Berkeley: University of California Press, 1983.

———. *Khubilai Khan: His Life and Times*. Berkeley: University of California Press, 1988.

Rowe, William T. *Crimson Rain: Seven Centuries of Violence in a Chinese County*. Stanford, CA: Stanford University Press, 2007.

———. *Saving the World: Chen Hongmou and Elite Consciousness in Eighteenth-Century China*. Stanford, CA: Stanford University Press, 2001.

Sanft, Charles. "Communication and Cooperation in Early Imperial China: The Qin Dynasty and Publicity." Submitted as *Habilitationsschrift* at Westfälische Wilhelms-Universität Münster, 2010.

Schafer, Edward. "The Yeh chung chi." *T'oung Pao*, 76.4–5 (1990): 147–207.

Scheidel, Walter. "From the 'Great Convergence' to the 'First Great Divergence': Roman and Qin-Han State Formation and Its Aftermath." In *Rome and China: Comparative Perspectives on Ancient World Empires*, edited by Walter Scheidel, 11–23. Oxford: Oxford University Press, 2009.

———, ed. *Rome and China: Comparative Perspectives on Ancient World Empires*. Oxford: Oxford University Press, 2009.

Schirokauer, Conrad. "Neo-Confucians under Attack: The Condemnation of *Wei-hsueh*." In *Crisis and Prosperity in Sung China*, edited by John W. Haeger, 163–198. Tucson: University of Arizona Press, 1975.

Schirokauer, Conrad, and Robert R. Hymes. "Introduction." In *Ordering the World: Approaches to State and Society in Sung Dynasty China*, edited by Robert R. Hymes and Conrad Schirokauer, 1–58. Berkeley: University of California Press, 1993.

Schneewind, Sarah, ed. *Long Live the Emperor: Uses of the Ming Founder across Six Centuries of East Asian History*. Ming Studies Research Series. Minneapolis, MN: Society for Ming Studies, 2008.

———. "Visions and Revisions: Village Policies of the Ming Founder in Seven Phases." *T'oung Pao* 87.4–5 (2001): 317–359.

Schram, Stuart R. *The Thought of Mao Tse-Tung*. Cambridge: Cambridge University Press, 1989.

Schwarcz, Vera. *The Chinese Enlightenment: Intellectuals and the Legacy of the May Fourth Movement of 1919*. Berkeley: University of California Press, 1985.

Shambaugh, David. "Introduction: The Evolving and Eclectic Modern Chinese State." In *The Modern Chinese State*, edited by David Shambaugh, 1–14. Cambridge: Cambridge University Press, 2000.

Shang jun shu zhuizhi 商君書錐指. Annotated by Jiang Lihong 蔣禮鴻. Beijing: Zhonghua shuju, 1996.

Shapiro, Sydney, trans. *Outlaws of the Marsh*. Beijing: Foreign Languages Press, 1993.

Shek, Richard, and Tetsurō Noguchi. "Eternal Mother Religion: Its History and Ethics." In *Heterodoxy in Late Imperial China*, edited by Liu Kwang-Ching and Richard Shek, 241–280. Honolulu: University of Hawai'i Press, 2004.

Shelach, Gideon. "Collapse or Transformation? Anthropological and Archaeological Perspectives on the Fall of Qin." In *The Birth of Empire: The State of Qin Revisited*, edited by Yuri Pines, Lothar von Falkenhausen, Gideon Shelach, and Robin D. S. Yates. Berkeley: University of California Press, forthcoming.

Shiji 史記, by Sima Qian 司馬遷 et al. Annotated by Zhang Shoujie 張守節, Sima Zhen 司馬貞, and Pei Yin 裴駰. Beijing: Zhonghua shuju, 1997.

Shui hu zhuan 水滸傳 [Rongyu tang 容與堂 ed.], attributed to Shi Nai'an 施耐庵 and Luo Guanzhong 羅貫中. Collated by Ling Geng 凌賡, Heng He 恆鶴, and Diao Ning 刁寧. Reprint. Shanghai: Shanghai guji chubanshe, 1993.

Smith, Paul J. "Irredentism as Political Capital: The New Policies and the Annexation of Tibetan Domains in Hehuang (the Qinghai-Gansu Highlands) under Shenzong and His Sons, 1068–1126." In *Emperor Huizong and Late Northern Song China*, edited by Patricia Ebrey and Maggie Bickford, 78–130. Cambridge, MA: Harvard University Asia Center, 2006.

———. "Shen-Tsung's Reign and the New Policies of Wang An-Shih, 1067–1085." In *The Cambridge History of China*, vol. 5, *Part One: The Sung Dynasty and Its Precursors, 907–1279*, edited by Denis Twitchett and Paul Jakov Smith, 347–483. Cambridge: Cambridge University Press, 2009.

———. "State Power and Economic Activism during the New Policies, 1068–1085: The Tea and Horse Trade and the 'Green Sprouts' Loan Policy." In *Ordering the World: Approaches to State and Society in Sung Dynasty China*, edited by Robert R. Hymes and Conrad Schirokauer, 76–127. Berkeley: University of California Press, 1993.

Smolin, Georgij Ia. "Problemy obshchego i osobennogo v istorii krest'ianskikh vojn v feodal'nom Kitae (K razrabotke poniatiia 'krest'ianskaia vojna')" In *Istoriografiia i istochnikovedenie istorii stran Azii i Afriki*, edited by L. A. Berezny, 6 (1982): 104–140.

Solomon, Richard H. *Mao's Revolution and the Chinese Political Culture*. Berkeley: University of California Press, 1971.

Somers, Robert M. "The End of the T'ang." In *The Cambridge History of China*, vol. 3, *Sui and T'ang China, 589–906 AD, Part I*, edited by Denis C. Twitchett, 682–789. Cambridge: Cambridge University Press, 1979.

Song shu 宋書, by Shen Yue 沈約. Beijing: Zhonghua shuju, 1997.

Spence, Jonathan D. *Emperor of China: Self-Portrait of K'ang-Hsi*. New York: Knopf, 1974.

———. "The Kang-hsi Reign." In *The Cambridge History of China*, vol. 9, *Part One: The Ch'ing Empire to 1800*, edited by Denis Twitchett and John K. Fairbank, 120–182. Cambridge: Cambridge University Press, 2002.

———. *The Search for Modern China*. New York: Norton, 1990.

———. *Treason by the Book: Traitors, Conspirators and Guardians of an Emperor*. New York: Viking, 2001.

Standen, Naomi. "The Five Dynasties." In *The Cambridge History of China*, vol. 5, *Part One: The Sung Dynasty and Its Precursors, 907–1279*, edited by Denis Twitchett and Paul Jakov Smith, 38–132. Cambridge: Cambridge University Press, 2009.

———. *Unbounded Loyalty: Frontier Crossings in Liao China*. Honolulu: University of Hawai'i Press, 2007.

———. "What Nomads Want: Raids, Invasions and the Liao Conquest of 947." In *Mongols, Turks and Others: Eurasian Nomads and the Sedentary World*, edited by Reuven Amitai and Michal Biran, 129–174. Leiden: Brill, 2005.

Sun Yat-sen. *San min chu i: The Three Principles of the People*. Translated by Frank W. Price. Edited by L. T. Chen (陳立廷). Chungking : Ministry of Information of China, 1943.

Tackett, Nicolas. "Great Clansmen, Bureaucrats, and Local Magnates: The Structure and Circulation of the Elite in Late-Tang China." *Asia Major*, 3rd ser., 21.2 (2008): 101–152.

———. "The Transformation of Medieval Chinese Elites (850–1000 C.E.)." PhD diss., Columbia University, 2006.

Tao, Jing-shen. "Barbarians or Northerners: Northern Sung Images of the Khitans." In *China among Equals: The Middle Kingdom and Its Neighbors, 10th–14th Centuries*, edited by Morris Rossabi, 66–86. Berkeley: University of California Press, 1983.

———. *Two Sons of Heaven: Studies in Sung-Liao Relations*. Tucson: University of Arizona Press, 1988.

Taylor, Romeyn. "Official and Popular Religion and Organization of Chinese Society in the Ming." In *Orthodoxy in Late Imperial China*, edited by Liu Kwang-Ching, 126–157. Berkeley: University of California Press, 1990.

Teiwes, Frederick C. "The Establishment and Consolidation of the New Regime, 1949–1957." In *The Politics of China, 1949–1989*, edited by Roderick MacFarquhar, 5–86. Cambridge: Cambridge University Press, 1993.

Teng Xincai 滕新才. "Lun Huang Chao de xingge tezheng ji qi yingxiang" 論黃巢的性格特徵及其影響. In *Zhongguo gudai minben sixiang yu nongmin wenti* 中國古代民本思想與農民問題, edited by Meng Xiangcai 孟祥才, 130–144. Ji'nan: Shandong daxue chubanshe, 2003.

Ter Haar, Barend J. "Rethinking 'Violence' in Chinese Culture." In *Meanings of Violence: A Cross Cultural Perspective*, edited by Göran Aijmer and Jos Abbink, 123–140. Oxford: Berg, 2000.

———. *The White Lotus Teachings in Chinese Religious History*. Leiden: Brill, 1992.

Tong, James W. *Disorder under Heaven: Collective Violence in the Ming Dynasty*. Stanford, CA: Stanford University Press, 1991.

Townsend, James. "Chinese Nationalism." *Australian Journal of Chinese Affairs* 27 (1992): 97–130.

Tu Wei-ming. "The Creative Tension between *Jen* and *Li*." *Philosophy East and West* 18.1–2 (1968): 29–39.

———. "The Structure and Function of the Confucian Intellectual in Ancient China." In idem, *Way, Learning and Politics: Essays on the Confucian Intellectual*, 13–28. Albany: State University of New York Press, 1993.

Twitchett, Denis C. *Financial Administration under the T'ang Dynasty*. 2nd ed. Cambridge: Cambridge University Press, 1970.

———. "Hsüan-tsung (reign 712–756)." In *The Cambridge History of China*, vol. 3, *Sui and T'ang China, 589–906 AD, Part I*, edited by Denis C. Twitchett, 333–463. Cambridge: Cambridge University Press, 1979.

———. "The T'ang Imperial Family." *Asia Major*, 3rd ser., 7.2 (1994): 1–61.

Twitchett, Denis, and Klaus-Peter Tietze. "The Liao." In *The Cambridge History of China*, vol. 6, *Alien Regimes and Border States, 907–1368*, edited by Herbert Franke and Denis Twitchett, 43–153. Cambridge: Cambridge University Press, 1994.

Van de Ven, Hans J. *War and Nationalism in China 1925–1945*. New York: Routledge, 2003.

Vankeerberghen, Griet. *The Huainanzi and Liu An's Claim to Moral Authority*. Albany: State University of New York Press, 2001.

Vervoorn, Aat. *Men of the Cliffs and Caves: The Development of the Chinese Eremitic Tradition to the End of the Han Dynasty*. Hong Kong: Chinese University Press, 1990.

Wagner, Donald B. *Iron and Steel in Ancient China*. Leiden: Brill, 1993.

Wagner, Rudolf G. " 'In Guise of a Congratulation': Political Symbolism in Zhou Xinfang's Play *Hai Rui Submits His Memorial*." In *Using the Past to Serve the Present: Historiography and Politics in Contemporary China*, edited by Jonathan Unger, 46–103. Armonk, NY: Sharpe, 1997.

Wakeman, Frederic, Jr. *The Fall of Imperial China*. New York: Free Press, 1975.

———. *The Great Enterprise: The Manchu Reconstruction of Imperial Order in Seventeenth-Century China*. Berkeley: University of California Press, 1985.

———. "The Price of Autonomy: Intellectuals in Ming and Qing Politics." In idem, *Telling Chinese History: A Selection of Essays*, selected and edited by Lea H. Wakeman, 135–173. Berkeley: University of California Press, 2009.

Waley, Arthur, trans. *The Book of Songs: The Ancient Chinese Classic of Poetry*. Edited with additional translations by Joseph R. Allen. New York: Grove Press, 1996.

Walton, Linda. *Academies and Society in Southern Sung China*. Honolulu: University of Hawai'i Press, 1999.

Wang Fuzhi 王夫之. *Du Tongjian lun* 讀通鑑論. Beijing: Zhonghua shuju 1998.

Wang Hui 王輝 and Cheng Xuehua 程學華. *Qin wenzi jizheng* 秦文字集證. Taipei: Yinwen, 1999.

Wang Gungwu. *Divided China: Preparing for Reunification, 883–947*. Hackensack, NJ: World Scientific Pub., 2007. (Revised edition of *The Structure of Power in North China during the Five Dynasties*, 1957.)

———. "The Rhetoric of a Lesser Empire: Early Sung Relations with Its Neighbors." In *China among Equals: The Middle Kingdom and Its Neighbors, 10th–14th Centuries*, edited by Morris Rossabi, 47–65. Berkeley: University of California Press, 1983.

Wang Yi 王毅. *Zhongguo huangquan zhidu yanjiu—yi 16 shiji qianhou Zhongguo zhidu xingai ji qi fali wei jiaodian* 中國皇權制度研究—以 16世紀前後中國制度形態及其法理為焦點. Beijing: Beijing daxue chubanshe, 2007.

Wang Zhongluo 王仲犖. *Wei Jin Nanbeichao shi* 魏晉南北朝史. Shanghai: Shanghai renmin chubanshe, 1998.

Wassertrom, Jeffrey N., and Elizabeth J. Perry, eds. *Popular Protest and Political Culture in Modern China*. 2nd ed. Boulder, CO: Westview, 1994.

Watson, Burton, trans. *Records of the Grand Historian: Han Dynasty*. 2 vols. Hong Kong: Columbia University Press, 1993.

———, trans. *Records of the Grand Historian*, vol. 3, *Qin Dynasty*. Hong Kong: Chinese University of Hong Kong Press, 1993.

Wechsler, Howard J. *Offerings of Jade and Silk: Ritual and Symbol in the Legitimation of the T'ang Dynasty*. New Haven, CT: Yale University Press, 1985.

———. "T'ai-tsung (Reign 626–49): The Consolidator." In *The Cambridge History of China*, vol. 3, *Sui and T'ang China, 589–906 AD, Part I*, edited by Denis C. Twitchett, 188–241. Cambridge: Cambridge University Press, 1979.

Weinstein, Stanley. *Buddhism under the Tang*. Cambridge: Cambridge University Press, 1987.

Wilbur, Martin C. *The Nationalist Revolution in China, 1923–1928*. Cambridge: Cambridge University Press, 1984.

Will, Pierre-Étienne. *Bureaucracy and Famine in Eighteenth-Century China*. Translated by Elborg Forster. Stanford, CA: Stanford University Press, 1990.

Will, Pierre-Étienne, and R. Bin Wong. *Nourish the People: The State Civilian Granary System in China, 1650–1850*. Ann Arbor: University of Michigan Press, 1991.

Wittfogel, Karl A. *Oriental Despotism: A Comparative Study of Total Power*. New Haven, CT: Yale University Press, 1957.

Wong, R. Bin. "Food Riots in the Qing Dynasty." *Journal of Asian Studies* 41.4 (1982): 767–788.

Wong Kwok-Yiu 王國堯. " 'Hide-and-Seek'—On the Reclusion and Political Activism of the Mid-Tang *Yinshi* ('Hermit') Fu Zai." *Oriens Extremus* 46 (2007): 147–183.

Worthy, Edmund H., Jr. "Diplomacy for Survival: Domestic and Foreign Relations of Wu-Yüeh, 907–978." In *China among Equals: The Middle Kingdom and Its Neighbors, 10th–14th Centuries*, edited by Morris Rossabi, 17–46. Berkeley: University of California Press, 1983.

Wu Fusheng. *Written at Imperial Command: Panegyric Poetry in Early Medieval China*. Albany: State University of New York Press, 2008.

Xiong, Victor Cunrui. *Emperor Yang of the Sui Dynasty: His Life, Times, and Legacy*. Albany: State University of New York Press, 2006.

Xunzi jijie 荀子集解. Compiled by Wang Xianqian 王先謙. Beijing: Zhonghua shuju, 1992.

Yan Buke 閻步克. *Shidafu zhengzhi yansheng shi gao* 士大夫政治演生史稿. 3rd ed. Beijing: Beijing daxue, 2003.

Yantie lun jiaozhu 鹽鐵論校注. Compiled and annotated by Wang Liqi 王利器. Beijing: Zhonghua shuju, 1996.

Yao Xinzhong. *The Introduction to Confucianism*. Cambridge: Cambridge University Press, 2000.

Yü Ying-shih (Yu Yingshi). "Han Foreign Relations." In *The Cambridge History of China*, vol. 1, *The Ch'in and Han Empires 221 B.C.–A.D. 220*, edited by Denis Twitchett and Michael Loewe, 377–462. Cambridge: Cambridge University Press, 1986.

Yu Yingshi 余英時. *Shi yu Zhongguo wenhua* 士與中國文化. Shanghai: Shanghai renmin chubanshe, 1987.

———. *Zhu Xi de lishi shijie: Songdai shidafu zhengzhi wenhua yanjiu* 朱熹的歷史世界: 宋代士大夫政治文化的研究. Reprint. Beijing: Sanlian, 2004.

Zelin, Madeleine. *The Magistrate's Tael: Rationalizing Fiscal Reform in Eighteenth-Century Ch'ing China*. Berkeley: University of California Press, 1984.

———. "The Yung-cheng Reign." In *The Cambridge History of China*, vol. 9, *Part One: The Ch'ing Empire to 1800*, edited by Denis Twitchett and John K. Fairbank, 183–229. Cambridge: Cambridge University Press, 2002.

Zhang Chunlong 張春龍. "Liye Qinjian zhong huji he renkou guanli jilu" 里耶秦簡中戶籍和人口管理記錄. In *Liye gucheng: Qin jian yu Qin wenhua yanjiu* 里

耶古城·秦簡與秦文化研究, edited by Zhongguo shehuikexueyuan Kaogu Yan-jiusuo 中國社會科學院考古研究所 et al., 188–195. Beijing: Kexue chubanshe, 2009.

Zhang Fentian 張分田. *Zhongguo diwang guannian—shehui pubian yishi zhong de 'zun jun—zui jun' wenhua fanshi* 中國帝王觀念—社會普遍意識中的"尊君—罪君"文化範式. Beijing: Zhongguo renmin daxue chubanshe, 2004.

———. *Min ben sixiang yu Zhongguo gudai zhengzhi sixiang* 民本思想與中國古代政治思想. Tianjin: Nankai daxue chubanshe, 2009.

Zhang Rongming 張榮明. *Yin Zhou zhengzhi yu zongjiao* 殷周政治與宗教. Taipei: Wunan tushu gongsi, 1997.

Zhang Xiangming. "A Preliminary Study of the Punishment of Political Speech in the Ming Period." *Ming Studies* 62 (2010): 56–91.

Zhanguo ce zhushi 戰國策注釋. Annotated by He Jianzhang 何建章. Beijing: Zhonghua shuju, 1991.

Zheng Xiaowei. "Loyalty, Anxiety, and Opportunism: Local Elite Activism during the Taiping Rebellion in Eastern Zhejiang, 1851–1864." *Late Imperial China* 30.2 (2009): 39–83.

Zheng Yongnian. *Technological Empowerment: The Internet, State, and Society in China.* Stanford, CA: Stanford University Press, 2008.

Zhou Lasheng 周腊生. "Da Xi, Taiping tianguo keju shulue" 大西、太平天國科舉述略. *Xiaogan zhiye jishu xueyuan yuan xuebao* 孝感職業技術學院學報 4 (2001): 32–36.

Zhou Liangxiao 周良霄. *Huangdi yu huangquan* 皇帝與皇權. Rev. ed. Shanghai: Shanghai guji chubanshe, 2006.

Zizhi tongjian 資治通鑒, by Sima Guang 司馬光. Annotated by Hu Sanxing 胡三省. Beijing: Zhonghua shuju, 1992.

Zürcher, Erik. *The Buddhist Conquest of China: The Spread and Adaptation of Buddhism in Early Medieval China.* Leiden: Brill, 1972.

———. "Prince Moonlight: Messianism and Eschatology in Early Medieval Chinese Buddhism." *T'oung Pao* 68.1–3 (1982): 1–75.

Index

118; reforms in, 170. *See also* academies; examinations

egalitarianism, 5, 79, 135, 141–144, 157–159, 182, 203n17. *See also* equality

Eisenstadt, Shmuel N., 198n63, 202n71

elite, educated. *See* intellectuals

elite, local, 4–5, 77, 104–105, 128–133, 146, 158, 160, 198–99n1; abuse of power by, 122–123, 149–150; aristocratic, 105–106; co-optation of, 105, 109–110, 119–126, 129–130; and family values, 126–129; in Han, 108–111; as mediators, 120–121; militia of, 150; in Ming, 123–125, 128–129, 201n47; and modernization, 131–133; and Neo-Confucianism, 117–119; absent in Qin, 106–107; in Qing, 125–126, 129, 201n51; and regionalism, 25, 30–31; in Song, 113–119; suppression of, 109–110, 122–125, 130, 201n47; in Tang, 111–113; in the twentieth century, 165–166, 175–180, 206n27. *See also* aristocracy; intellectuals; *shi*; subelites; "voluntarism" of the literati

elitism, 135, 139, 141, 172, 178, 180, 182. *See also* hierarchy; "superior men"

Elman, Benjamin, 91, 199–200n22

emperor, 2, 4, 20, 23–25, 170, 191n3; bifurcation between institutional and individual power of, 46, 54–55, 66–67, 71–74, 195n66; constrained by bureaucracy, 45, 63–68, 71, 194n53, 195n66; child emperors, 59, 68, 74; criticism of, 44, 77, 95, 97–100, 197n32; despotism of, 45, 56, 60, 63–65, 68, 72, 93–94, 98, 123–124; as essential feature of Chinese political culture, 74–75; impartiality of, 90; and intellectuals, 85–100; and landownership, 45, 62–63; in modern age, 168–169, 176; nomadic, 69–71, 195n62, 195n64; overburdened by his tasks, 63–66; passivity of, 45, 56, 64–68, 70–71, 73–74; political roles of, 45, 64–66, 73, 89, 194n51, 194n52; religious authority of, 44–45, 57, 60–62, 193n39; ritual role of, 45, 56–57, 64–65, 73, 191n2, 194n57; as a sage, 45, 54, 72, 98; sacredness of, 44–45, 57–62, 193n31, 193n35; symbolic position of, 44–45, 57–63, 191n2; and "ten abomi-

nations," 58–59; title, explained, 54; training of, 66–67, 194n55; and unity, political, 27, 29–30, 44, 74; universal rule of, 32–37, 39–40. *See also* khan; monarch; remonstrance; succession struggles; True Monarch

Emperor An of Jin (晉安帝, r. 397–403 and 404–419 CE), 62

Emperor Huizong of Song (宋徽宗, r. 1101–1125), 40, 117, 191n74

Emperor Kangxi. *See* Kangxi Emperor

Emperor Qianlong. *See* Qianlong Emperor

Emperor Shizong of Ming (明世宗, r. 1521–1567), 73, 97–99, 198n55, 198n57

Emperor Shun of Han (漢順帝, r. 125–144), 198n53

Emperor Taizong of Tang (唐太宗, r. 626–649), 26, 67, 194n56. *See also* Li Shimin

Emperor Wen of Sui (隋文帝, r. 581–604), 194n51

Emperor Wu of Han (漢武帝, r. 141–87 BCE), 132, 190n58; Confucianism promoted by, 87–88, 93, 197n29, 197n30; image of, 88, 197n32; and intellectuals, 86–89, 94; and local magnates, 109–110, 112; territorial expansion under, 35

Emperor Wu of Liang (梁武帝, r. 502–549), 61, 193n40

Emperor Wuzong of Ming (明武宗, r. 1505–1521), 195n66

Emperor Xiaowen of Northern Wei (北魏孝文帝, r. 471–499), 38, 62–63, 111

Emperor Xizong of Ming (明熹宗, r. 1621–1627), 99

Emperor Yang of Sui (隋煬帝, r. 605–617), 149, 204n38

Emperor Yongzheng. *See* Yongzheng Emperor

empire, Chinese, 5–6; collapse of, 162–164, 170; in comparative perspective, 7–9, 11, 186n14, 186n15; durability of, 1–4, 11, 74, 100–103, 130–131, 135, 159–161; ideological prowess of, 3–4, 17, 19–20, 25, 41, 130, 185n5; magnitude of, 21–22, 35, 119, 185n4; and modern nation-state, 9, 165–166, 183; and steppe empires, 37–38. *See also* emperor; foreign policy; intellectuals; stability; unity

Springs-and-Autumns period (Chunqiu 春秋, 770–453 BCE), 13–15, 33, 48, 78–79, 105, 126, 137–138, 185n4, 187n7, 192n7

stability, 1, 3, 9, 40, 62, 74, 90, 123, 150, 162, 175–176; versus efficiency, 24, 67, 69; and intellectuals, 101–102; and local elites, 113, 132; and monarch's activism, discouraged, 66–67, 69–71; and multistate system, 13; versus progress, 8, 129–133, 163, 180–182; and rebellions, 134, 156, 158; under regional regimes, 28–30, 43; and unity, 16–18, 20–21, 29–32, 42–43, 85, 167–169

Stalinism, 164

Standen, Naomi, 29, 188n41

students: in imperial academies, 92, 96, 124; modern, 173–174; status privileges of, 113, 124

subcounty units, 22, 121, 123–124

subelites, 148

succession struggles, 29, 46, 69–71

Sui dynasty (隋, 581–618), 26, 65, 111, 149, 189n47, 194n51

Sun En (孫恩), rebellion leader (399–402), 153

Sun Yat-sen (孫逸仙, a.k.a. Sun Zhongshan 孫中山, 1866–1925), 165, 169, 176, 205n4

"superior men" (junzi 君子), 78–79, 85, 88, 94, 98–99, 118, 139, 141–142, 177

Taiping Dao (太平道). See Yellow Turbans

Taiping (太平) rebellion (1850–1864), 134, 143, 144, 153, 157, 160, 203n25, 205n60

Taiwan (Republic of China), 167–169, 182

Tang dynasty (唐 618–906), 25, 38, 42, 65, 67, 96, 194n51; and aristocracy, 111–113, 133, 199n20; collapse of, 28, 71, 153; decentralization under, 24, 26–28, 193n37; Liao as heirs of, 39; local administration in, 24, 26; rebellions under, 153, 157, 160; recruitment of officials in, 111–112, 199n18; territorial expansion in, 32, 36. See also An Lushan; Emperor Taizong; Huang Chao; Later Tang dynasty

Tanguts, 39, 191n71. See also Xi Xia

taxation, 31, 121–124, 141, 157–158; in Han, 110, 199n14

temples: Confucian, 93, 120

Tengri, supreme God of the nomads, 37, 69

theocracy, 164

Three Bonds (san gang 三綱), 126–128, 141

Tiananmen incident, 1989, 170, 174, 185n3, 206n12

tianzi (天子). See "Son of Heaven"

Tibet, 36, 164. See also Tibetans

Tibetans, 39. See also Tibet

Toghon Temür, Yuan emperor (r. 1333–1368), 70, 195n62

Treaty of Shanyuan, 1005, 39–40

tribute system, 35–36, 190nn59–60

True Monarch, 50–53, 68–69, 72, 80; and the First Emperor, 54–56; and unity, 19, 29, 39; universal rule of, 32, 35–36, 190n58; yearned for, 100

True Way. See The Way

Tu Wei-ming, 5, 139

Tuoba (拓拔), 62. See also Northern Wei dynasty

Turks, 39

Uighurs, 27, 39, 188n35

unity, political, 1; and cultural, 102, 130; deterministic explanations of rejected, 11; and dynastic legitimacy, 20–21; as fundamental political desideratum, 3, 5, 11–12, 41–43, 46; and historiographic biases, 42; ideological justifications for, 17–19; and intellectual uniformity, 85–87, 90–91; in modern age, 165–169, 182; and monarchism, 19, 44, 74; and nomads, 34, 36–41, 191n77; quest for, during the periods of disunion, 13, 15, 17–18, 29–30; sustainability of, 20–21, 25; territorial scope of, 32–37. See also All-under-Heaven; centralization; disintegration; multistate system; stability

Versailles Treaty (1919), 172

Vietnam, 36

violence, 135, 139; in conquest, 41; in Cultural Revolution, 179; in dynastic struggles, 12, 69; by elites, 122; by government, 153; by rebels, 141, 143, 147, 150, 153–157, 204n49